*They Knew
The Prophet*

They Knew The Prophet

Compiled by
HYRUM L. ANDRUS and
HELEN MAE ANDRUS

BOOKCRAFT
SALT LAKE CITY, UTAH

Library of Congress Catalog Card Number: 74-75538
ISBN 0-88494-210-4

Seventh Printing, 1985

Printed in the United States of America

To

John, Richard and David

Preface

They Knew the Prophet is a compilation of statements by people who were associated with Joseph Smith and later recalled historical incidents in his life, some of his teachings, and their impressions of him. The list in this volume is not complete, but is a selection of many of the more interesting and representative statements. Some of these statements are combined expressions by a given individual taken from several sources. In their compilation extraneous materials have been deleted, introductory and transitional phrases have been added, major spelling errors have been corrected, and punctuation has been altered where necessary for clarity. In all the statements, however, the original meaning and (as far as possible) wording have been preserved. In one or two instances, such as in the case of Mrs. Palmer, the report has been changed from the second to the first person.

Most of the statements included in this volume may be classified as memoirs, and are subject to the limitations historians impose on this class of information. But they also have the value of giving personal accounts of those who witnessed history in the making. Above all, they reflect the lasting impressions Joseph Smith made on his associates.

The compilers are indebted to several institutions and people for their contributions to this work, including the staff members of the Church Historian's Library and the Brigham Young University Library. Particular thanks is given to Steve Farnes, who has worked as a student assistant in gathering many of these statements. Don Norton of the English Department at Brigham Young University read the manuscript for grammatical accuracy and prepared the index.

The following secretaries have assisted in typing the manuscript: Kaye Cook, Denise Mortensen, Lorraine Indermill, Wendy Gause, Sue Beck, Terry Anderson, Ivy Yau, Beth Lunt, Miriam Dew, and Jeanine Molberg. They also have our special thanks.

Finally, special thanks is given to Bookcraft editor H. George Bickerstaff for his perceptive efforts in the final preparation of the manuscript and to Marvin W. Wallin, manager of Bookcraft, for his encouragement and assistance in the publication of this book.

HYRUM L. ANDRUS
HELEN MAE ANDRUS

Contents

Mrs. Palmer   1

Orlando Saunders   2

Thomas H. Taylor   3

Dr. John Stafford   4

Joseph Knight, Jr.   5

Newell Knight   6

Addison Everett 14

Mary A. Noble 15

Edwin Holden 16

Levi W. Hancock 17

Mary Elizabeth Rollins Lightner 22

Zebedee Coltrin 27

Joel Hills Johnson 29

Luke S. Johnson 29

Lucy Diantha Morley Allen 31

Lorenzo Snow 32

Brigham Young 34

Heber C. Kimball 36

Elizabeth Ann Whitney 39

Lydia Bailey Knight 42

Louisa Y. Littlefield 46

Harrison Burgess 46

George A. Smith 47

Daniel Tyler 49

John M. Chidester 55

Eliza R. Snow 56

Parley P. Pratt 58

Oliver B. Huntington 60

Philo Dibble 66

Daniel D. McArthur 73

James Henry Rollins 74

James B. Bracken, Sr. 78

Calvin W. Moore 79

Wilford Woodruff 80

Edward Stevenson 85

Benjamin F. Johnson 88

Samuel Miles 98

Jesse N. Smith 99

Sariah A. Workman 99

Susan E. J. Martineau 99

Henry William Bigler 100

John W. Hess 101

David Osborn 101

Mosiah L. Hancock 102

Orange L. Wight 104

Anson Call 105

Alexander McRae 108

Peter Hardeman Burnett 112

George Miller 113

Wandle Mace 115

William G. Nelson 118

Mercy R. Thompson 119

Christopher Merkley 121

Bathsheba W. Smith 122

Sarah Ann Gregory Hales 124

Benjamin Brown 125

Rachel Ridgeway Grant 126

Margarette McIntire Burgess 127

William Huntington 128

Sarah M. Kimball 130

William Farrington Cahoon 132

Howard Coray 133

Lucy Walker Kimball 137

William Moore Allred 140

Joseph Taylor, Sr. 141

James Leech 141

Jesse W. Crosby 143

John Lyman Smith 146

Henrietta Cox 147

William Holmes Walker 147

Andrew Workman 150

Lucy M. Smith 150

Eunice Billings Snow 152

James Palmer 154

Emmeline Blanche Wells 156

"Aunt" Jane James 158

William Taylor 160

William E. Jones 162

James P. Terry 162

Angus M. Cannon 163

Joseph Lee Robinson 164

Jane Snyder Richards 165

Mary Ann Winters 166

Mary C. Westover 167

Mary Alice Cannon Lambert 168

John F. Bellows 169

Edwin Rushton 170

Sarah M. Pomeroy 171

Charles Lambert 172

Emily D. Partridge Young 173

Christopher Layton 174

Helen Mar Whitney 175

John M. Bernhisel 176

Andrew J. Stewart 178

Gilbert Belnap 180

Mary Ellen Kimball 182

Dan Jones 183

John Taylor 188

Index 203

Mrs. Palmer

My father owned a farm near that of the Smith family, in New York. My parents were friends of the Smith family, which was one of the best in that locality—honest, religious and industrious, but poor. The father of the family was above the average in intelligence. I have heard my parents say that he bore the appearance of having descended from royalty. Mrs. Smith was called "Mother Smith" by many. Children loved to go to her home.

My father loved young Joseph Smith and often hired him to work with his boys. I was about six years old when he first came to our home. I remember going into the field on an afternoon to play in the corn rows while my brothers worked. When evening came, I was too tired to walk home and cried because my brothers refused to carry me. Joseph lifted me to his shoulder, and with his arm thrown across my feet to steady me, and my arm about his neck, he carried me to our home.

I remember the excitement stirred up among some of the people over Joseph's First Vision, and of hearing my father contend that it was only the sweet dream of a pure minded boy. One of our church leaders came to my father to remonstrate against his allowing such close friendship between his family and the "Smith Boy," as he called him. My father defended his own position by saying that Joseph was the best help he had ever found. He told the churchman that he always fixed the time of hoeing his large field to that when he could secure the services of Joseph Smith, because of the influence that boy had over the wild boys of the neighborhood, and explained that when these boys, or young men, worked by themselves much time would be spent in arguing and quarreling, which often ended in a ring fight. But when Joseph Smith worked with them, the work went steadily forward, and he got the full worth of the wages he paid.

I remember the churchman saying, in a very solemn and impressive tone, that the very influence the boy carried was the danger they feared for the coming generation, that not only the young men, but all who came in contact with him, would follow him, and *he must be put down.*

Not until Joseph had had a second vision and begun to write a book which drew many of the best and brightest people of the churches away did my parents come to a realization of the fact that their friend, the churchman, had told them the truth. Then, my family cut off their friendship for all the Smiths, for *all* the family followed Joseph. Even the father, intelligent man that he was, could not discern the evil he was helping to promote.

My parents then lent all the aid they could in helping to crush Joseph Smith; but it was too late. He had run his course too long. He could not be put down.

There was never a truer, purer, nobler boy than Joseph Smith, before he was led away by superstition.

> "Stories from the Notebook of Martha Cox, Grandmother of Fern Cox Anderson," Church Historian's Library, Salt Lake City, Utah; Lee C. LaFayette, "Recollections of Joseph Smith," Church Historian's Library, Salt Lake City, Utah.

Orlando Saunders

"Were you acquainted with the Smiths, Mr. Saunders?"

"Yes, sir; I knew all of the Smith family well. They have all worked for me many a day. They were very good people. Young Joe (as we called him then) has worked for me, and he was a good worker."

"In what respect did they differ from other people, if at all?"

"I never noticed that they were different from other neighbors. They were the best family in the neighborhood in case of sickness; one was at my house nearly all the time when my father died. I always thought them honest. They were owing me some money when they left here. One of them came back in about a year and paid me."

"How well did you know young Joseph Smith?"

"Oh, just as well as one could, very well. He has worked for me many a time, and been about my place a great deal. He stopped with me many a time, when through here, after they went west to Kirtland. He was always a gentleman when about my place."

"What did you know about his finding that book, or the plates in the hill over here?"

"He always claimed that he saw the angel and received the book."

Interview with E. L. and William H. Kelley, March 1881, published in *The Saints' Herald,* Plano, Illinois, XXVIII (June 1, 1881), p. 165; *Juvenile Instructor,* XVII (October 1, 1882), pp. 301-302.

Thomas H. Taylor

To our inquiries if he was acquainted with the Smiths, and the early settlers throughout that part sometimes called Mormons, Mr. Taylor said: "Yes, I knew them very well. They were very nice men, too. The only trouble was they were ahead of the people; and the people, as in every such case, turned out to abuse them, because they had the manhood to stand for their own convictions. I have seen such work all through life."

"What did the Smiths do that the people abused them so?"

"They did not do anything. Why! these rascals at one time took Joseph Smith and ducked him in the pond that you see over there, just because he preached what he believed, and for nothing else. And if Jesus Christ had been there, they would have done the same to Him. Now I don't believe like he did; but every man has a right to his religious opinions, and to advocate his views, too. If people don't like it, let them come out and meet him on the stand, and show his error. Smith was always ready to exchange views with the best men they had."

"Why didn't they like Smith?"

"To tell the truth, there was something about him they could not understand. Some way he knew more than they did, and it made them mad."

"But a good many tell terrible stories, about them being rogues, and liars, and such things. How is that?"

"Oh! they are a set of d - - - - d liars. I have had a home here, and been here, except when on business, all my life—ever since I came to this country—and I know these fellows. They make these lies on Smith, because they love a lie better than the truth. I can take you to a great many old settlers here who will substantiate what I say."

"Well, that is very kind, Mr. Taylor, and fair; if we have time we will call around and give you the chance; but we are first going to see these fellows who, so rumor says, know so much against them."

"All right; but you will find they don't know anything against those men when you put them down to it. They could never sustain anything against Smith."

> Interview with E. L. and William H. Kelley, March 1881, published in *The Saint's Herald,* Plano, Illinois, XXVIII, (June 1, 1881), p. 167; *Juvenile Instructor,* XVII (October 1, 1882), p. 302.

Dr. John Stafford

"Joseph Smith was a real clever, jovial boy. I lived a mile from the Smiths. They were peaceable. The old woman had a great deal of faith that their children were going to do something great. Joe was quite illiterate. After they began to have school at their house, he improved greatly."

"Did they have school in their own house?"

"Yes, sir, they had school in their house, and studied the Bible."

"Who was their teacher?"

"They did not have any teacher; they taught themselves."

"If young Smith was as illiterate as you say, Doctor, how do you account for the Book of Mormon?"

"Well, I can't; except that Sidney Rigdon was connected with them."

"What makes you think he was connected with them?"

"Because I can't account for the Book of Mormon any other way."

"Was Rigdon ever around there before the Book of Mormon was published?"

"No, not as we could ever find out."

"Well, you have been looking out for the facts a long time, have you not, Doctor?"

"Yes, I have been thinking and hearing about it for the last fifty years, and lived right among all their old neighbors there most of the time."

"And no one has ever been able to trace the acquaintance of Rigdon and Smith, until after the Book of Mormon was published, and Rigdon was proselyted by Parley P. Pratt, in Ohio?"

"Not that I know of."

> Interview with E. L. and William H. Kelley, March 1881, published in *The Saints' Herald,* Plano, Illinois, XXVIII (June 1, 1881), p. 167; *Juvenile Instructor,* XVII (October 1, 1882), p. 301.

Joseph Knight, Jr.

My father bought three farms on the Susquehanna River, in Broome County, New York. In 1827, he hired Joseph Smith, Jr. Joseph and I worked and slept together. My father said that Joseph was the best hand he ever hired. We found him a boy of truth. He was about twenty-one years of age.

I think it was in November, 1827, he made known to my father and me that he had seen a vision, that a personage had appeared to him and told him where there was a gold book of ancient date buried, and if he would follow the directions of the angel he could get it. We were told it in secret. My father and I believed what he told us. I think we were the first after his father's family.

At last he got the plates, and rode in my father's wagon and carried them home.

Joseph then commenced to translate the plates. Father and I often went to see him, to carry him some things to live upon. After many trials and troubles, he got the plates translated. By this time, my mother and many of my relations believed.

Joseph and Oliver came to Colesville, in May, 1830, where we lived, and Oliver baptized my father's family, and a few of my relatives. When we were going from the water, we were met by many of our neighbors, who pointed at us and asked if we had been washing our sheep. Before Joseph could confirm us, he was taken by the officers to Chenango County for trial, for saying that the Book of Mormon was a revelation from God.

My father employed two lawyers to plead for him, and they cleared him. That night our wagons were turned over and wood piled on them, and some sunk in the water. Rails were piled against our doors, and chains sunk in the stream, and a great deal of mischief done. Before Joseph got to my father's house, he was taken again to be tried in Broome County. Father employed the same lawyers, who cleared him there.

Four weeks passed before Joseph could get a chance to confirm us. Then we had the greatest time I ever saw. The house was filled with the Holy Ghost, which rested upon us.

> Joseph Knight, Jr., Folder, Church Historian's Library, Salt Lake City, Utah.

Newell Knight

My father lived at Colesville, Broome County, New York. He was a sober, honest man, generally respected and beloved by his neighbors and acquaintances. The business in which he was engaged often required him to have hired help, and among the many he from time to time employed was a young man by the name of Joseph Smith, Jun., to whom I was particularly attached. His noble deportment, his faithfulness and his kind address could not fail to win the esteem of those who had the pleasure of his acquaintance. One thing I will mention, which seemed to be a peculiar characteristic with him in all his boyish sports and amusements: I never knew any one to gain advantage over him, and yet he was always kind and kept the good will of his playmates.

We were frequently visited by my young friend, Joseph Smith, who would entertain us with accounts of the wonderful things which had happened to him. It was evident to me that great things were about to be accomplished through him—that the Lord was about to use him as an instrument in His hands to bring to pass the great and mighty work of the last days. This chosen instrument told us of God's manifestations to him, of the discovery and receiving of the plates from which the Book of Mormon was translated, of his persecutions for the gospel's sake, and of many other items of his eventful life.

So honest and plain were all his statements that there was no room for any misgivings with me on the subject. Besides, I found by reading and searching the Bible that there would be a great falling away from the gospel as preached and established by Jesus and His apostles, that in the last days God would set His hand again to restore that which was lost.

On the first day of June, 1830, the first conference was held by the Church, at Fayette, New York. Our number consisted of about thirty, besides many others who came to learn of our principles, or were already believers, but had not been baptized.

Soon after conference Joseph Smith came to Colesville to make us a visit. There were many in our neighborhood who believed and were anxiously waiting for an opportunity to be baptized. Meeting was appointed for the Sabbath, and on Saturday afternoon we erected a dam across a stream which was close by, with the intention of baptizing those who applied on Sunday. But during the night a mob collected and tore away the dam.

Early on Monday morning we were on the alert, and before our enemies were aware of it, Oliver Cowdery proceeded to baptize Emma Smith, Hezekiah Peck and wife, Joseph Knight and wife, Levi Hall, Polly Knight and Julia Stringham. But before the baptism was entirely finished, the mob began to collect again. We retired to my father's house, and the mob, which numbered about fifty, surrounded the house, raging with anger, and apparently wishing to commit violence against us. So violent and troublesome were they that the brethren were obliged to leave my father's house, and they succeeded in reaching mine. The mob, who soon found where they had gone, followed them and it was only by great prudence on our part and help from our Heavenly Father that they were kept from laying violent hands upon us.

A meeting had been appointed for the evening to confirm those who had been baptized in the morning. The time appointed had arrived, and our friends had nearly all collected together, when, to our great surprise and sorrow, the constable came and

arrested Brother Joseph Smith, Jun., on a warrant charging him
with being a disorderly person, and of setting the country in an
uproar by preaching the Book of Mormon.

The constable, soon after he had arrested Joseph, told him
that the plan of those who had got out the warrant for his arrest
was to get him into the hands of the mob who were now lying
in ambush for him, and that he, the constable, was determined to
save Joseph from them, as he found him to be a different person
to what he had been represented. This proved true, for they had
not proceeded far from the house when the wagon in which Joseph
and the constable were riding was surrounded by the mob, who
seemed only to await some signal from the constable. But to their
great discomfiture, he gave the horses the whip and was soon
out of their reach.

As the constable was driving briskly along, one of the wagon
wheels came off, which accident left them almost in the hands of
the mob who had pursued them closely. But the constable was
an expert man and managed to get the wheel on again before
the mob overtook him, and soon left them in the rear once more.

He drove on to the town of South Bainbridge, Chenango
County, where he lodged Joseph in an upper room of a tavern; and
in order that all might be safe for himself and Joseph, he slept
during the night with his feet against the door, and kept a loaded
gun by him (Joseph occupied a bed in the same room), and
declared that if they were unlawfully molested he would fight for
Joseph and defend him to the utmost of his ability.

On the following day a court was convened for the purpose
of investigating the charges which had been made against Joseph
Smith, Jun. On account of the many scandalous reports which
had been put in circulation, a great excitement prevailed. My
father, Joseph Knight, Sen., did not let the opportunity pass of
doing all in his power to assist this persecuted boy. He went to
two of his neighbors, James Davidson and John Reid, Esqs.,
respectable farmers who were well versed in the laws of their
country, and retained them in behalf of Joseph during his trial.

The trial commenced among a crowded multitude of spectators. Among the witnesses called up against Joseph was one
Josiah Stoal, a gentleman for whom Joseph formerly worked. He
was examined as follows:

Question—"Did not the prisoner, Joseph Smith, have a horse
from you?"

Answer—"Yes."

Q.—"Did he not go to you and tell you an angel had appeared unto him and told him to get the horse from you?"

A.—"No, he told me no such thing."

Q.—"Well, how did he get the horse from you?"

A.—"He bought it from me the same as any other man would do."

Q.—"Have you had your pay?"

A.—"That is not your business."

The question being repeated, the witness replied, "I hold his note for the price of the horse, which I consider as good as the money; for I am well acquainted with Joseph Smith, Jun., and know him to be honest, and, if he wishes, I am ready to let him have another horse on the same terms."

Mr. Jonathan Thompson was next called and examined.

Question—"Has not the prisoner, Joseph Smith, Jun., had a yoke of oxen of you?"

Answer—"Yes."

Q.—"Did he not obtain them from you by telling you that he had had a revelation to the effect that he was to have them?"

A.—"No, he did not mention a word of the kind concerning the oxen; he purchased them the same as any other man would."

After several more similar attempts the court was detained for a time in order that two young ladies, daughters of Josiah Stoal, with whom Joseph had at times kept company, might be sent for, in order, if possible, to elicit something from them which could be made a pretext against Joseph.

The young ladies came and were each examined as to his character and conduct in general, but in particular as to his behavior towards them in public and private. They both bore such testimony in Joseph's favor as to leave his enemies without a cause for complaint. Several attempts were made to prove something against Joseph, and even circumstances which were alleged to have taken place in Broome County were brought forward. But these Joseph's lawyers would not admit against him, in consequence of which his persecutors managed to detain the court until they had succeeded in obtaining a warrant from Broome

County. This warrant they served upon him at the very moment
he had been acquitted by the court.

The constable who served this second warrant upon Joseph
had no sooner arrested him than he began to abuse him. So
heartless was he that, although Joseph had been kept all day in
court without anything to eat since the morning, he hurried him
off to Broome County, a distance of about fifteen miles, before
allowing him to eat. The constable took him to a tavern where
were gathered a number of men who used every means to abuse,
ridicule, and insult him. They spit upon him, pointed their fingers
at him, saying, "Prophesy! prophesy!" Thus did they imitate those
who crucified the Savior of mankind, not knowing what they did.

The tavern was but a short distance from Joseph's own house.
He wished to spend the night with his wife, offering to give any
bail desired for his appearance. But this was denied him. He
applied for something to eat. The constable ordered him some
crusts of bread and some water, which was the only fare he
received that night. At length he retired to bed. The constable
made him lie next to the wall. He then laid himself down, threw
his arms around Joseph, as if fearing that he intended to escape;
and in this manner was Joseph compelled to spend the night.

Next day he was brought before the magistrate's court of
Colesville, Broome County, and placed on trial. His friends and
lawyers were again at his side, and his former persecutors were
arrayed against him with the rage and fury of demons visible
upon their countenances, and manifested in their actions. Many
witnesses were again examined, some of whom swore to the most
palpable falsehoods, just as those had done who appeared against
him the previous day. But they contradicted themselves so plainly
that the court would not admit their testimony. Others were called
who showed by their zeal that they were willing to prove anything
against him. But all they could do was to tell some things that they
had heard somebody else say about him.

They proceeded for a considerable time in this frivolous and
vexatious manner, when finally I was called upon and examined
by Lawyer Seymour, who had been sent for specially for this
occasion. One lawyer, Burch, was also retained on the prosecution.
But Mr. Seymour seemed to be a more zealous Presbyterian, and
seemed more anxious and determined that the people should not be
deluded by any one professing godliness and not denying the
power thereof.

As soon as I had been sworn, Mr. Seymour proceeded to interrogate me as follows:

Question—"Did the prisoner, Joseph Smith, Jun., cast the devil out of you?"

Answer—"No, sir."

Question—"Why, have you not had the devil cast out of you?"

Answer—"Yes, sir."

Question—"And had not Joseph Smith some hand in it being done?"

Answer—"Yes, sir."

Question—"And did he not cast him out of you?"

Answer—"No, sir. It was done by the power of God, and Joseph Smith was the instrument in the hands of God on this occasion. He commanded him to come out of me in the name of Jesus Christ."

Question—"And are you sure it was the devil?"

Answer—"Yes, sir."

Question—"Did you see him after he was cast out of you?"

Answer—"Yes sir, I saw him."

Question—"Pray, what did he look like?"

(Here one of the lawyers on the part of the defense told me I need not answer that question.) I replied: "I believe, I need not answer you that question, but I will do it if I am allowed to ask you one, and you can answer it. Do you, Mr. Seymour, understand the things of the Spirit?"

"No," answered Mr. Seymour. "I do not pretend to such big things."

"Well, then," I replied, "it will be of no use for me to tell you what the devil looked like, for it was a spiritual sight and spiritually discerned, and, of course, you would not understand it were I to tell you of it."

The lawyer dropped his head, while the loud laugh of the audience proclaimed his discomfiture.

Mr. Seymour now addressed the court and in a long and violent harangue endeavored to blacken the character of Joseph, and bring him in guilty of the charges preferred against him.

Messrs. Davidson and Reid followed on Joseph's behalf. They held forth in true colors the nature of the prosecution, the malignity of intention, and the apparent disposition of the prosecution to persecute their client rather than to do him justice. They took up the different arguments that had been brought forward by the lawyers for the prosecution, and having shown their utter futility and misapplication they proceeded to scrutinize the evidence which had been adduced, and each in his turn thanked God that he had been engaged in so good a cause as that of defending a man whose character stood so well the test of such a strict investigation.

In fact these men, although not regular lawyers, were, upon this occasion, able to put to silence their opponents, and convince the court that Joseph Smith, Jun., was innocent. They spoke like men inspired of God, while those who were arrayed against Joseph trembled under the sound of their voices and shook before them as criminals before the bar of justice. Disappointment and shame were depicted on the faces of the assembled multitude, who now began to learn that nothing could be sustained against Joseph.

The constable, who had arrested Joseph and treated him in so cruel and heartless a manner, came forward and apologized and asked his forgiveness for the ill-treatment he had given him. So much was this man changed that he told Joseph the mob had resolved if the court acquitted him that they would take him, tar and feather him, and ride him on a rail; and further, that if Joseph wished, he would lead him out another way, so that he could escape in safety.

After all the efforts of the people and court to sustain the charges brought against Joseph proved an entire failure, he was discharged and succeeded in making good his escape from the mob through the instrumentality of his new friend, the constable.

After a few days the Prophet, accompanied by Oliver Cowdery, came to my house, intending to confirm those who had been baptized. These servants of God had scarcely arrived when the mob began to collect, and so violent were they that it was thought best for Joseph and Oliver to make their escape lest they should suffer at the hands of our enemies. They left without taking any refreshment, the mob closely pursuing them, and it was ofttimes as much as Joseph and Oliver could do to escape them. However, by traveling all night, excepting a short time when they were forced to lie down and rest themselves under a tree, alternately watching and sleeping, they managed to get beyond the reach of their pursuers.

In the beginning of August, 1830, I, in company with my wife, went to make a visit to Brother Joseph Smith, Jun., who then resided at Harmony, Pennsylvania. We found him and his wife well, and in good spirits. We had a happy meeting. It truly gave me joy to again behold his face. As neither Emma, the wife of Joseph Smith, nor my wife had been confirmed, we concluded to attend to that holy ordinance at this time, and also to partake of the sacrament before we should leave for home. In order to prepare for this, Brother Joseph set out to procure some wine for the occasion. But he had gone only a short distance when he was met by a heavenly messenger who informed him that it did not matter what the Saints ate and drank when they partook of the sacrament, but that they should not purchase wine or strong drink from their enemies.

In obedience to this revelation, we prepared some wine of our own make and held our meeting, consisting of only five persons namely, Joseph Smith and wife, John Whitmer, and myself and wife. We partook of the sacrament, after which we confirmed the two sisters into the Church, and spent the evening in a glorious manner. The Spirit of the Lord was poured out upon us. We praised the God of Israel and rejoiced exceedingly.

About the last of August, 1830, I took my team and wagon to Harmony to move Joseph and his family to Fayette, New York. After arranging my affairs at home, I again set out for Fayette to attend our second conference, which had been appointed to be held at Father Whitmer's, where Joseph then resided. On my arrival I found Brother Joseph in great distress of mind on account of Hiram Page, who had managed to get up some dissension of feeling among the brethren by giving revelations concerning the government of the Church and other matters which he claimed to have received through the medium of a stone he possessed. He had quite a roll of papers full of these revelations, and many in the Church were led astray by them. Even Oliver Cowdery and the Whitmer family had given heed to them, although they were in contradiction to the New Testament and the revelations of these last days. Joseph was perplexed and scarcely knew how to meet this new exigency. That night I occupied the same room that he did, and the greater part of the night was spent in prayer and supplication. After much labor with these brethren, they were convinced of their error and confessed the same, renouncing the revelations as not being of God, but acknowledging that Satan had conspired to overthrow their belief in the true plan of salvation. In consequence of these things, Joseph inquired of the Lord before conference commenced and received a revelation in which the Lord explicitly stated His mind and will concerning the receiving of revelation. (See D&C 28.)

During this time we had much of the power of God manifested among us, and it was wonderful to witness the wisdom that Joseph displayed on this occasion, for truly God gave unto him great wisdom and power, and it seems to me that none who saw him administer righteousness under such trying circumstances could doubt that the Lord was with him. He acted not with the wisdom of man, but with the wisdom of God. The Holy Ghost came upon us and filled our hearts with unspeakable joy. Before this memorable conference closed, three other revelations besides the one already mentioned were received from God by our prophet, and we were made to rejoice exceedingly in His goodness.

> "Newel Knight's Journal," in *Scraps of Biography* (*Faith Promoting Series,* Volume 10) (Salt Lake City, 1883), pp. 47-65.

Addison Everett

In a conversation I heard between Joseph and Hyrum Smith, Oliver Cowdery was spoken of. Joseph said, "Poor boy!"

He then said that at Colesville, New York, in 1829, he and Oliver were under arrest on a charge of deceiving the people. When they were at the justice's house for trial in the evening, all were waiting for Mr. Reid, Joseph's lawyer. While waiting, the justice asked Joseph some questions, among which was this: "What was the first miracle Jesus performed?"

Joseph replied, "He made this world, and what followed we are not told."

Mr. Reid came in and said he wanted to speak to his clients in private and that the law allowed him that privilege, he believed. The judge pointed to a door to a room in the back part of the house and told them to step in there. As soon as they got into the room, the lawyer said there was a mob outside in front of the house. "If they get hold of you they will perhaps do you bodily injury; and I think the best way for you to get out of this is to get right out there," pointing to the window and hoisting it.

They got into the woods in going a few rods from the house. It was night and they traveled through brush and water and mud, fell over logs, etc., until Oliver was exhausted. Then Joseph helped him along through the mud and water, almost carrying him.

They traveled all night, and just at the break of day Oliver gave out entirely and exclaimed, "Oh, Lord! Brother Joseph, how long have we got to endure this thing?"

They sat down on a log to rest, and Joseph said that at that very time Peter, James and John came to them and ordained them to the apostleship.

They had sixteen or seventeen miles to go to get back to Mr. Hale's, his father-in-law's, but Oliver did not complain any more of fatigue.

> Letter of Addison Everett to Oliver B. Huntington, February 17, 1881, *Young Woman's Journal,* II (November, 1890), pp. 76-77.

Mary A. Noble

About 1828, my father, Alva Beaman, became acquainted with Father Joseph Smith, the father of the Prophet. We frequently would go to Palmyra to see Father Smith and his family during this time. Brother Joseph Smith came in possession of the plates that contained the Book of Mormon. As soon as it was noised around that there was a Golden Bible found, for that was what it was called at the time, the minds of the people became excited, and rose to such a pitch that a mob collected to search the house of Father Joseph Smith to find the records. My father was there at the time and assisted in concealing the plates in a box, in a secluded place, where no one could find them, although he did not see them.

In the spring of 1834, Brother Joseph Smith came from Kirtland, Ohio, to my father's New York estate, which he had purchased at Avon, Livingston County. This was the first time I ever beheld a prophet of the Lord, and I can truly say at the first sight that I had a testimony within my bosom that he was a man chosen of God to bring forth a great work in the last days. His society I prized. His conversation was meat and drink to me. The principles that he brought forth and the testimony that he bore of the truth of the Book of Mormon made a lasting impression upon my mind.

While he was there, Sidney Rigdon, Joseph and Brigham Young, Luke and Lyman Johnson, and twelve or fourteen of the traveling elders had a council at my father's place. I, in company with my sisters, had the pleasure of cooking and serving the table and waiting on them, which I considered to be a privilege and a blessing.

Brother Joseph and Elder Rigdon held a meeting in Geneva, which was called the Orton neighborhood, in a barn. Elder Rigdon preached, Brother Joseph bore testimony of the truth of the Book of Mormon, and of the work that had come forth in these last days. Never did I hear preaching sound so glorious to me as that did. I realized it was the truth of heaven, for I had a testimony of it myself. Many very interesting interviews we had with them while they were at my father's house.

> Journal of Mary A. Noble, included in the journal of Joseph Bates Noble, Brigham Young University Library, pp. 16, 18, 19.

Edwin Holden

The first time I saw Joseph Smith was in 1831, in Genesee, New York State, about twenty-five miles from the famous hill, Cumorah. On hearing that two men were there calling themselves "Mormons," I determined to see them. I rode on horseback fifteen miles from the place I was living to see them—Joseph Smith and Sidney Rigdon. When I got to the place, I learned that they were going to hold a meeting in a barn. It was so crowded that it was with much difficulty I got inside; and by a great effort climbed up on one of the beams of the roof. There I could see and hear them distinctly.

In 1838, after the Church moved to Missouri, Joseph and some of the young men were playing various outdoor games, among which was a game of ball. By and by they began to get weary. He saw it, and calling them together he said: "Let us build a log cabin."

So off they went, Joseph and the young men, to build a log cabin for a widow woman. Such was Joseph's way, always assisting in whatever he could.

The Juvenile Instructor, XXVII (March 1, 1892), p. 153.

Levi W. Hancock

On the 4th of June, 1831, we all met in Kirtland, in a school house built of logs. Here the Elders were seated on slab benches, and the meeting was opened as usual.

Joseph Smith began to speak. He said that the kingdom that Christ spoke of, that was like a grain of mustard seed, was now before him, and some should see it put forth its branches, just as the Savior had said.

He looked at Lyman Wight and said, "You shall see the Lord and meet him near the corner of the house."

The Prophet laid his hands upon him and blessed him with the visions of heaven.

Joseph Smith then stepped out on the floor and said, "I now see God, and Jesus Christ at his right hand. Let them kill me; I should not feel death as I am now."

Joseph put his hands upon Harvey Whitlock and ordained him to the office of high priest in the High Priesthood. He turned as black as Lyman was white. His fingers were set like claws. He went around the room and showed his hands and tried to speak. His eyes were in the shape of oval O's.

Hyrum Smith said, "Joseph, that is not of God."

Joseph said, "Do not speak against this."

"I will not believe," said Hyrum, "unless you inquire of God and he owns it."

Joseph bowed his head, and in a short time got up and commanded Satan to leave Harvey, laying his hands upon his head at the same time.

At that very instant an old man said to weigh two hundred and fourteen pounds, sitting in the window, turned a complete summersault in the house and came down with his back across a bench, and lay helpless.

Joseph told Lyman to cast Satan out. He did. The man's name was Leman Copley, formerly a Quaker.

The evil spirit left him, and as quick as lightning Harvey Green fell bound and screamed like a panther. Satan was cast out of him, but immediately entered someone else. This continued all day and the greater part of the night.

But to return to the meeting, Joseph said, "Now if you elders have sinned, it will do you no good to preach, if you have not repented. Heman Basset, you sit still. The devil wants to sift you."

He then ordained Jacob Scott and some others to the High Priesthood. He came to Zebedee Coltrin and myself, and told us that we had another calling as high as any man in the house. [They were made members of the First Council of Seventy in 1835.] I was glad for that, for I was so scared I would not stir without his liberty, for all the world. I knew the things I had seen were not made.

Joseph Smith called Lyman Wight to lay his hands on his head and say what God should tell him to say. He did, and the blessing was so long I cannot write it.

After this we went down to the house and heard Harvey Whitlock say that when Hyrum Smith said it was not of God, he disdained him in his heart, and when the devil was cast out he was convinced it was Satan that was in him, and then he knew it. I also heard Harvey Green say that he could not describe the awful feeling he experienced while in the hands of Satan.

On June the fifth we all assembled on the hill, in a field where there was a large concourse of people collected. The Prophet Joseph said that from that time on the Elders would have large congregations to speak to, and they must soon take their departure into the regions west.

After I returned from a mission, the Prophet told me about being mobbed in Hiram, and how they pulled the hair out of his head. Then he showed me the place where they had pulled the hair out. He said they poured aqua fortis down him, he thought.

I said, "While I was in Cleveland, I heard some laughing about it. They said the devil must have gotten the better of the

Lord that time. I told them I thought he did once before when they killed the Son of God, and his disciples too. I did not consider that proved him an impostor."

I never saw men so much confounded. I said no more, but all eyes were on me while I stayed at the house.

The Prophet was often in trouble. If his friends gave him money, he was stripped of it all by his enemies. I know, for I did all I could do to uphold that good man. My heart would ache for him. He had to stand against thousands of his pretended friends who sought to overthrow him. It was terrible the abuse he suffered.

Bishop Newel K. Whitney also was cursed by some when he did his best to uphold Joseph. He would suffer himself to be slandered to save the Prophet from trouble.

The Prophet called me to go on a mission with Evan Green. The snow came and it began to get cold to travel, but we went as far as we could get, and returned back. Joseph talked plain to me for not pressing forward into Pennsylvania. I told him that I was to blame, for I had had a dream that troubled me.

He said, "Don't let that trouble you. I have had dreams as bad as you ever had. You do as I now tell you to and you will come out all right."

He gave me to understand how the Comforter would comfort the mind of man when asleep. He said, "Go again," and we started forthwith for Pennsylvania.

We went from neighborhood to neighborhood preaching. We were treated very well through the land about. When the time came for us to open the door to baptism, Lyman Johnson came along. We asked him to preach. He opened the door and baptized all we had labored with, except two who chose to have me baptize them. Lyman returned to Kirtland and never mentioned Evan or Levi or their good works.

I asked the Prophet Joseph about such a case. He said the laborer who first labored with the people would in the end get the blessing.

On the first of May, 1834, I started for Cartage County, some forty miles from Kirtland, to go with Zion's Camp. I was appointed cook for Sylvester Smith's mess. In this way we traveled, being directed by the Prophet in peace, until Sylvester lost the spirit of peace and became dissatisfied with John Carter, and called him an old jackass and many other names, which soon brought dissatisfaction in our tent. Some dared to express their feelings, until Joseph rebuked them and told them that Sylvester was guilty of sowing the seeds of discord.

Sylvester said, if Joseph was a prophet he was not afraid, and would contradict him in the face of all present.

Joseph said, "If I have not told you the truth, then God never spoke by me," and walked off.

We all said, "That is enough."

We believed Joseph. Sylvester became more calm and acted like a saint, and for some time we had peace. We did not stop, but continued on our march westward until we got in Illinois. Joseph then said, "I want you to remember what I say to you. The Lord is going to give us dry weather now until we get through. He has given rains that there might be water on the prairies. You will see the movings of the Lord in our favor all the way through."

One morning, many went to see a big mound about a mile below the crossing. I did not go on it, but saw some bones that were brought back with a broken arrow. They were laid down by our camp. Joseph Smith said, "This land was called the land of desolation, and Onedagus was the king, and a good man was he. There in that mound did he bury his dead, and did not dig holes as the people do now, but they brought their dirt and covered them until you see they have raised it to be about one hundred feet high. The last man buried was Zelf. He was a white Lamanite who fought with the people of Onedagus for freedom. When he was young, he was a great warrior and had his thigh broken, and it never was set. It knitted together as you see on the side. He fought after it got strength, until he lost every tooth in his head save one, when the Lord said he had done enough and suffered him to be killed by that arrow you took from his breast."

We continued our march westward. I had made me an elder fife, and played some marches on the way to the camp, being led by Sylvester Smith. As soon as we came in sight of camp, a dog came. He began to bark and ran to Sylvester and tried to bite him. It made Sylvester mad, and he said he would kill that dog.

Joseph said he should not, and he would whip any man who would do it. If Sylvester had a good spirit he could get along without being bit. It was a man's being overcome with such a spirit that caused him always to try to take vengeance and seek an opportunity to do it, and take life. Such a spirit kept men in misery.

Sylvester would not believe it. Joseph said, "If you do not get rid of that feeling, you will have your flesh eaten off from you and you cannot help it."

He would not believe Joseph yet.

Once after this, Joseph on the same principle said, "If a man should have to fight in self defense and kill his enemy, he should say in his heart, 'I wish it might have been otherwise, but you sought to take my life and would not let me alone and I was obliged to take yours.'"

He said, "If you ever go to battle and are prospered over your enemies and slay them, I fear you will be tempted to boast. If you should boast of your own strength, I fear God will leave you."

The greatest miracle in our favor was when we had got between the two branches of Fishing River, on a high ridge by a log meetinghouse. We had been told that morning by a colored woman who came to the fence where we were walking, that there were three hundred men who were armed and equipped to fall on us that night and cut us off. Men came riding by who cussed and swore that before morning we would all be in hell, for there was an army before and behind, and death was our portion.

Jenkins Salsbury wanted Joseph to let him fight.

"No," said he, "the Lord will give us a bramble to keep off the dogs this night."

In a short time it commenced thundering and the clouds arose. I went into the tent and lay down and knew no more till I found myself one third buried in water. The tent had blown down and all hands were gone. I soon found they had gone to the old church for shelter, where I also went. The lightning flashed and thunder roared one continual sound. The flashes were so connected that one could hardly hear any interval between the flash and the peal of thunder, as if the marshal bands of the whole earth had assembled and were beating the sounds of war.

We lay on the benches dripping with water until daylight, when we were called to go and discharge our pieces and load anew, which we did. To our astonishment, two thirds, if not more, went off.

It was a pleasant morning. We got our breakfast and soon learned that the two branches of Fishing River were so high we could not cross over. The branch west had raised upwards of forty feet and all boats were gone. We turned our course northward about three miles and camped near an old acquaintance of some in our camp. Next day we were visited by a committee from the mob. Lyman Wight explained to them the cause of our coming, and others spoke, which appeared to give satisfaction.

After the meeting, those of the community went away, and Joseph said, "Let us help this man right up his corn." We all went into our friend's field and straightened up the corn that the storm had laid low.

> "Life story of Levi W. Hancock," Brigham Young University Library, pp. 47-49, 73-75, 76, 77, 78, 79-80, 81-82.

Mary Elizabeth Rollins Lightner

After many people were converted at Kirtland, John Whitmer came and brought a Book of Mormon. There was a meeting that evening, and we learned that Brother Morley had the book in his possession—the only one in that part of the country. I went to his house before the meeting and asked to see the book. As I looked at it, I felt such a desire to read it that I could not refrain from asking him to let me take it home while he attended meeting. He finally said, "Child, if you will bring this book home before breakfast, tomorrow morning, you may take it."

My uncle and aunt were Methodists, so when I got into the house, I exclaimed, "Oh, Uncle, I have got the 'Golden Bible.'"

We took turns reading it until late at night.

As soon as it was light enough to see, I was up and learned the first verse in the book. When I reached Brother Morley's house, he remarked, "I guess you did not read much in it."

I showed him how far we had read.

He was surprised, and said, "I don't believe you can tell me one word of it."

I then repeated the first verse, also the outline of the history of Nephi.

He gazed at me in surprise and said, "Child, take this book home and finish it. I can wait."

About the time I finished the last chapter, the Prophet Joseph Smith arrived in Kirtland. Brother Whitney brought the Prophet Joseph to our house and introduced him to the older ones of the family. He saw the Book of Mormon on the shelf and asked how that book came to be there. He said, "I sent that book to Brother Morley."

Uncle told him how his niece had obtained it.

He asked, "Where is your niece?"

I was sent for. When he saw me, he looked at me so earnestly I felt almost afraid, and I thought, "He can read my every thought." I thought how blue his eyes were. After a moment or two, he came and put his hands on my head and gave me a great blessing, the first I ever received, and made me a present of the book, and said he would give Brother Morley another.

Joseph came in time to rebuke the evil spirits and set the Church in order. We all felt that he was a man of God, for he spoke with power, as one having authority in very deed.

A few evenings after his visit to our house, Mother and I went over to the Smith house. There were other visitors. The whole Smith family, excepting Joseph, was there. As we stood talking to them, Brother Joseph and Martin Harris came in, with two or three others. When the greetings were over, Brother Joseph looked around very solemnly. It was the first time some of them had ever seen him. He then said, "There are enough here to hold a little meeting."

A board was put across two chairs to make seats. Martin Harris sat on a little box at Joseph's feet. They sang and prayed; then Joseph got up to speak. He began very solemnly and very earnestly. All at once his countenance changed and he stood mute. He turned so white he seemed perfectly transparent. Those who looked at him that night said he looked like he had a searchlight within him, in every part of his body. I never saw anything like it on earth. I could not take my eyes away from him. He got so white that anyone who saw him would have thought he was transparent. I remember I thought we could almost see the bones through the flesh of his face. I shall remember it and see it in my mind's eye as long as I remain upon the earth.

He stood some moments looking over the congregation, as if to pierce each heart, then said, "Do you know who has been in your midst this night?"

One of the Smiths said, "An angel of the Lord."

Joseph did not answer. Martin Harris was sitting at the Prophet's feet on a box. He slid to his knees, clasped his arms around the Prophet's knees and said, "I know, it was our Lord and Savior, Jesus Christ."

Joseph put his hand on Martin's head and answered, "Martin, God revealed that to you. Brothers and Sisters, the Savior has been in your midst this night. I want you all to remember it. There is a veil over your eyes, for you could not endure to look upon Him. You must be fed with milk and not strong meat. I want you to remember this as if it were the last thing that escaped my lips. He has given you all to me, and commanded me to seal you up to everlasting life, that where He is there you may be also. And if you are tempted of Satan say, 'Get thee behind me, Satan, for my salvation is secure.'"

Then he knelt and prayed, and such a prayer I never heard before or since. I felt he was talking to the Lord, and the power rested upon us all. The prayer was so long that some of the people got up and rested, then knelt again.

In the fall of 1831, we left Kirtland for Jackson County, Missouri. One evening, the brethren came to Uncle's house to converse upon the revelations that were being printed. They felt to rejoice that they were counted worthy to be the means of publishing them to the world. While talking, they were filled with the Spirit and spoke in tongues. I was called upon to interpret. I felt the spirit of it in a moment.

On one occasion after interpreting something about the Saints going to be driven, there was a great cry raised by the High Council. They wrote the Prophet and said I was talking with an evil spirit. Joseph answered, "What she has said is true and correct. Interpretations rightly belong to the Priesthood, but you did not ask for it. She did and received it."

I was a very inquisitive girl, and after becoming well acquainted with the Prophet, I asked many questions. As I grew older, he told me more serious things. He said, "John the Revelator was caught up to the third heaven, but I know one who was caught up to the seventh heaven and saw and heard things not lawful for me to utter."

I stayed with Uncle Gilbert most of the time until Zion's Camp came up in 1834. Many of the brethren stopped with us, including the Prophet Joseph. One morning Joseph came while we were eating breakfast of cold mush. My stepfather liked cold mush, so had told Mother not to fix anything else. When Joseph came in, Mother and I looked at each other and must have shown it, for he asked for some, first saying, "Brother Burk, that mush looks good. I like mush."

Of course he was asked to have some. He ate heartily, but we thought he did it to lessen our embarrassment.

After the Saints settled in Illinois, my husband, Mr. Lightner, got a job cutting cordwood about fifteen miles up the river from Nauvoo. He got a log house and I prepared to move there. The Prophet felt very sad when he knew we were going to leave, and with tears running down his cheeks he prophesied that if we left the Church we would have plenty of sorrow; that we would make property on the right and lose it on the left, we would have sickness on sickness, and lose our children; that I would have to work harder than I ever dreamed; then he added, "And at last when you are worn out and old you will get back to the Church."

I thought these were hard sayings for it seemed as though things had already been about as hard as could be, and I felt to doubt them. But the sequel proved them true. It all came to pass as he predicted.

Before leaving Nauvoo, there was a general parade of the Legion. Since I was living as a neighbor, Emma came to borrow my dining room table, as the officers were to dine with them. The Prophet came also a few minutes later. He spoke to his wife, then said, "I want you and you (pointing to my aunt, brother Henry and wife, and myself) to go and be baptized." He added that he had been commanded to baptize us that day.

Emma said, "What Joseph, why is this? They have always been good members of the Church, and another thing, the officers will be here for dinner soon."

He answered, "Never mind, they can wait."

Then Emma said, "Well, you certainly are not going in those clothes."

To this he replied, "No, but you all be ready by the time I return."

As we lived on the bank of the river, we were soon there. Mr. Lightner carried the baby. Mr. Lightner had never been baptized, and perhaps the Prophet thought he would want to be at that time, for the rest of us had of course been baptized some time before, in the year the Church was organized.

After we were baptized and confirmed, he turned to my husband and said, "Now, Adam, it's your turn."

Mr. Lightner said, "No, Joseph, I'll wait till I quit smoking. I don't feel worthy. I will some other time."

I thought Joseph could persuade him, as he tried hard.

As we walked back to the house, my husband went ahead with the baby. Joseph walked by me and said, "Mary, that man will never be baptized in this life, unless it is a few moments before he dies."

Though he was only then twenty-one and lived to be seventy-three, crossing the plains, enduring all the hardships, and seeing the prophecies of Joseph fulfilled, and often saying he would be baptized, still he never was. He was the kind that looks at the acts of men and lets that influence him, instead of looking at the principles. A few minutes before his death, he seemed to want something and looked all around, then finally settled back and said, "It's too late now."

I thought he may have been wondering if he could yet be baptized. So in all of the fifty-two years, the Prophet's prophecy held good.

I heard Joseph say, "I have rolled this kingdom off of my shoulders on to the shoulders of the Twelve and they can carry out this work and build up His kingdom."

Said he: "I am tired, I have been mobbed, I have suffered so much. Some of the brethren think they can carry this work out better than I can, far better. I have asked the Lord to take me out of this world. I have stood all I can. I have to seal my testimony to this generation with my blood. I have to do it, for this work will never progress until I am gone, for the testimony is of no force until the testator is dead. People little know who I am when they talk about me, and they never will know until they see me weighed in the balance in the kingdom of God. Then they will know who I am, and see me as I am. I dare not tell them, and they do not know me."

These words were spoken with such power that they penetrated the heart of every soul that believed on him.

Diary of Mary Elizabeth Rollins Lightner; *Young Woman's Journal,* XVI (December, 1905), pp. 556-557; *The Utah Genealogical and Historical Magazine,* XVII (July, 1926), pp. 193-195; Remarks of Mary E. Lightner, April 14, 1905, at Brigham Young University.

Zebedee Coltrin

About ten days after I was confirmed a member of the Church by Lyman Wight, I first saw the Prophet Joseph at a prayer meeting at the home of Father Morley. He was then a beardless young man.

During the meeting, the powers of darkness were made manifest in a remarkable degree, causing some to make horrid noises, and others to throw themselves violently around. Joseph said this was a fulfillment of the scriptures where it says "That the man of sin should be revealed."

When Lyman Wight was ordained a high priest, Joseph told him he should see the heavens opened, and after he was ordained he stood on his feet and testified that he could see the heavens open and could see Jesus standing at the right hand of God.

Harvey Whitlock was ordained next with the same promise, but afterwards he seemed paralyzed. His mouth was in the shape of an italic *"O"* and his arm was stretched as if nailed to a cross. Joseph rebuked the power that had seized him, and it left him, and he testified, as Lyman had done, that he saw the heavens open, and Jesus standing on the right hand of the Father. This was the beginning in our day of ordinations to the office of high priest.

At Father Billings' home, a revelation was given where some of the men undertook to correct the language of a revelation as being ungrammatical. Joseph rebuked them and said that every word of that revelation had been dictated by Jesus Christ. There were twelve persons present, who were all the elders then belonging to the Church, with the exception of those in Missouri. Joseph thanked God that he had as many members as Jesus had in the beginning when he first organized the Church.

At Kirtland, we were called to the School of the Prophets. At one time Joseph was in the translating room, and myself and others were talking about the gift of tongues, when the gift of tongues fell upon me and I spoke under its influence. Joseph came into the room and said, "God bless you Brother Coltrin, that is the Spirit of God." He told me to continue, and the gift of tongues and of prophesying rested on the greater part of the brethren present, and we continued speaking in tongues and prophesying through that day and the greater part of the night.

At another time after fasting and prayer, Joseph told us that we should see the glory of God, and I saw a personage passing through the room as plainly as I see you now. Joseph asked us if we knew who it was, and answered himself: "That is Jesus our elder Brother, the Son of God."

Once after returning from a mission to Kirtland, I met Brother Joseph, who asked me if I did not wish to go with him to a conference at New Portage, Ohio. The party consisted of Presidents Joseph Smith, Sidney Rigdon, Oliver Cowdery and me. Next morning at New Portage, I noticed that Joseph seemed to have a far off look in his eyes, or was looking at a distance. Presently he stepped between Brother Cowdery and me, and taking us by the arm said, "Let's take a walk."

We went to a place where there was some beautiful grass, and grapevines and swamp birch interlaced. President Joseph Smith then said, "Let us pray."

We all three prayed in turn—Joseph, Oliver and me. Brother Joseph then said, "Now brethren, we will see some visions."

Joseph lay down on the ground on his back and stretched out his arms, and we laid on them. The heavens gradually opened, and we saw a golden throne, on a circular foundation, and on the throne sat a man and a woman, having white hair and clothed in white garments. Their heads were white as snow, and their faces shone with immortal youth. They were the two most beautiful and perfect specimens of mankind I ever saw. Joseph said, "They are our first parents, Adam and Eve."

Adam was a large broad shouldered man, and Eve, as a woman, was as large in proportion.

In the Kirtland Temple I have seen the power of God as it was on the day of Pentecost, and cloven tongues of fire have rested on the brethren, and they have spoken in other tongues as the Spirit gave them utterance. I saw the Lord high and lifted up. The angels of God rested upon the Temple and we heard their voices singing heavenly music.

> Address of Zebedee Coltrin at a meeting of high priests, Spanish Fork, Utah, February 5, 1878, High Priests' record of Spanish Fork Branch, from April 29, 1866 to December 1, 1898, Church Historian's Library, Salt Lake City, Utah; Minutes of the Salt Lake City School of the Prophets, October 10-11, 1883, Church Historian's Library, Salt Lake City, Utah.

Joel Hills Johnson

I attended the conference held in the town of Orange, in Ohio, in the month of October, 1831, where I first beheld the face of the Prophet and Seer, Joseph Smith. When I was introduced to him, he laid his hands upon my shoulders and said to me, "I suppose you think that I am great, green, lubberly fellow."

His expression was an exact representation of his person, being large and tall and not having a particle of beard about his face. I conversed very freely with him upon many subjects relative to his mission, and received much instruction, and was highly edified and blessed of the Lord during the conference, and returned home rejoicing.

> Diary of Joel Hills Johnson, Brigham Young University Library.

Luke S. Johnson

Soon after Joseph Smith moved to Ohio from the state of New York, my father, mother and Ezra Booth, a Methodist minister, went to Kirtland, to investigate Mormonism. For about two years my mother had been laboring under an attack of chronic rheumatism in the shoulder, so that she could not raise her hand to her head. The Prophet laid hands upon her, and she was healed immediately.

My father was satisfied in regard to the truth of Mormonism, and was baptized by Joseph Smith, Jr., in the winter of 1830-1. He furnished him and his family a home while he revised a portion of the Bible.

In the fall of 1831, while Joseph was yet at my father's place, a mob of forty or fifty came to his house. A few entered his room in the middle of the night, and Carnot Mason dragged Joseph out of bed by the hair of his head. He was then seized by as many as could get hold of him, and taken about forty rods from the house, stretched on a board, and tantalized in the most insulting and brutal manner. They tore off the few night clothes that he had on, for the purpose of emasculating him, and had Dr. Dennison there to perform the operation. But when the doctor saw the Prophet stripped and stretched on the plank, his heart failed him, and he refused to operate; the mob then scratched his body all over, saying, "Damn you, this is the way the Holy Ghost falls upon you."

In attempting to force open his jaws and pour a vial of some obnoxious drug into his mouth, they broke one of his front teeth.

The mob became divided, and did not succeed; but poured tar over him and then stuck feathers in it and left him, and went to an old brick yard to wash themselves and bury their filthy clothes. At this place a vial was dropped, the contents of which ran out and killed the grass. About the same time, part of the mob went to the house that Sidney Rigdon occupied and dragged him out, and besmeared him with tar and feathers. My father, hearing the outcry of the family, went to the door, but finding it held by someone on the outside, he called for his gun, when those who held the door left. He pursued and was knocked down; his collar bone was broken. He was taken back to the house, and hands laid upon him by David Whitmer, and he was immediately healed. A few minutes after this accident, we heard the voice of Joseph calling for a blanket. Some person handed him one, and he came in, the tar trickling down his face. His wife was very much alarmed, supposing it to be blood, until he came near enough to see that it was tar. My mother got some lard and rubbed it upon him to get the tar off, which they succeeded in removing.

Waste, who was the strongest man on the Western Reserve, had boasted that he could take Joseph out alone. At the time they were taking him out of the house, Waste had hold of one foot. Joseph drew up his leg and gave him a kick, which sent him sprawling in the street. He afterwards said that the Prophet was the most powerful man he ever had hold of in his life.

At a conference in Orange, Cuyahoga County, Ohio, I was ordained a high priest by Joseph Smith. At this conference, the eleven witnesses to the Book of Mormon, with uplifted hands, bore their solemn testimony to the truth of that book, as did also the Prophet Joseph.

A Baptist clergyman from the state of New York, who had been acquainted with the Prophet Joseph in his early life, called upon him and stayed all night. Joseph made the minister welcome and treated him hospitably and respectfully. But when breakfast was over next morning, he called Joseph a hypocrite, a liar, an impostor and a false prophet, and called upon him to repent. Joseph boxed his ears with both hands and, turning his face towards the door, kicked him into the street. The clergyman immediately went before a magistrate and swore out a writ against Joseph for assault and battery.

I saw the operation, and as an officer of the law I followed the minister into the Squire's office and demanded a writ for his apprehension, for provoking an assault. The clerk filled up the writ I called for first. The minister, fearing trouble, paid for his writ and withdrew without it, and made his way posthaste for Cuyahoga County. I followed him on horseback, making him travel pretty lively until he got a few rods over the line, where I overtook him and said, "Sir, you are lucky to have got over the line, and out of my jurisdiction, or I should have arrested you."

> Handwritten account by Luke Johnson, Church Historian's Library, Salt Lake City, Utah.

Lucy Diantha Morley Allen

When Joseph and family came to Kirtland they lived for a time with Isaac Morley, my father. He later built a small house for them on his farm. The twins were born there. My elder sister and I kept house for Emma Smith while she was ill.

Later, Joseph went to Hiram, about thirty miles distant, to organize a branch of the Church. While he was absent from

Kirtland, evil spirits molested the inexperienced Saints, and Bishop Partridge could not manage the people.

When the Prophet returned and learned the condition, he called a meeting in a little school house on Isaac Morley's farm.

Joseph arose and said in a powerful voice, "Let the spirits be made manifest."

Immediately, some began to sing, some to shout, some to cry, etc. When Joseph rebuked them, all became quiet except two, whom he rebuked separately.

We moved to Far West, where I married Joseph Allen, a member of Zion's Camp, who stood guard for the Prophet many times. I've seen the Prophet wrestle, and run, and jump, but have never seen him beaten. In all that he did he was manly and almost godlike. The only words that express his looks and actions are: "Surely he was a man of God."

Young Woman's Journal, XVII (December, 1906), pp. 537-538.

Lorenzo Snow

The first time I saw Joseph Smith I was seventeen years of age. It was in the fall of 1831. He was going to hold a meeting in Hiram, Portage County, Ohio, about four miles from my father's home. Having heard many stories about him, my curiosity was considerably aroused and I thought I would take advantage of this opportunity to see and hear him.

When we reached there, the people were already assembled in a small bowery. There were about two hundred or two hundred and fifty people present. The meeting had already commenced, and Joseph Smith was standing in the door of Father Johnson's house looking into the bowery and addressing the people.

I made a critical examination as to his appearance, his dress, and his manner as I heard him speak. He was only twenty-five years of age and was not, at that time, what would be called a fluent speaker. His remarks were confined principally to his own experiences, especially the visitation of the angel, giving a strong and powerful testimony in regard to these marvelous manifestations. He simply bore his testimony to what the Lord had manifested to him, to the dispensation of the gospel which had been committed to him, and to the authority that he possessed.

At first he seemed a little diffident and spoke in rather a low voice. But as he proceeded, he became very strong and powerful and seemed to affect the whole audience with the feeling that he was honest and sincere. It certainly influenced me in this way, and it made impressions upon me that remain until the present day.

As I looked upon him and listened, I thought to myself that a man bearing such a wonderful testimony as he did, and having such a countenance as he possessed, could hardly be a false prophet. He certainly could not have been deceived, it seemed to me. If he was a deceiver, he was deceiving the people knowingly; for when he testified that he had had a conversation with Jesus, the Son of God, and had talked with Him personally, as Moses talked with God upon Mount Sinai, and that he had also heard the voice of the Father, he was telling something that he either knew to be false or to be positively true.

When I went to Kirtland some three or four years later, I was on the street with my sister, Eliza, when Joseph Smith came along. He was in a great hurry, and stopped just long enough to be introduced and shake hands. He turned to my sister and said, "Eliza, bring your brother over to the house to dinner."

She was then boarding at his home and teaching his private school. As he left us I watched him just as far as I could see him, then I turned to my sister and said: "Joseph Smith is a most remarkable man; I want to get better acquainted with him. Perhaps, after all, there is something more to Joseph Smith and to Mormonism than I have ever dreamed."

Accordingly, the next time I saw the Prophet was at his own house in Kirtland. He sat down at one end of the table and I sat next to him. He seemed to have changed considerably in his appearance since I first saw him at Hiram, four and a half years before. He was very ready in conversation, and had apparently lost that reserve and diffident feeling that he seemed to have before. He was free and easy in his conversation with me, making me feel perfectly at home in his presence. In fact, I felt as free with him as if we had been special friends for years.

I became perfectly acquainted with the Prophet. I sat at his table frequently, and had many conversations with him. I listened to the teaching of the gospel and received these truths with an open heart. I was exceedingly anxious to know without doubt that Joseph Smith was a true prophet.

I heard the Prophet discourse upon the grandest of subjects. At times he was filled with the Holy Ghost, speaking as with the voice of an archangel and filled with the power of God. His whole person shone, and his face was lightened until it appeared as the whiteness of the driven snow. Finally, I was convinced of the truth sufficiently to want to be baptized, to get a knowledge for myself of the testimony that Joseph Smith had seen God. After my baptism, everything that I had thought about in a religion was changed. Every part of my system became convinced, through the power of the Holy Ghost, that God is my Father, that Jesus Christ is my Elder Brother, and that Joseph Smith is His prophet.

The Improvement Era, XL (February, 1937), pp. 82-84.

Brigham Young

In the Fall of 1832, Brothers Heber C. Kimball, Joseph Young and myself started for Kirtland to see the Prophet Joseph. We went to his father's house and learned that he was chopping wood. We immediately went to the woods, where we found the Prophet and two or three of his brothers.

Here my joy was full at the privilege of shaking the hand of the Prophet of God, and I received the sure testimony, by the spirit of prophecy, that he was all that any man could believe him to be, as a true prophet. He was happy to see us, and made us welcome.

In the evening a few of the brethren came in, and we conversed together upon the things of the kingdom. Joseph called upon me to pray. In my prayer I spoke in tongues, which gift I had previously received and exercised. As soon as we arose from our knees, the brethren flocked around him and asked his opinion concerning the gift of tongues that was upon me. He told them that it was the pure Adamic language. Some said to him they expected he would condemn the gift Brother Brigham had, but he said, "No, it is of God, and the time will come when Brother Brigham Young will preside over this Church."

The latter part of this conversation was in my absence.

When Zion's Camp went to Missouri in 1834, there were no apostles or seventies in the Church. After we returned, my brother, Joseph Young, and myself had been singing after preaching in a meeting. Brother Joseph Smith said, "Come, go down to my house with me."

We went and sang to him a long time, and talked with him. He then opened the subject of the Twelve and Seventies for the first time I ever thought of it. He said, "Brethren I am going to call out Twelves Apostles. We will get together by-and-by and select Twelve Apostles, and select a Quorum of Seventies from those who have been up to Zion, out of the camp boys."

In 1835, about the last of January, or in February, we held our meetings from day to day, and Brother Joseph called out Twelve Apostles at that time. He had a revelation when we were singing to him.

Those who were acquainted with him knew when the spirit of revelation was upon him, for his countenance wore an expression peculiar to himself while under that influence. He preached by the spirit of revelation, and taught in his council by it, and those who were acquainted with him could discover it at once, for at such times there was a peculiar clearness and transparency in his face.

When I saw Joseph Smith, he took heaven, figuratively speaking, and brought it down to earth; and he took the earth, brought it up, and opened up, in plainness and simplicity, the things of God. The excellency of the glory of the character of Brother Joseph Smith was that he could reduce heavenly things to the understanding of the finite. When he preached to the people—revealed the things of God, the will of God, the plan of salvation, the purposes of Jehovah, the relation in which we stand to Him and all the heavenly beings—he reduced his teachings to the capacity of every man, woman, and child, making them as plain as a well-defined pathway. This should have convinced every person that ever heard of him of his divine authority and power, for no other man was able to teach as he could, and no person can reveal the things of God, but by the revelations of Jesus Christ.

When you hear a man pour out eternal things, how well you feel! to what a nearness you seem to be brought with God! What a delight it was to hear Brother Joseph talk upon the great principles of eternity.

Who can say aught against Joseph Smith? I do not think that a man lives on the earth that knew him any better than I did, and I am bold to say that, Jesus Christ excepted, no better man ever lived or does live upon this earth. I feel like shouting Hallelujah all the time, when I think that I ever knew Joseph Smith, the Prophet.

> *Millennial Star,* XXI (July 11, 1863), p. 439; *Journal of Discourses,* III, p. 51; IV, p. 54; V, p. 332; VIII, p. 206; IX, pp. 89, 332.

Heber C. Kimball

In September, 1832, Brothers Brigham and Joseph Young and myself went to Kirtland, Ohio. We saw Brother Joseph Smith and had a glorious time, during which Brother Brigham spoke in tongues, this being the first time Joseph had heard the gift. The Prophet rose up and testified that it was from God. The gift then fell upon him, and he spoke in tongues himself.

At that time, our enemies were threatening destruction upon us, and we had to establish a guard night after night. For weeks we were not permitted to take off our clothes, and were obliged to lay with our firelocks in our arms to preserve Brother Joseph's life and our own.

Our brethren in Jackson County, Missouri, also suffered great persecution. In 1833, about twelve hundred were driven, plundered and robbed. Their houses were burned, and some of the brethren were killed. The next spring, Joseph gathered together as many of the brethren as he could, with what means they could spare, to go to Zion, to render assistance. We gathered clothing and other necessaries to carry to our brethren.

Our wagons were about full of baggage, etc. Consequently, we had to travel on foot. Every night before we went to bed, we united in our tent and offered up our prayers before the Lord for protection. This was done by all of the companies at the sound of the trumpet; and at the sound of the trumpet in the morning every man was upon his knees, each one in every tent being called upon in his turn to be mouth in prayer.

When we came to Belle Fountain, we discovered refractory feelings in Sylvester Smith. Finding quite a rebellious spirit in him, and to some extent in others, the Prophet declared that as a result they would meet with misfortune, difficulties and hindrances. *"And you will know it before you leave this place,"* he said, while exhorting them to humble themselves before the Lord and become united.

On the following morning when we arose, we found almost every horse in the camp so badly foundered that we could scarcely lead them a few rods to water. When Brother Joseph learned the fact, he explained that it was for a witness that God overruled and had his eye upon them. He then said that all those who would humble themselves before the Lord should know that the hand of God was in this misfortune, and their horses should be restored to health immediately. By twelve o'clock the same day the horses were as nimble as ever, with the exception of one of Sylvester Smith's, which soon afterwards died.

On the 21st of June, Colonel Sconce and two other leading men from Ray County, Missouri, came to see us. Said he, "I see that there is an Almighty power that protects you, for I started from Richmond, Ray County, with a company of armed men, having a fixed determination to destroy you, but was kept back by the storm and was not able to reach you."

When he came into camp, he was seized with such a trembling that he was obliged to sit down. When he desired to know our intentions, Brother Joseph arose and began to speak, and the power of God rested upon him. He gave a relation of the sufferings of our people in Jackson County, and what we had suffered from our enemies for our religion; and that he had come one thousand miles to assist our brethren, to bring them clothing, and to reinstate them upon their own lands; that we had no intention to molest or injure any people, but only to administer to the wants of our afflicted brethren. After he got through with his address, the power of which melted them into compassion, they arose and offered him their hands and said they would use their influence to allay the excitement which everywhere prevailed against us. They accordingly rode day and night to pacify the people.

Brother Joseph called the camp together and told us that in consequence of the disobedience of some who had not been willing to listen to his words, but had been rebellious, God had decreed that sickness should come upon us. "I am sorry," he said, "but I cannot help it."

When he spoke these things it pierced me like a dart, having a testimony that so it would be.

About twelve o'clock at night the destroyer came upon us and we began to hear the cries of those who were seized. Even those on guard fell, and we had to exert ourselves considerably to attend to the sick, for they were stricken down on every hand.

Brother Joseph, seeing the sufferings of his brethren, stepped forward to rebuke the destroyer, but was immediately seized with the disease, and I assisted him a short distance from the place, when it was with difficulty he could walk.

In the winter of 1834-5, I attended a theological school in Kirtland. On one occasion I was called upon to speak on the principle of faith. I referred to an original circumstance which took place in my family. My wife, when going out to make a call, gave my little daughter a charge not to touch the dishes which she had left on the table. But she broke a number by letting the table leaf fall. She then went out under an apple tree and prayed that her mother's heart would be softened, that she might not whip her. Her mother was very punctual to fulfil her promises. But when she returned she had no disposition to chastise the child. Afterwards the child told her mother that she had prayed to God that she might not whip her.

Joseph wept like a child on hearing this simple narrative and its application, and said it was well timed.

While I was in the Kirtland Temple, June 4, 1837, the Prophet Joseph came to me and said, "Brother Heber, the Spirit of the Lord has whispered to me, saying: 'Let my servant, Heber, go to England and proclaim my gospel, and open the door of salvation to that nation.' "

A short time previous to starting, I was laid prostrate on my bed from a stitch in my back, which suddenly seized me while chopping and drawing wood for my family. I could not stir a limb without calling out from the severeness of the pain. Joseph, hearing of it, came to see me, bringing Oliver Cowdery and Bishop Partridge with him. They prayed for and blessed me, Joseph being mouth, beseeching God to raise me up. The Prophet then took me by the right hand and said, "Brother Heber, I take you by the right hand in the name of Jesus Christ of Nazareth, and by virtue of the Holy Priesthood vested in me I command you in the name of Jesus Christ to arise, and be thou made whole."

I arose from my bed, put on my clothes and felt no more of the pain afterwards.

Woman's Exponent, IX (August 1, 1880), p. 39; (September 15, 1880), p. 59; (November 1, 1880), p. 82; (November 15, 1880), p. 90; X (May 15, 1881), p. 186.

Elizabeth Ann Whitney

Joseph Smith, with his wife, Emma, and a servant girl, came to Kirtland in a sleigh early in 1831; they drove up in front of my husband's store. Joseph jumped out and went in; he reached his hand across the counter to my husband and called him by name. My husband spoke, saying: "I could not call you by name as you have me."

He answered, "I am Joseph the Prophet; you have prayed me here, now what do you want of me?"

My husband brought them directly to our own house. I remarked to my husband that this was the fulfillment of the vision we had seen of a cloud as of glory resting upon our house. During the time they resided with us, many of the revelations were given which are recorded in the Doctrine and Covenants.

My husband traveled with Joseph the Prophet through many of the Eastern cities, bearing testimony and collecting means toward building a temple in Kirtland, and also toward purchasing lands in Missouri. During this journey the Prophet Joseph often prophesied of the destruction that ultimately would come upon the cities of the Eastern States, and especially New York, that in that city there would not be left a vestige of its grandeur. He said that wars would soon commence in our own land, which last has since transpired. He said to my husband, "If they reject us they shall have our testimony, for we will write it and leave it upon their doorsteps and window sills."

He prophesied of the desolation by fire, by storms, by pestilence and by earthquakes.

After their return from the East, they traveled together up to Missouri, and while upon this journey my husband had his ankle broken. Through the power of the administration of the gospel ordinance and faith, he was relieved from all pain.

My husband was ordained a bishop. We had always been in the habit of entertaining our friends and acquaintances generously and hospitably, but after we received the gospel we did not feel like using our means and time in a way that would only benefit those who had an abundance of this world's means. According to our Savior's pattern and agreeable to the Prophet Joseph's and our own ideas of true charity, we determined to make a Feast for the Poor, such as we knew could not return the same to us: the lame, the halt, the deaf, the blind, the aged and infirm.

This feast lasted three days, during which time all in the vicinity of Kirtland who would come were invited, and entertained as courteously and generously as if they had been able to extend hospitality instead of receiving it. The Prophet Joseph and his two counselors were present each day, talking, blessing, and comforting the poor, by words of encouragement and their most welcome presence.

The Prophet Joseph often referred to this particular Feast, during his lifetime, and testified of the great blessing he felt in associating with the meek and humble ones whom the Lord has said that "He delights to own and bless."

Great manifestations of power were witnessed in the Kirtland Temple. It seemed as though it was illuminated, and many and powerful were the manifestations to those who were humble and participated in the ordinances bestowed upon the faithful Saints in that house.

The first patriarchal blessing meeting over which Joseph Smith, Sen., presided was one of the most striking features of that particular period of time. In this meeting I received the gift of singing inspirationally, and the first song of Zion ever given in the pure language was sung by me then, and interpreted by Parley P. Pratt. It describes the manner in which the ancient patriarchs blessed their families, and gives some account of Adam-ondi-Ahman. The Prophet Joseph promised me that I should never lose this gift if I would be wise in using it; and his words have been verified.

About 1837, the Prophet Joseph called upon my husband to go to Far West to preside. My friends, who knew what delicate health I had, and how unaccustomed I was to any hardships, looked upon it as almost certain death for me to go. But I had unbounded faith in the promises of Joseph, that I should be able to go in safety, and my trust in God was firm and unshrinking.

Early in the Spring of 1840 we went to Nauvoo. Here we were all sick with ague, chills and fever, and were only just barely able to crawl around and wait upon each other. Under these trying circumstances my ninth child was born. Joseph, upon visiting us and seeing our change of circumstances, urged us at once to come and share his accommodations. We went to live in the Prophet Joseph's yard in a small cottage; we soon recruited in health, and the children became more like themselves.

One day while coming out of the house into the yard the remembrance of a prophecy Joseph Smith had made to me, while living in our house in Kirtland, flashed through my mind like an electric shock. It was this: that even as we had done by him, in opening our doors to him and his family when he was without a home, even so should we in the future be received by him into his house. We afterwards moved upstairs over the brick store.

During our residence in the brick store the Relief Society was organized, March 17, 1842, and I was chosen counselor to the President of the society, Mrs. Emma Smith. I was also set apart under the hand of Joseph Smith the Prophet to administer to the sick and comfort the sorrowful. Several other sisters were also set apart to administer in these holy ordinances.

The Relief Society then was small in numbers, but the Prophet foretold great things concerning the future of this organization, many of which I have lived to see fulfilled; but there are many things which yet remain to be fulfilled in the future.

President Joseph Smith had great faith in the sisters' labors, and ever sought to encourage them in the performance of the duties which pertained to these societies, which he said were not only for benevolent purposes and spiritual improvement, but were actually to save souls. And my testimony to my sisters is that I have seen many demonstrations of the power and blessing of God through the administration of the sisters.

Woman's Exponent, VII (September 1, 1878), p. 51; (October 1, 1878), p. 71; (November 1, 1878), p. 83; (November 15, 1878), p. 91; (December 15, 1878), p. 105; (February 15, 1879), p. 191.

Lydia Bailey Knight

One day in October, 1833, a wagonload of people stopped at the door of Freeman Nickerson's home. They had with them two strange men—Joseph Smith and Sidney Rigdon. Although so remote from the States, rumors of a new prophet and a "golden bible" had reached Mount Pleasant, Brunt County, Ontario, Canada, and had been wondered over and commented upon.

Freeman had been told that his parents had joined the new church, and he was rather disgusted with the news. His father was indeed full of the gospel he had embraced, and was so anxious for the eternal welfare of his sons in Canada that he had hitched up his carriage, gone on a visit to Kirtland, Ohio, and prevailed upon the Prophet Joseph Smith and Elder Sidney Rigdon to accompany him on a visit to his sons, Moses and Freeman, in Mount Pleasant.

"Well, Father," said Freeman, when told who the two strangers were, "I will welcome them for your sake. But I would just about as soon you had brought a nest of vipers and turned them loose upon us."

Moses and Freeman were wealthy merchants and men of influence in Mount Pleasant. On the evening of the arrival, after the bustle of welcome and a warm supper were over, everyone was too tired to talk, so all retired to rest.

Next morning many were the curious glances that I cast at this strange man who dared to call himself a prophet. I saw a tall, well-built form, with the carriage of an Apollo; brown hair, handsome blue eyes, which seemed to dive down to the innermost thoughts with their sharp, penetrating gaze; a striking countenance, and with manners at once majestic yet gentle, dignified yet exceedingly pleasant.

Elder Rigdon was a middle-aged man of medium height, stout and quite good-looking, but without the noble grandeur that was so distinguishing a mark of the Prophet.

The Elders were very wise. They said nothing about their views or doctrines, but waited patiently until some one should express an interest.

As evening drew near, Mr. Nickerson became anxious to hear something of the newcomer's faith.

"Oh," said he to his wife, "just let him talk; I'll silence him, if he undertakes to talk about the Bible. I guess I know as much about the scriptures as he does."

As soon as supper was over, he invited his visitors and family to go upstairs to the parlor, where he said they would have some talk. "Now Mr. Smith," he said, "I wish you and Mr. Rigdon to speak freely. Say what you wish and tell us what you believe. We will listen."

Turning to his wife, he whispered, "Now you'll see how I shall shut him up."

The Prophet commenced by relating the scenes of his early life. He told how the angel visited him, of his finding the plates and the translation of them, and gave a short account of the matter contained in the Book of Mormon.

As the speaker continued his wonderful narrative, I was listening and watching him intently. I saw his face become white and a shining glow seemed to beam from every feature.

As his story progressed, he would often allude to passages of scripture. Then Mr. Nickerson would speak up and endeavor to confound him. But the attempt was soon acknowledged even by himself to be futile.

The Prophet bore a faithful testimony that the priesthood was again restored to the earth, and that God and His Son had conferred upon him the keys of the Aaronic and Melchizedek Priesthoods. He stated that the last dispensation had come, and the words of Jesus were now in force: "Go ye into all the world and preach the gospel to every creature. He that believeth and is baptized shall be saved; but he that believeth not shall be damned."

Elder Rigdon spoke after the Prophet ceased. He related some of his early experiences, and told those present that he had received a testimony for himself of the truth of what Joseph had said. "God," said Elder Rigdon, "is no respecter of persons, but will give to all that ask of Him a knowledge of the things Joseph Smith has declared unto you, whether they are true or false, of God or of man."

After both men were through speaking, many questions were asked by all present, for information. The listeners were honest-hearted people, and when truth is told to such they are constrained to accept and believe.

"And is this, then," said Mr. Nickerson, "the curious religion the newspapers tell so much about? Why, if what you have said is not good sound sense, then I don't know what sense is."

A feeling of agreeable disappointment was felt by Mr. Nickerson and family, that these strange men were so different from the various representations of them.

Next day, notice was sent out that there would be public preaching in the Nickerson Brothers' new store-house. A large and attentive audience was present. Elder Sidney Rigdon spoke to the people with great clarity on the first principles of the gospel, and closed with a strong testimony to the truth of so-called "Mormonism."

The Prophet then arose and poured forth a golden stream of words, many of which were verily pearls without price, setting forth the restoration of the gospel and the great work that had commenced on the earth. With power he exhorted everyone who was present to seek for the truth of his and his companion's words from the source of all light, all truth, and all religion, and a knowledge of the truth of the same should surely follow.

Great was the excitement among the peaceful dwellers in Mount Pleasant.

The day following, a meeting was again held, and after it was over the Prophet baptized twelve persons, including myself, Mr. Nickerson and all of his household. I, who was always sober and full of reflection, received the glad message with trembling joy. I was filled with a bright, peaceful influence and was full of gratitude that God had spared me to hear and accept His glorious gospel. As a lonely girl, I had thought of death and its rest with a longing heart. But here was life—life eternal. After I was baptized, I was constrained to cry aloud, "Glory to God in the highest. Thanks be to His holy name that I have lived to see this day and be a partaker of this great blessing."

In the evening, the new members of the Church assembled in Mr. Nickerson's house for confirmation. God bestowed His Spirit very freely, and the Prophet gave much valuable instruction.

Two more persons came to the Prophet and requested baptism at the meeting the next day. It was attended to and a branch of the Church was organized. Freeman Nickerson was ordained as the presiding elder.

That evening (the seventh day the Prophet had been there) the family were all seated around the wide, old-fashioned fireplace in the parlor, listening to the Prophet's words and full of rejoicing.

"I would be so glad if someone who had been baptized could receive the gift of tongues as the ancient saints did and speak to us," said Moses Nickerson.

"If one of you will rise up and open your mouth it shall be filled, and you shall speak in tongues," replied the Prophet.

Everyone then turned, as by a common instinct, to me and said with one voice, "Sister Lydia, rise up."

And then the great glory of God was manifested to this weak but trusting girl. I was enveloped as with a flame, and, unable longer to retain my seat, I arose and my mouth was filled with the praises of God and His glory. The spirit of tongues was upon me, and I was clothed in a shining light, so bright that all present saw it with great distinctness above the light of the fire and the candles.

While the visitors were preparing for their departure, Joseph paced back and forth in the sitting room, in deep study. Finally he spoke up and said, "I have been pondering on Sister Lydia's lonely condition, and wondering why it is that she has passed through so much sorrow and affliction and is thus separated from all her relatives. I now understand it. The Lord suffered it even as He allowed Joseph of old to be afflicted, who was sold by his brethren as a slave into a far country, and through that became a savior to his father's house and country."

Turning to me, he continued, "Sister Lydia, great are your blessings. The Lord, your Savior, loves you and will overrule all your past sorrows and afflictions for good unto you. You shall yet be a Savior to your father's house."

Immediately after that the party set out, and left behind many warm and faithful friends. The good work continued, and numbers came forward and were baptized.

"Lydia Knight's History," pp. 14-23, in *Journal History,* October 19, 1833, Church Historian's Library, Salt Lake City, Utah.

Louisa Y. Littlefield

A prominent trait of Joseph Smith's character, which was perhaps more marked in his early career than was the case after public cares and responsibilities multiplied upon him from so many sources, was his natural fondness for children. In Kirtland, when wagon loads of grown people and children came in from the country to meeting, Joseph would make his way to as many of the wagons as he could and cordially shake the hand of each person. Every child and young babe in the company were especially noticed by him and tenderly taken by the hand, with his kind words and blessings. He loved innocence and purity, and he seemed to find it in the greatest perfection with the prattling child.

The Juvenile Instructor, XXVII, (January 1, 1892), p. 24.

Harrison Burgess

In September 1834, I started with my father's family for Kirtland, Ohio. On our journey we accidently met with the Prophet Joseph Smith in Springfield, Pennsylvania. I there saw him for the first time and heard him preach.

I was in a meeting in the upper part of the Kirtland Temple, with about a hundred of the high priests, seventies and elders. The Saints felt to shout "Hosannah," and the Spirit of God rested upon me in mighty power. I beheld the room lighted up with a peculiar light such as I had never seen before—soft and clear—and the room looked to me as though it had neither roof nor floor to the building. I beheld Joseph and Hyrum Smith, and Roger Orton, enveloped in the light.

Joseph exclaimed aloud, "I behold the Saviour, the Son of God."

Hyrum: "I behold the angels of heaven."

Brother Orton exclaimed, "I behold the chariots of Israel."

All those who were in the room felt this power of God to that degree that many prophesied, and the power of God was made manifest, the remembrance of which I shall never forget while I live upon the earth.

The winter of 1836, I attended a high school, together with Brother Joseph and Hyrum, and most of the heads of the Church. The evenings were mostly spent in meetings for instruction on the principles of our faith and religion.

Harrison Burgess file, Church Historian's Library, Salt Lake City, Utah.

George A. Smith

On the first day of May, 1833, my father and his family started for Kirtland. We were heartily welcomed by Cousin Joseph, the Prophet. It was the first time I had seen him.

I was selected by President Joseph Smith, Jr., to accompany him to Missouri as a member of Zion's Camp, being then in my seventeenth year. My father furnished me with a musket, generally known as a Green's Arm, a pair of pantaloons made of bed ticking, a pair of cotton shirts, a straw hat, cloth coat and vest, a blanket, a pair of new boots, and an extra shirt and pantaloons which my mother packed up in a knap sack made of apron check.

The first day we traveled twenty-seven miles and slept in the barn of Mr. Ford, in the town of Streetsborough. My new boots blistered my feet severely, and Joseph gave me a pair of his own, a great relief to me.

President Joseph selected me to be of his mess. I slept in his tent, lying directly at his feet, and heard many of his counsels and instructions to the officers of the camp. Zebedee Coltrin was cook. After my day's walk, it was my duty to bring water, make fires and wait upon the cook.

The camp was organized into tens. Joseph Smith was acknowledged Commander-in-Chief, and Lyman Wight was the Second Officer. Joseph selected two companies of ten men each as his life guard. I was appointed his armor bearer, and the rest of the journey I took care of and kept his arms loaded and in good order. They consisted of a brace of fine silver-mounted, brass-barrelled horse pistols which had been taken from a British officer in the War of 1812, a rifle, also a sword. I generally accompanied him wherever he went, carrying these arms with me. This gave me a better opportunity of hearing the counsels and instructions of the Prophet than I had had previously.

The Prophet Joseph took a full share of the fatigues of the journey, in addition to the care of providing for the camp, and presiding over it. He walked most of the time and had a full share of blistered, bloody, and sore feet, which was the natural result of walking twenty-five to forty miles a day in the hot season of the year.

But during the entire trip he never uttered a murmur or complained, while most of the men in the camp complained to him of sore toes, blistered feet, long drives, scanty supply of provisions, poor quality of bread, bad corn dodger, frowsy butter, strong honey, strong bacon and cheese. Joseph had to bear with us and tutor us like children. There were many in the camp, however, who never murmured, and who were always ready and willing to do as our leader desired.

During our noon meal, near the place where the town of Pittsfield stands, Joseph stood on a wagon while he made a speech to the camp. He said: "The Lord is displeased with us. Our murmuring and fault finding and want of humility has kindled the anger of the Lord against us. A severe scourge will come upon the camp, and many will die like sheep with rot, and we cannot help it. It must come. But by repentance and humility and the prayer of faith, the chastisement may be alleviated, but cannot be entirely turned away, for as the Lord lives, this camp must suffer a severe scourge for their wickedness and rebellion. I say it in the name of the Lord."

This prophecy struck me to the heart. I thought we should probably get into battle with the mob and some of us get killed. Little thought I that within four weeks a dozen of my brethren would be laid in the ground without coffins, by the fell hand of the plague. But it was so, and I learned ever after to heed the counsels of the Prophet, and not murmur at the dispensations of Providence.

When several men died, Joseph said to me, "If your work had been finished, you would have had to tumble into the ground without a coffin."

I told him it did seem as if it would have been better for me to have died than my Cousin Jesse, as he had a good education, and many other qualifications to benefit the Church which I did not possess.

The Prophet replied, "You do not know the mind of the Lord in these things."

On May 30, 1835, I was appointed on a mission to preach the gospel in the East. My circumstances were so reduced that I could not procure clothes to go in. Joseph and Hyrum gave me some gray cloth to make me a coat and a snuff-colored vest and pantaloons. Brother Charles Thompson cut them out, and Sister Eliza Brown made them up for me. Elder Brigham Young gave me a pair of shoes.

I called to see Cousin Joseph. He gave me a Book of Mormon, shook hands with me and said: "Preach short sermons, make short prayers, and deliver your sermons with a prayerful heart."

This advice I have always denominated my collegiate education.

Later, while on a mission to England, I went with Elder Richards to visit Elder Theodore Turley, in Stafford jail. We shook hands with him through a large iron grating, which forcibly brought to mind a circumstance which occurred when Elder Turley and myself parted with the Prophet Joseph Smith in Nauvoo. Joseph had blessed us and said: "Keep up good courage, boys. Some of you will look through grates before you come back!"

At the close of another conversation with the Prophet, he wrapped his arms around me and squeezed me to his bosom and said: "George A., I love you, as I do my own life."

I felt so affected I could hardly speak, but replied, "I hope, Brother Joseph, that my whole life and actions will ever prove my feelings and the depth of my affection towards you."

Zora Smith Jarvis, "George A. Smith Family," pp. 46, 49, 50, 51, 52, 64, 71, 86, 87.

Daniel Tyler

My first impression of the Prophet was that he was a meek, humble, sociable and very affable man, as a citizen, and one of the most intelligent of men, and a great prophet. My subsequent acquaintance with him more than confirmed my most favorable impressions in every particular. He was a great statesman, philosopher and philanthropist, logician, and last, but not least, the greatest prophet, seer and revelator that ever lived, save Jesus Christ only.

A short time prior to his arrival at my father's house, my mother, Elizabeth Comins Tyler, had a remarkable vision. Lest it might be attributed to the evil one, she related it to no person, except my father, Andrew Tyler, until the Prophet arrived, on his way to Canada, I think. She saw a man sitting upon a white cloud, clothed in white from head to foot. He had a peculiar cap, different from any she had ever seen, with a white robe, under-clothing, and moccasins. It was revealed to her that this person was Michael, the Archangel.

The Prophet informed her that she had had a true vision. He had seen the same angel several times. It was Michael, the Archangel.

During his short stay, he preached at my father's residence. He read the third chapter of John and explained much of it, making it so plain that a child could not help understanding it, if he paid attention. I recollect distinctly the substance of his remarks on the third verse—"Except a man be born again he cannot *see* the Kingdom of God."

The birth here spoken of, the Prophet said, was not the gift of the Holy Ghost, which was promised after baptism, but was an illumination of the mind by the Spirit which attended the preaching of the gospel by the elders of the Church. The people wondered why they had not previously understood the plain declarations of scripture as explained by the Elders, as they had read them hundreds of times. When they afterward read the Bible, it was a new book to them. This was being born again to *see* the kingdom of God. They were not in it, but could see it from the outside, which they could not do until the Spirit of the Lord took the veil from before their eyes. It resulted in a change of heart, but not of state; they were converted, but were yet in their sins. For instance, although Cornelius had seen an holy angel, and on the preaching of Peter the Holy Ghost was poured out upon him and his household, they were only born again to *see* the kingdom of God. Had they not been baptized afterwards they would not have been saved. (See Acts, 10th chapter.)

Explaining the fifth verse, he said, "To be born of water and of the Spirit means to be immersed in water for the remission of sins and receive the gift of the Holy Ghost thereafter."

The latter was given by the laying on of the hands of one having authority given him of God.

The joy that filled my juvenile soul no one can realize, except those who have had a foretaste of heavenly things. It seemed as though the gates of heaven were opened, and that a living stream flowed directly to the holy man of God. It also filled the house where we were sitting.

The Prophet Joseph Smith was a great reconciler of discrepancies in passages of scripture which were or seemed to be in conflict with each other. Until I heard the great expounder of Bible doctrines explain the following passages I concluded there must be a wrong translation in one verse or the other. One verse read: "I indeed baptize you with water unto repentance, but he that cometh after me is mightier than I, whose shoes I am not worthy to bear; he shall baptize you with the Holy Ghost and with fire."—Matthew iii, 11.

Here we have baptism with water, baptism with the Holy Ghost, and baptism with fire, three in number. The question naturally arises, how can this passage be reconciled with the following: "There is one . . . Lord, one faith, *one baptism.*"— Ephesians iv., 4-6.

Joseph Smith reconciled these two scriptural passages. He said: "There is but one baptism; it takes the baptism of water, of the Holy Ghost, and of fire to constitute one full baptism."

At the time William Smith and others rebelled against the Prophet at Kirtland, I attended a meeting "on the flats" where Joseph presided. Entering the school house a little before the meeting opened and gazing upon the man of God, I perceived sadness in his countenance and tears trickling down his cheeks. A few moments later a hymn was sung and he opened the meeting by prayer. Instead of facing the audience, however, he turned his back and bowed upon his knees, facing the wall. This, I suppose, was done to hide his sorrow and tears.

I had heard men and women pray—especially the former— from the most ignorant, both as to letters and intellect, to the most learned and eloquent. But never until then had I heard a man address his Maker as though He was present listening as a kind father would listen to the sorrows of a dutiful child. Joseph was at that time unlearned, but that prayer, which was to a considerable extent in behalf of those who accused him of having gone astray and fallen into sin, was that the Lord would forgive them and open their eyes that they might see aright. That prayer, I say, to my humble mind, partook of the learning and eloquence of heaven. There was no ostentation, no raising of the voice as by enthusiasm, but a plain conversational tone, as a man would address a present friend. It appeared to me as though, in case the veil were taken away, I could see the Lord standing facing His humblest of all servants I had ever seen. It was the crowning of all the prayers I ever heard.

When Joseph arose and addressed the congregation, he spoke of his many troubles, and said he often wondered why it was that he should have so much trouble in the house of his friends, and he wept as though his heart would break. Finally he said, "The Lord once told me that if at any time I got into deep trouble and could see no way out of it, if I would prophesy in His name, he would fulfill my words." He then said, "I prophesy in the name of the Lord that those who have thought I was in transgression shall have a testimony this night that I am clear and stand approved before the Lord."

The next Sabbath his brother William and several others made humble confessions before the public.

In a discourse in Far West, Missouri, Joseph Smith said, "Many of the elders of this Church will yet be martyred."

When the massacre took place at Brother Haun's mill, I felt in hopes that that was the fulfillment of the prediction. Subsequently, when he and his brother Hyrum were martyred in Carthage jail, I hoped that that would be the entire amount of those who would seal their testimony with their blood; but alas, several have since had their blood shed for the testimony of Jesus.

Everyone has probably heard or read of the terrible massacre at Haun's Mill. Brother Haun owned a grist mill which took his name. From two to four days prior to the massacre, the citizens of the little settlement assembled in a mass meeting and appointed Brother Haun a committee of one to go to the city for advice to know what to do. The whole country was under arms and excitement. The Apostle David W. Patten, with Brothers Gideon Carter and O'Banion, had already sealed their testimony with their blood.

Brother Haun repaired to the city, and as the Prophet was but a private citizen and minister of the gospel, in the legal sense, he first went to Captain John Killian, of the Caldwell County Militia, informed him of his appointment, and inquired what he and his brethren should do.

"Move into the city," was the prompt reply.

Brother Haun: "What! and leave the mill?"

Captain Killian: "Yes, and leave the mill."

Brother Haun: "What! to the mob?"

Captain Killian: "Yes, to the mob."

Brother Haun then left the Captain and went to Brother Joseph and asked him the same questions, and received the same answers.

"But Brother Joseph," responded the mill-owner, "we think we are strong enough to defend the mill and keep it in our own hands."

"Oh, well," replied he, "if you think you are strong enough to hold the mill you can do as you think best."

What more could he say? The Prophet's method had always been when his counsel was asked to give it freely and leave parties to receive or reject it. He could not, nor would not if he could, take away people's agency.

Brother Haun returned and reported that Brother Joseph's counsel was for them to stay and protect or hold the mill.

Soon after the Prophet's arrival in Nauvoo from Missouri prison, Brother Isaac Behunnin and I made him a visit at his residence. His persecutions were the topic of conversation. He repeated many false, inconsistent and contradictory statements made by apostates, frightened members of the Church and outsiders. He also told how most of the officials who would fain have taken his life when he was arrested turned in his favor on forming his acquaintance. He laid the burden of the blame on false brethren.

Those who testified against him through fear subsequently returned to the Church, some of them weeping and expressing a willingness that the Lord would remove them by death if that would remove the stain they had brought upon themselves by swearing falsely to shield themselves from the threatened death if they said aught in the Prophet's favor.

One scene was particularly touching, and showed the goodness of the Prophet's heart. A man who had stood high in the Church while in Far West was taken down with chills or ague and fever. While his mind as well as body was weak, disaffected parties soured his mind and persuaded him to leave the Saints and

go with them. He gave some testimony against the Prophet. While
the Saints were settling in Commerce, having recovered from his
illness, he removed from Missouri to Quincy, Illinois. There he
went to work chopping cordwood to obtain means to take himself
and family to Nauvoo, and provide a present to the injured man
of God if, peradventure, he would forgive and permit him to
return to the fold as a private member. He felt that there was
salvation nowhere else for him, and if that was denied him, all was
lost as far as he was concerned. He started with a sorrowful heart
and downcast look.

While on the way, the Lord told Brother Joseph he was
coming. The Prophet looked out of the window and saw him
coming up the street. As soon as he turned to open the gate,
the Prophet sprang up from his chair and ran and met him in the
yard, exclaiming, "O Brother, how glad I am to see you!"

He caught him around the neck, and both wept like children.

Suffice it to say that proper restitution was made, and the
fallen man again entered the Church by the door, received his
priesthood again, went upon several important missions, gathered
with the Saints in Zion, and died in full faith.

When the Prophet had ended telling how he had been treated,
Brother Behunnin remarked, "If I should leave this Church, I
would not do as those men have done. I would go to some remote
place where Mormonism had never been heard of, and no one
would ever learn that I knew anything about it."

The great Seer immediately replied: "Brother Behunnin, you
don't know what you would do. No doubt these men once thought
as you do. Before you joined this Church you stood on neutral
ground. When the gospel was preached, good and evil were set
before you. You could choose either or neither. There were two
opposite masters inviting you to serve them. When you joined
this Church you enlisted to serve God. When you did that, you
left the neutral ground, and you never can get back on to it.
Should you forsake the Master you enlisted to serve, it will be by
the instigation of the evil one, and you will follow his dictation
and be his servant."

On one occasion, when the Nauvoo Legion was on parade,
the heavens began to blacken as if to rain. The people began to
get uneasy, and some were preparing to leave. Joseph arose in
his saddle and shouted, "Attention, Legion! Don't break the ranks

—it is not going to rain. If it rains enough to wet through your shirt sleeves, the Lord never spoke by my mouth!"

It had already begun to sprinkle rain, but it ceased, the clouds passed away, and drill continued as long as it was desirable.

> *The Juvenile Instructor,* XXVII (February 1, 1892), pp. 93-95; (February 15, 1892), pp. 127-128; (August 15, 1892), pp. 491-492; XXVIII (May 15, 1893), p. 332.

John M. Chidester

My first recollection of seeing the Prophet Joseph Smith was at a place about sixty or seventy miles from Kirtland, where two companies of Zion's Camp met. My impression on beholding the Prophet and shaking hands with him was that I stood face to face with the greatest man on earth.

Zion's Camp, in passing through the state of Indiana, had to cross very bad swamps. Consequently we had to attach ropes to the wagons to help them through, and the Prophet was the first man at the rope in his bare feet. This was characteristic of him in all times of difficulty.

We continued our journey until we reached the Wakandaw River, having traveled twenty-five miles without resting or eating. We were compelled to ferry this stream; and we found on the opposite side of it a most desirable place to camp, which was a source of satisfaction to the now weary and hungry men. On reaching this place, the Prophet announced to the Camp that he felt impressed to travel on; and taking the lead, he invited the brethren to follow him.

This caused a split in the camp. Lyman Wight and others at first refused to follow the Prophet, but finally came up. The sequel showed that the Prophet was inspired to move on a distance of some seven miles. It was reported to us afterwards that about eight miles below where we crossed the river a body of men was organized to come upon us that night.

When we reached Salt Creek, Missouri, Allred settlement had prepared a place in which to hold meeting. Joseph and Hyrum Smith and others were on the stand at the meeting when some strangers came in and were very anxious to find out which of them were Joseph and Hyrum, as they had pledged themselves to shoot them on sight. But the Prophet and his brother slipped away unobserved, being impressed that there was danger of their lives being taken.

The Juvenile Instructor, XXVII, (March 1, 1892), p. 151.

Eliza R. Snow

In the autumn of 1829, I heard of Joseph Smith as a prophet to whom the Lord was speaking from the heavens; and that a sacred record containing a history of the origin of the aborigines of America was unearthed. A prophet of God, the voice of God revealing to man as in former dispensations—this was what my soul had hungered for. But could it possibly be true? I considered it a hoax—too good to be true.

In the winter of 1830 and 31, Joseph Smith called at my father's home. As he sat warming himself, I scrutinized his face as closely as I could without attracting his attention, and decided that his was an honest face. My adopted motto, *"Prove all things and hold fast to that which is good,"* prompted me to investigation, as incredulous as I was.

On the 5th of April, 1835, I was baptized by a "Mormon" Elder.

In the Spring of 1836, I taught a select school for young ladies, and boarded with the Prophet's family.

Early in 1837, I again resided in the family of Joseph Smith, taught his family school, and had ample opportunity to mark his "daily walk and conversation" as a prophet of God. The more I became acquainted with him the more I appreciated him as such. His lips ever flowed with instruction and kindness; and, although very forgiving, indulgent, and affectionate in his temperament, when his godlike intuition suggested that the welfare of his brethren or the interests of the kingdom of God demanded it, no fear of censure, no love of approbation, could prevent his severe and cutting rebuke.

Though his expansive mind grasped the great plan of salvation and solved the mystic problem of man's destiny—though he had in his possession keys that unlocked the past and the future with its succession of eternities, in his devotion he was as humble as a little child. As a philanthropist, his soul was broad as eternity. In the cause of truth and righteousness—in all that would benefit his fellow man, his integrity was as firm as the pillars of heaven. He knew that God had called him to the work, and all the powers of earth and hell combined failed either to deter or divert him from his purpose. With the help of God and his brethren, he laid the foundation of the greatest work ever established by man— a work extending not only to all the living, and to all the generations to come, but also to the dead.

He boldly and bravely confronted the false traditions, superstitions, religious bigotry and ignorance of the world—proved himself true to every heaven-revealed principle—true to his brethren and true to God, then sealed his testimony with his blood.

In Nauvoo I first understood that the practice of plural marriage was to be introduced into the Church. The subject was very repugnant to my feelings—so directly was it in opposition to any educated prepossessions that it seemed as though all the prejudices of my ancestors for generations past congregated around me. But when I reflected that I was living in the Dispensation of the Fulness of Times, embracing all other dispensations, surely plural marriage must necessarily be included, and I consoled myself with the idea that it was far in the distance, and beyond the period of my mortal existence. It was not long, however, before the announcement reached me that the "set time" had come—that God had commanded His servants to establish the order, by taking additional wives. I was sealed to the Prophet Joseph Smith for time and eternity.

While my brother Lorenzo Snow was absent on his first mission to Europe, these changes had taken place with me, of which I supposed him to be entirely ignorant. Not knowing how my brother would receive it, I did not feel at liberty, and did not wish to assume the responsibility of instructing him in the principle of plural marriage, and either maintained silence, or, to his indirect questioning, gave evasive answers, until I was forced, by his cool and distant manner, to feel that he was growing jealous of my sisterly confidence—that I could not confide in his brotherly integrity. I could not endure this—something must be done. I informed my husband of the situation, and requested him to open the subject to my brother. A favorable opportunity soon presented, and, seated together on the lone bank of the Mississippi River, they had a most interesting conversation. The Prophet afterwards told me that he found that my brother's mind had been previously enlightened on the subject in question, and was ready to receive whatever the spirit of revelation from God should impart. That Comforter which Jesus said should *"lead into all truth"* had penetrated his understanding, and while in England had given him an intimation of what at that time was, to many, *a secret.* This was the result of living near the Lord, and holding communion with Him.

It was at the private interview referred to above that the Prophet Joseph unbosomed his heart and described the trying mental ordeal he experienced in overcoming the repugnance of his feelings, the natural result of the force of education and social custom, relative to the introduction of plural marriage. He knew the voice of God—he knew the commandment of the Almighty to him was to go forward, to set the example, and establish celestial plural marriage. He knew that he had not only his own prejudices and prepossessions to combat and to overcome, but those of the whole Christian world; but God, who is above all, had given the commandment, and He must be obeyed. Yet the Prophet hesitated and deferred from time to time, until an angel of God stood by him with a drawn sword, and told him that, unless he moved forward and established plural marriage, his priesthood would be taken from him and he should be destroyed! This testimony he not only bore to my brother, but also to others—a testimony that cannot be gainsayed.

> Eliza R. Snow, "Life Sketch," handwritten manuscript, Church Historian's Library, Salt Lake City, Utah; *Woman's Exponent,* II (January 1, 1874), p. 117; *Biography and Family Record of Lorenzo Snow* (Salt Lake City, 1888), pp. 68-70.

Parley P. Pratt

Joseph Smith returned from Pennsylvania to his father's residence in Manchester, near Palmyra, in the fall of 1830, and here I had the pleasure of seeing him for the first time. He received me with a hearty welcome, and with that frank and kind manner so universal with him in after years.

President Joseph Smith was in person tall and well built, strong and active; of light complexion, light hair, blue eyes, very little beard, and of an expression peculiar to himself, on which the eye naturally rested with interest, and was never weary of beholding. His countenance was ever mild, affable, beaming with intelligence and benevolence; mingled with a look of interest and an unconscious smile, or cheerfulness, and entirely free from all restraint or affectation of gravity; and there was something connected with the serene and steady penetrating glance of his eye, as if he would penetrate the deepest abyss of the human heart, gaze into eternity, penetrate the heavens, and comprehend all worlds.

He possessed a noble boldness and independence of character; his manner was easy and familiar; his rebuke terrible as the lion; his benevolence unbounded as the ocean; his intelligence universal, and his language abounding in original eloquence peculiar to himself—not polished—not studied—not smoothed and softened by education and refined by art; but flowing forth in its own native simplicity, and profusely abounding in variety of subject and manner. He interested and edified, while, at the same time, he amused and entertained his audience; and none listened to him that were ever weary with his discourse. I have ever known him to retain a congregation of willing and anxious listeners for many hours together, in the midst of cold or sunshine, rain or wind, while they were laughing at one moment and weeping the next. Even his most bitter enemies were generally overcome, if he could once get their ears.

In short, in him the characters of a Daniel and a Cyrus were wonderfully blended. The gifts, wisdom and devotion of a Daniel were united with a boldness, courage, temperance, perseverance and generosity of a Cyrus. His works will live to endless ages, and unnumbered millions yet unborn will mention his name with honor, as a noble instrument in the hands of God, who, during his short and youthful career, laid the foundation of that kingdom spoken of by Daniel, the prophet, which should break in pieces all other kingdoms and stand forever.

One of those tedious nights while prisoners in Richmond, Missouri, we had lain as if in sleep till the hour of midnight had passed, and our ears and hearts had been pained, while we had listened for hours to the obscene jests, the horrid oaths, the dreadful blasphemies and filthy language of our guards, as they recounted to each other their deeds of rapine, murder, robbery, etc., which they had committed among the "Mormons" while at Far West and vicinity. They even boasted of defiling by force wives, daughters and virgins, and of shooting or dashing out the brains of men, women and children.

I had listened till I became so disgusted, shocked, horrified, and so filled with the spirit of indignant justice that I could scarcely refrain from rising upon my feet and rebuking the guards; but had said nothing to Joseph, or any one else, although I lay next to him and knew he was awake. On a sudden he arose to his feet, and spoke in a voice of thunder, or as the roaring lion, uttering, as near as I can recollect, the following words:

"SILENCE, ye fiends of the infernal pit. In the name of Jesus Christ I rebuke you, and command you to be still; I will not live another minute and hear such language. Cease such talk, or you or I die THIS INSTANT!"

He ceased to speak. He stood erect in terrible majesty. Chained, and without a weapon; calm, unruffled and dignified as an angel, he looked upon the quailing guards, whose weapons were lowered or dropped to the ground; whose knees smote together, and who shrinking into a corner, or crouching at his feet, begged his pardon, and remained quiet till a change of guards.

I have seen the ministers of justice, clothed in magisterial robes and criminals arraigned before them, while life was suspended on a breath, in the courts of England; I have witnessed a Congress in solemn session to give laws to nations; I have tried to conceive of kings, of royal courts, of thrones and crowns; and of emperors assembled to decide the fate of kingdoms; but dignity and majesty have I seen but once, as it stood in chains, at midnight, in a dungeon in an obscure village of Missouri.

Autobiography of Parley P. Pratt, pp. 45-46, 209, 210-211.

Oliver B. Huntington

Soon after Joseph settled in Kirtland, members of the Church began to gather to that place. The name of Joseph Smith and his power with God aroused everybody either for good or for bad. Mrs. John Johnson, who lived at the town of Hiram, forty miles distant from Kirtland, heard of the wonderful man that could receive revelations from God, heal the sick and see angels. She had a stiff arm that she wanted healed and made useful like the other, so she induced her husband to take a journey to Kirtland to see the Prophet.

Joseph asked her if she believed that God could make him instrumental in healing her arm which had been stiff a long time.

She answered that she believed her arm could be healed.

The Prophet only remarked that he would visit her the next day.

The next day Joseph came to Bishop Newell K. Whitney's home where Mr. Johnson and his wife were staying. There were a Campbellite doctor and a Methodist preacher in the room. He took Mrs. Johnson by the hand and without sitting down or standing on ceremonies, and after a very short mental prayer, pronounced her arm whole in the name of Jesus Christ. He left the house immediately.

When he was gone, the preacher asked if her arm was well. She immediately stretched out her arm straight, remarking at the same time, "It's as well as the other."

The next day the preacher came to the house of Philo Dibble, who lived a little out of town, and related what he saw, and then tried to account for it upon natural principles, saying that when Joseph pronounced that arm whole in the name of Jesus Christ, it frightened her so badly that it threw her in a heavy perspiration and relaxed the cords, and the result was that she could straighten her arm.

When the knowledge of the miracle was had among the Saints, some of the brethren asked the Prophet if the arm would remain sound. Joseph answered, "The arm is as sound as the other and is as liable to accidents or to be hurt as the other."

Joseph Smith said that some people entirely denounce the principle of self-aggrandizement as wrong. "It is a correct principle," he said, "and may be indulged upon only one rule or plan —and that is to elevate, benefit and bless others first. If you will elevate others, the very work itself will exalt you. Upon no other plan can a man justly and permanently aggrandize himself."

At another time he was speaking of works that tend to save and elevate the human family. He spoke earnestly of improving one's time in this life. Said he, "A man can do as much in this life in one year as he can do in ten years in the spirit world without the body."

On another occasion, he was asked the meaning of the words of the Savior: "Make to yourselves friends of the mammon of unrighteousness, that when ye fail they may receive you into everlasting habitations."

His answer was this, as near as I can get the words, but the meaning I give, for I marveled when I heard him say: "Every man will fail sometime. Be charitable and liberal with your substance, for it is only a secondary consideration—the use you make of it is the primary consideration. You may do good to some one who is down today and who will rise and be on top of the wheel when you are down, for every man will fail sometime."

He said that he would compare our existence to a wheel that was forever revolving. We are on the outside of the wheel, and sometimes we are on the top and sometimes on the down side.

I heard the Prophet reply to the question: "Will there ever be any more offering of sheep and heifers and bullocks upon altars, as used to be required of Israel?"

He said: "Yes, there will; for there were never any rites, ordinances or laws in the priesthood of any gospel dispensation upon this earth but what will have to be finished and perfected in this the last dispensation of time—the dispensation of all dispensations."

Another question was, "If a person does a good act, a kindness, or perhaps a charitable act, to a very bad, wicked man, will that person receive a reward of good for that act as if he had done it to a good man?"

Joseph said, "Yes, he will receive a reward for that good act to a wicked man, as surely as if he did it to a good man, but not as quick."

These were the words of Joseph Smith, for they were so strange to me that I could never forget my thought: "It's strange that the reward should come quicker if done to a good man."

I heard him say that he hoped the spirit of invention and improvement would rest upon the Saints, as it was upon the Gentiles, for unless it did there would many useful and important inventions be lost to the world when the great destruction of nations comes. It would then probably take hundreds of years to reproduce them again among men; yes, and perhaps thousands of years before they would get back upon the earth.

When the Saints were driven from the state of Missouri it was a very surprising circumstance that we could not undertsand. We naturally asked ourselves the question, "Where can we find another Holy land? How or when shall we get back to the consecrated spot for the New Jerusalem, that is to be built?"

Our only hope was that as God had given us a prophet he would certainly tell us how to manage and where to go, or what to do.

Oh! what confidence we had in that man! What comfort we derived through our faith in God and Joseph Smith. How little we knew of the great future, and for that one thing I feel very thankful!

Joseph finally led us to Nauvoo. Under his all-inspiring words, we quickly resolved, "We will stay here as long as Joseph wants us to—he knows what is best."

In a few months there was quite a town built up out of as near nothing as God ever made anything.

My father was living in a good hewed log house in 1840, when one morning as the family all sat at breakfast old Father Joseph Smith, the father of the Prophet, came and sat down by the fireplace, after declining to take breakfast with us. There he sat some little time in silence, looking steadily in the fire. At length he observed that we had been driven from Missouri to this place. He then asked this question, "And how long, Brother Huntington, do you think we will stay here?"

As he asked this question, I noticed a strange, good-natured expression creep over his whole being—an air of mysterious joy.

Father answered, after a moment's hesitation, "Well, Father Smith, I can't begin to imagine."

"We will just stay here seven years," he answered. "The Lord has told Joseph so—just seven years. Now this is not to be made public; I would not like to have this word go any further."

The Patriarch leaned and relied upon his son Joseph in all spiritual matters as much as boys generally do upon their parents for temporalities.

There were two or three minutes of perfect silence. Then the old gentleman with more apparent secret joy and caution in his countenance said, "And where do you think we will go to when we leave here, Brother Huntington?"

Father did not pretend to guess—unless we went back to Jackson County.

"No," said the old Patriarch, his whole being seeming to be alive with animation. "The Lord has told Joseph that when we leave here we will go into the Rocky Mountains, right into the midst of the Lamanites."

This information filled our hearts with unspeakable joy, for we knew that the Book of Mormon and this gospel had been brought to light more for the remnants of Jacob upon this continent than for the Gentiles.

Father Smith again enjoined upon us profound secrecy in this matter, and I don't think it was ever uttered by one of Father Huntington's family.

The history of Nauvoo shows that we located in Nauvoo in 1839 and left it in 1846.

Joseph Smith once undertook to plead law. This is impressed upon my mind, never to be blotted out or dimmed by time, not so much for the law he quoted, but for the great prophecy he uttered and the divine appearance of the man while he spoke the word of the Lord.

Soon after we settled in Commerce, three of our brethren were kidnapped by Missourians, taken to Missouri and starved and whipped until they were hardly able to run at all. But they managed to get away and returned home.

One of the men who did the wicked, cruel deed was found, years after, in disguise, parading the streets of Nauvoo.

The kidnapper was brought before an alderman for trial, and Joseph acted as prosecuting attorney. When he had just started to set forth the crime that the defendant was arraigned for, he suddenly left the law and declared the word of God with regard to the state of Missouri and its inhabitants. He told what the Saints had suffered at the hands of Missouri and the injustice and cruelty of their sufferings. He went on to tell what Missouri should be called to endure in order to pay the penalty for wrongs inflicted, and for the blood of the Saints they had shed.

A portion of the words of the prophecy I will quote verbatim: "She shall drink out of the same cup, the same bitter dregs we have drunk, poured out, out, out! and that by the hand of the enemy—a race meaner than themselves."

All the time he was delivering the word of the Lord, his face shone as if there was a light within him, and his flesh was translucent. The time thus occupied was considerable, for he pronounced two other very remarkable prophecies.

When he had done prophesying, he stopped speaking entirely, while he wiped a flood of perspiration from his face and gave vent to his pent-up breath with a long blow, kind of a half-whistle.

After a minute or two he remarked: "Well, where that meaner race is coming from God only knows. It is not the Negroes, for they don't know enough, and are gentlemen by the side of their masters. It is not the Indians, for they are chosen people of God and a noble race of men. But as sure as God ever spoke by me that shall come to pass."

I have lived to see that prophecy literally fulfilled in the Rebellion, when every family in that part of that state that the Saints used to occupy was killed or compelled to leave their homes by the Bushwhackers or Guerillas under Quantrell—a generation of vipers raised up mostly after the prophecy was uttered.

The place or country where Noah's ark was built was designated in my hearing by the Prophet Joseph Smith as being in or near South Carolina.

He advised the elders all to keep daily journals. "For," said he, "your journals will be sought after as history and scripture. That is the way the New Testament came, what we have of it, though much of the matter there was written by the apostles from their memory of what had been done, because they were not prompt in keeping daily journals."

I have kept a journal as he directed.

On one occasion while the Prophet was waiting for his boots to be repaired by my brother Dimick in Nauvoo, he indulged in recounting personal services rendered him by Dimick. He exhibited his gratitude and greatness of soul in this way. He said, "Now, Dimick, in return for such acts, you may ask of me what you will and it shall be given you, even if it be to the half of my kingdom."

Dimick told it to me, and said that in thinking what he should ask for, decided he would not ask for anything that would impoverish Joseph. Nor would he ask for worldly honors or goods, but made this request: "Brother Joseph, I desire that where you and your father's house are (having reference to eternity), there I and my father's house may be also."

Joseph sat in meditation but a moment, and then said, "Dimick, in the name of Jesus Christ, it shall be even as you ask."

On another occasion, when Joseph was sitting in Dimick's shop waiting for something, he got on a wonderful strain of relating the history of the world in the past, recounting many strange things I never had read or heard of before. When he came to the present times, he did not stop, but went on and related the principal events that will transpire in the history of the world down to the time when the angel will declare that time shall be no longer.

Although I did not see the events with my natural eyes, the vividness of their appearance to my mind was next to reality. He declared the succession of events with as great clearness as one of us can repeat the events of our past lives.

After the Prophet had crossed the Mississippi River to go west before his martyrdom, he went to the house of Joseph Hancock and told him where he was going, and that he wanted him to go along as a hunter to kill game for the company. Brother Hancock was a great hunter. Brother Hancock's horse was on the open prairie, and could not be caught only by several men on horseback driving it into a yard.

He replied to Joseph that he would go if he could catch his horse.

The Prophet said that if he would go right after the horse, he could catch it. Brother Hancock went out immediately and had no trouble in walking up to the horse on the broad prairie, the first and only time he ever did.

The Young Woman's Journal, II, (December, 1890), pp. 124-125; (February, 1891), pp. 225-226; (April, 1891), pp. 314-315; (May, 1891), p. 366; (July, 1891), pp. 466-468; IV (March, 1893), pp. 274-275; (April, 1893) pp. 320-321; (June, 1893), pp. 424-425.

Philo Dibble

I saw Joseph Smith the Prophet when he first came to Kirtland. There was a branch of the Church raised up in Kirtland before he came, and at the time he arrived a variety of false spirits were manifested, such as caused jumping, shouting, falling down, etc. Joseph said, as soon as he came, "God has sent me here, and the devil must leave here, or I will."

Those delusive spirits were not seen nor heard any more at that time.

On invitation of Father Johnson, of Hiram, Ohio, Joseph removed his family to his home, to translate the New Testament.

At this time Sidney Rigdon was left to preside at Kirtland and frequently preached to us. Upon one occasion he said the keys of the kingdom were taken from us. On hearing this, many of his hearers wept, and when some one undertook to dismiss the meeting by prayer he said praying would do them no good, and the meeting broke up in confusion.

Brother Hyrum came to my house the next morning and told me all about it, and said it was false, and that the keys of the kingdom were still with us. He wanted my carriage and horses to go to the town of Hiram and bring Joseph. The word went abroad among the people immediately that Sidney was going to expose "Mormonism."

Joseph came up to Kirtland a few days afterwards and held a meeting in a large barn. Nearly all the inhabitants of Kirtland turned out to hear him. The barn was filled with people, and others, unable to get inside, stood around the door as far as they could hear.

Joseph arose in our midst and spoke in mighty power, saying: "I can contend with wicked men and devils—yes, with angels. No power can pluck those keys from me, except the power that gave them to me; that was Peter, James and John. But for what Sidney has done, the devil shall handle him as one man handles another."

Thomas B. Marsh's wife went from the meeting and told Sidney what Joseph had said, and he replied: "Is it possible that I have been so deceived? But if Joseph says so, it is so."

About three weeks after this, Sidney was lying on his bed alone. An unseen power lifted him from his bed, threw him across the room, and tossed him from one side of the room to the other. The noise being heard in the adjoining room, his family went in to see what was the matter, and found him going from one side of the room to the other, from the effects of which Sidney was laid up for five or six weeks. Thus was Joseph's prediction in regard to him verified.

The vision of the three degrees of glory which is recorded in the Doctrine and Covenants was given at the house of "Father

Johnson," in Hiram, Ohio, and during the time that Joseph and Sidney were in the Spirit and saw the heavens open there were other men in the room, perhaps twelve, among whom I was one during a part of the time—probably two-thirds of the time. I saw the glory and felt the power, but did not see the vision.

Joseph wore black clothes, but at this time seemed to be dressed in an element of glorious white, and his face shone as if it were transparent, but I did not see the same glory attending Sidney.

The events and conversation, while they were seeing what is written (and many things were seen and related that are not written) I will relate as minutely as is necessary.

Joseph would, at intervals, say: "What do I see?" as one might say while looking out the window and beholding what all in the room could not see. Then he would relate what he had seen or what he was looking at.

Then Sidney replied, "I see the same."

Presently Sidney would say, "What do I see?" and would repeat what he had seen or was seeing.

And Joseph would reply, "I see the same."

This manner of conversation was repeated at short intervals to the end of the vision, and during the whole time not a word was spoken by any other person. Not a sound or motion was made by anyone but Joseph and Sidney, and it seemed to me that they never moved a joint or limb during the time I was there, which I think was over an hour, and to the end of the vision.

Joseph sat firmly and calmly all the time in the midst of a magnificent glory, but Sidney sat limp and pale, apparently as limber as a rag, observing which, Joseph remarked, smilingly, "Sidney is not used to it as I am."

I was with Joseph the morning after he was tarred and feathered by a mob in the town of Hiram, Ohio. After he had washed and dressed in clean clothes, I heard him say to Sidney Rigdon, who was also tarred and feathered, "Now, Sidney, we are ready to go on that mission."

He had reference to a command of God to go to Jackson County, Missouri, and which they had deferred to comply with until they should have accomplished some work which they had planned, but never did accomplish.

On one occasion Joseph was preaching in Kirtland, some time in the fall of 1833. Quite a number of persons were present who did not belong to the church. One man, more bitter and skeptical than others, made note with pencil and paper of a prophecy uttered on that occasion, wherein Joseph said, "Forty days shall not pass, and the stars shall fall from heaven."

Such an event would certainly be very unusual and improbable to the natural man, and the skeptic wrote the words as a sure evidence to prove Joseph to be a false prophet.

On the thirty-ninth day after the utterance of that prophecy, a man and brother in the Church by the name of Joseph Hancock, and another brother, were out hunting game and got lost. They wandered about until night, when they found themselves at the house of this unbeliever, who exultingly produced this note of Joseph Smith's prophecy and asked Brother Hancock what he thought of his prophet now that thirty-nine days had passed and the prophecy was not fulfilled.

The matter weighed upon the mind of Brother Hancock, who watched that night, and it proved to be the historical one, known in all the world as "the night of the falling of the stars."

He stayed that night at the house of the skeptical unbeliever, as it was too far from home to return by night. In the midst of the falling of the stars, he went to the door of his host and called him out to witness what he had thought impossible and the most improbable thing that could happen, especially as that was the last night in which Joseph Smith could be saved from the condemnation of being "a false prophet."

The whole heavens were lit up with the falling meteors, and the countenance of the new spectator was plainly seen and closely watched by Brother Hancock, who said that he turned pale as death and spoke not a word.

I was in Clay County, Missouri, when Zion's camp came up. I met them on Fishing River. There the power of the Lord was manifested by His sending a thunder storm, which raised Fishing River ten feet higher than it was ever known to rise before. I saw the cloud coming up in the west when I was ten miles from Fishing River in the middle of the afternoon. As it moved on eastwardly it increased in size and in blackness, and when it got over the camp it stopped. In the night, the rain and hail poured down in torrents, and the lightning flashed from the cloud continuously for three hours.

Just before night, two men came into camp and asked where Mr. Smith was. Joseph said, "I am the man." They then advised him to disband his camp, "for," said they, "the mobs are gathering, and there won't be one of you left tomorrow morning!"

Joseph smiled, and said, "I guess not."

Seeing that Joseph did not believe what they came to tell him, they went off vexed.

We learned afterwards that the hail was so heavy on the mob that they were forced to seek shelter, and the leader of them swore he would never go against the "Mormons" again.

While at Far West, Missouri, an election was held to elect an assessor. Isaac Higbee, myself and a Missourian were the candidates. The brethren held a caucus meeting and advised one of us to withdraw our name lest the Missourian might gain the election, and proposed that Higbee and I cast lots for it. Two tickets were put into a hat for us to draw from. There was a large crowd gathered around and Joseph Smith was among them. He said, "I am going to prophesy that Philo will get it."

Sure enough I drew it.

While celebrating the 4th of July, in 1838, at Far West, there came up a thunder shower, and the lightning struck our liberty pole and shivered it to pieces. Joseph walked around on the splinters and said: "As the pole was splintered, so shall the nations of the earth be!"

When the trouble with the mob commenced, Colonel G. W. Robinson took about one-half of the force to Adam-ondi-Ahman to defend that place. Joseph, Hyrum and Sidney also went with them, leaving me in command at Far West. The detachment returned in about four days.

A few days afterwards Joseph Smith and I took a walk out upon the prairie, and in the course of our conversation I suggested that he send for General Atchison to defend him in the suit then brought against him, as he was in command of the third division of the militia of the State of Missouri, and was a lawyer and a friend to law. Joseph made no reply, but turned back immediately to Far West, and a man was selected with the best horse to be found, to go to Liberty for General Atchison.

The next day General Atchison came to Far West with a hundred men and camped a little north of the town.

On consulting with Joseph Smith, Atchison told him that he did not want any one to go with them to his trial, which was to take place midway between Far West and Adam-ondi-Ahman. Joseph at first hesitated about agreeing to this, but Atchison reassured him by saying: "My life for yours!"

When they arrived at the place of trial quite a number of the mob had gathered, and on seeing Joseph they commenced to curse and swear. Atchison, however, checked them by saying: "Hold on, boys, if you fire the first gun there will not be one of you left!"

Joseph was cleared and came away unmolested. Soon afterwards the governor, thinking Atchison was too friendly towards the Saints, took his command from him and placed General Clark in command of the militia.

When Joseph first came to Nauvoo, then called Commerce, a Mr. White, living there, proffered to sell him his farm for twenty-five hundred dollars, five hundred dollars of the amount to be paid down, and the balance one year from that time. Joseph and the brethren were talking about this offer when some of them said: "We can't buy it, for we lack the money."

Joseph took out his purse, and emptying out its contents, offered a half dollar to one of the brethren, which he declined accepting, but Joseph urged him to take it, and then gave each of the other brethren a similar amount, which left him without any. Addressing the brethren he then said: "Now you all have money, and I have none; but the time will come when I will have money and you will have none!"

He then said to Bishop Knight, "You go back and buy the farm!"

The bargain was closed and the obligations drawn up, but how the money was going to be raised neither Brother Knight nor the other brethren could see.

The next morning Joseph and several of the brethren went down to Mr. White's to sign the agreement and make the first payment on the land. A table was brought out with the papers upon it, and Joseph signed them, moved back from the table and sat with his head down, as if in thought for a moment. Just then a man drove up in a carriage and asked if Mr. Smith was there. Joseph hearing it, got up and went to the door. The man said,

"Good morning, Mr. Smith; I am on a speculation today. I want to buy some land, and thought I would come and see you."

Joseph then pointed around where his land lay, but the man said: "I can't go with you today to see the land. Do you want any money this morning?"

Joseph replied that he would like some, and when the stranger asked how much, he told him, "Five hundred dollars."

The man walked into the house with Joseph, emptied a small sack of gold on the table, and counted out that amount. He then handed to Joseph another hundred dollars, saying: "Mr. Smith, I make you a present of this!"

After this transpired, Joseph laughed at the brethren and said: "You trusted in money; but I trusted in God. Now I have money and you have none."

In Nauvoo, I rented a house on the river bank. While there in business, I saw in vision my grave before me for two weeks; it mattered not whether my eyes were open or shut, it was there, and I saw no way of escape. One day Brother Joseph came and took dinner with us, and as we arose from the table I walked out upon the porch and sat down on a bench. Joseph and my wife followed me, and he came before me and said: "Philo, you must get away from here or you will die, as sure as God ever spoke by my mouth!"

He then turned to my wife and said: "And you will hardly escape by the skin of your teeth!"

I immediately stepped into Joseph's carriage and rode with him to the south part of town and rented another place, after which I settled up my business as fast as I could, and made arrangements to remove. Many hearing of Joseph's prediction about me said if they had been in my place they would have remained where I was and tested the truth of it. But I assured them if they had been in my place they would have done just as I did.

After I had settled my business and removed my family, we were one day at Joseph's house when he said to my wife: "You didn't believe what I told Philo the other day! Now, I will tell you what the Lord told me. He told me to go and tell Philo to come away from there, and if he obeyed he should live; if not, he should die; and I didn't want to see you a widow so soon again.

If Philo had remained there fourteen days longer, he would have been a corpse."

The Juvenile Instructor, XXVII, (January 1, 1892), pp. 22-23; (May 15, 1892), pp. 303-304; (June 1, 1892), p. 345; *Early Scenes in Church History (Faith Promoting Series,* volume 8) (Salt Lake City, 1882), pp. 79-96.

Daniel D. McArthur

To me, Joseph Smith seemed to possess more power and force of character than any ordinary man. I would look upon him when he was with hundreds of other men, and he would appear greater than ever. The more I heard his sayings and saw his doings, the more I was convinced that he had of a truth seen God the Father and His Son Jesus Christ, and also the holy angels of God. If I know anything on this earth, I surely know that he was a prophet.

When Joseph Smith first spoke to me, I was in the woods about half a mile south of Kirtland. He was on his horse and I was chopping wood. Said he, "Good afternoon."

I returned the compliment. He had a smile on his face, and I felt that he was going to say something else.

"You are not the young man who sold his wife for a bull-eye watch the other day, are you?" he asked.

I replied, "No, sir."

He went on laughing. There was a man who had sold his wife for a bull-eye watch a day or two before, and there was quite a talk about it in the neighborhood, so I suppose he thought he would have a little fun with me.

This same winter, 1836, he stated that he was out of firewood and that he had no time to get up any, for the officers of the law were continually on his track. So some of the brethren thought they would turn out and get him some wood.

When noon came, we were all called to dinner at Joseph's house. The table was loaded down with corn-meal mush and milk, and at the bidding of Joseph we all stepped forward to our places around the table, standing on our feet. Joseph asked Joshua Holman, who was one of the wood haulers, to ask a blessing upon the food. He went at his duty with all his soul. As he had been a Methodist exhorter before joining the Church, he commenced to call upon the great and mighty God who sat upon the top of a topless throne to look down and bless the food, and asked many other blessings to rest upon the Prophet, etc.

As soon as he closed, Joseph said, "Brother Joshua, don't let me ever hear you ask another such blessing."

Before we took our seats, he stated his reasons for making this remark and showed us how inconsistent such ideas were. He told us many things about God and who He was. Then we sat down to our mush and milk. After eating, the men went out to hitch up their teams, and Joseph took his hat and stepped out into the yard. We boys followed close at his heels. He turned around and said: "Boys, you think I am a prophet, and want to hear all I have to say. If I should tell you all I know that will come to pass within twelve years, perhaps there would not one of you believe it. You would apostatize from the Church. But I shall let you learn things as they happen, then most likely you will all stand in the Church."

This saying caused me to watch what transpired in the following twelve years. About the first thing that took place after that was the great apostasy in 1837. Next we were driven out of Kirtland; and Joseph was obliged to flee for his life. Next, Joseph and his brethren and the whole Church were driven out of Missouri. Later, Joseph and Hyrum were murdered. Afterwards, the entire Church was driven from Nauvoo. These things took place inside of twelve years, and ten thousand other things besides.

> *The Juvenile Instructor,* XXVII (February 15, 1892), pp. 128-129.

James Henry Rollins

I first met Joseph Smith in my Uncle Sidney Gilbert's house, the first day he arrived in Kirtland, in February, 1831. While he was in the house with my uncle and aunt, I saw a wagon turn over as it was coming down the slippery hill, and heard a woman and two or three children screaming. I ran in and told Joseph and my uncle about it, and Joseph ran without his hat to assist them. My first impression was that if any of the occupants were hurt seriously, Joseph could heal them. But none of them were hurt, and it turned out to be Joseph's own family.

Joseph and my uncle returned to the house. He asked my uncle if I was his son.

He said no, I was his wife's nephew.

"Well," he said, "The Lord has shown him great things."

I had seen Joseph and Hyrum in a vision, in December, 1830.

In 1831, I started for Missouri, and arrived about the 1st of January, 1832. Joseph Smith the Prophet came to Independence on his second visit there, about the last of April or the first of May, 1832. He came to my uncle's house and saluted my uncle and aunt. Then he came to me and said, "Henry, I want to baptize you, if possible, before I leave."

I was then working in my uncle's store, and, on Saturday, Joseph came into my uncle's store and asked him if I could go with him to the Whitmer settlement. He wanted to baptize me, but my uncle could not spare me.

When Joseph returned from the Whitmer settlement, he authorized Oliver Cowdery to baptize me, instead of himself, but Cowdery did not get to do it. I was finally baptized by John Corrill.

On June 1, 1834, the first news came of the arrival of Zion's Camp in Missouri. Joseph the Prophet and his brother William, with Dr. F. G. Williams and several others, stayed at our place. But the majority of the camp went to the farm of John Burk, where many were stricken with the cholera and died.

George A. Smith and Jesse Smith were about my own age. We three were out in the road trying to get a ball out of a pistol which had got wet at Fishing River. We were all three quite merry and were laughing a great deal, when Jesse made the remark, "We had not ought to be out here making so much noise, while there are so many of our brethren sick and dying in the house. We don't know how soon some of us may be taken."

We then went in the house. In a short time this noble boy was struck with the cholera. Joseph and his brethren worked over him, but fever took hold of him and with all they could do for him it availed them nothing. He died lying on the floor of our largest room.

Joseph took the death of this noble boy very hard, as he undoubtedly had been entrusted with his care by the boy's parents.

When the Saints were driven from Missouri, I was taken to Richmond. General Clark said, "You get down off the horse and go into the bull pen with the rest of them."

When I entered, I found forty or fifty brethren.

I was called the next morning, when court had convened. A pole was stretched across to keep us back from Judge King and his court. I stood close to this pole, at the back of Joseph and Hyrum and the lawyers, and Doniphan and Atchison. A man was brought in as a witness, who testified that I had burned his house. I spoke openly, as I stood behind Joseph and Hyrum, that he was a curly headed liar.

Joseph turned his head toward me and said, "Pshaw, Henry, don't say anything."

This saying caused some consolation in the court room.

After leaving Missouri, I went to my stepfather's farm, nine miles from Montrose, in Iowa territory. While there, I received a letter from the Prophet requesting me to come to Nauvoo immediately. I went and asked Joseph what he wanted of me.

He said for me to move to Nauvoo, that he wanted me there.

I did as he advised.

Soon after this I went to Joseph, where he resided down on the flats in a mansion, and asked him what he desired me to do. The next morning I went with him to his store. He asked Newell K. Whitney if he had any work for me to do.

He replied that there was nothing that he knew of then, that he had sufficient help at present.

Joseph then said, "I have work for you."

He took me through in the back of the store and showed me cords of hickory wood. He asked me if I was a good hand with the ax. I laughed and said, "Well, some little."

I chopped and piled up the wood the same day.

The next day he came to the store and unbarred the outside cellar door, and asked me if I thought I could straighten up things.

He was pleased with the change I made with the appearance of the cellar.

Early the next morning, Judge Cleveland brought a carload of hogs. Joseph asked me if I could cut them up and salt them. He said, "I want it done just as my wife Emma tells you."

She told me to cut out the bones and salt the pork in the barrels, then add brine and molasses; and after laying for a certain time, smoke them in the carriage house.

I said I was afraid, as it was getting quite warm in the day, that the flies would spoil them.

She said, "Fix them as I want it done, if they all spoil."

They did almost all of them spoil.

About this time, Lyman Wight, Amasa Lyman and Henry G. Sherwood came up the river with twenty-five barrels of Orleans sugar and several barrels of molasses.

Edward Hunter also came with a large supply of dry goods, from Philadelphia. Joseph told me to harness up his old Charlie to the buggy and take Brother Hunter around to view the city, to see Joseph's farm, and to answer all the questions he might ask.

A good deal of work was being done on the temple, and the workmen received orders on the store for their labor. It was very crowded for two or three days, and as I stood in the counting room door looking at faces in the house, the men came to me and asked if I could wait on them.

Joseph said to me, "Why don't you wait on these people?"

I told him that when I was ordered I would do so with pleasure.

He then said, "Go and wait on them."

I then went to work behind the counter on the grocery side, and paid off many orders.

When Joseph came in and saw us looking tired and pale, he told us to shut up the store that night and not open again for two or three days, which we did until we got rested.

During the spring and summer of 1844, previous to his death, the Prophet told me to assist in carrying water and other commodities to the room above the store. Afterwards I found out it was to give endowments to some of the brethren.

A few days after this as I was alone in the store, standing outside of the counter, Joseph came in with his cane in his hand and stepped directly opposite of me on the other side and eyed me for a moment. Then he walked across to where I stood and raised his right leg and laid it on my left shoulder. He then took it down, walked back to his first position, and he said, "I thought to break you down with the heft of my leg, but you are stiffer than I thought you were."

While I was in the store, Newell K. Whitney came in and said, "Joseph wants you to come up the river near the old printing office."

I went, supposing he would send me somewhere on an errand as he sometimes did. When I arrived I saw that he had been baptizing several individuals.

He said to me, "Do you remember, I promised to baptize you at Independence, Missouri. I want to fulfill that promise now, if you are willing."

I said, yes, I was very willing.

He then took me in the river and baptized me, after which I took a seat on a rock and he confirmed me and placed many blessings on my head.

A Sketch of the Life of James Henry Rollins, Church Historian's Library, Salt Lake City, Utah.

James B. Bracken, Sr.

In the fall of 1838, we went with David Patten to Adam-ondi-Ahman. When we got to the rock in the valley of Adam-ondi-Ahman, the Prophet Joseph told us it was the altar that Adam built. Joseph formed a circle of the brethren present, he himself in the center. He then drew his sword and called upon us to do likewise. This being done, we entered into a covenant never to accept terms of peace at the sacrifice of truth and right. That was the substance of the covenant.

Soon after Joseph's arrival in Far West, trouble commenced, and the same fall there were several thousand state troops sent to Far West with extermination orders from Governor Boggs. I never saw a nobler looking or acting man than Joseph Smith appeared on that occasion.

On one occasion when the mob was on us and some of the brethren did things they should not have done, such as appropriating to their own use things that did not belong to them, Joseph called us together and said that he felt to censure because of the acts of men. "Some," he said, "are doing things that will cause the blood of the brethren to be shed."

He referred to stealing.

I saw George M. Hinkle when he betrayed the Prophet, and took him into the camp of the mob. I also saw Joseph Smith a day or two later, when they brought him back and were taking him to Jackson County, when they said we would never see our Prophet any more. Many of the brethren tried to get to the wagon to shake hands with the Prophet but the mob would not allow that privilege, so the Prophet raised the wagon cover and put out his hand toward the brethren and said, "Good-bye," and passed on in silence.

> The Juvenile Instructor, XXVII, (April 1, 1892), p. 203; Statement by James B. Bracken, November 6, 1881, Church Historian's Library, Salt Lake City, Utah.

Calvin W. Moore

When I was a small boy, my impression of Joseph Smith was that he was a great man and a prophet of God. When I grew up and became older, I got a testimony for myself.

One time in the Kirtland Temple, at a fast meeting, Charles Hyde got up to talk, and the devil took hold of him and stopped him. Joseph laid his hands on him and rebuked the evil one, and Brother Hyde went on talking.

On another occasion, at a Sunday meeting, Joseph was speaking when a large, tall man came into the temple and walked up and down the aisles whittling and whistling. Joseph requested Bishop Knight, who was a smaller man, to put him out, and he took hold of the disturber and put him out just as the Prophet told him to do.

When Porter Rockwell was in jail, in Missouri, his mother went to see him at the jail, and the Missourians told her that if she would raise a certain amount of money and give it to them they would let her son go. Joseph started out to get the money. He came to a large crowd of young men who were wrestling, that being the popular sport in those days. Among the boys there was a bully, from LaHarpe I believe. He had thrown down every one on the ground who wrestled with him. When Joseph came to the crowd he told them what he wanted, passed around the hat, raised what money he could and then went into the ring to take part with the young men and boys in their games. So he was invited to wrestle with this bully.

The man was eager to have a tussle with the Prophet, so Joseph stepped forward and took hold of the man. The first pass he made, Joseph whirled him around and took him by the collar and seat of his trousers and walked out to a ditch and threw him in it. Then, taking him by the arm, he helped him up and patted him on the back and said, "You must not mind this. When I am with the boys I make all the fun I can for them."

The Juvenile Instructor, XXVII (April 15, 1892), p. 255.

Wilford Woodruff

My first introduction to the Prophet, in 1834, was rather singular. He had on a very old hat, and was shooting at a mark. He had a pistol in his hand. Said he, "Brother Woodruff, I've been out shooting at a mark. I wanted to see if I could hit anything. Have you any objection to it?"

"Not at all," said I. "There is no law against a man shooting at a mark, that I know of."

He invited me to his house. I accepted the invitation, and I watched him pretty closely to learn what I could. He remarked while passing to his house that this was the first hour he had spent in recreation for a long time.

Shortly after we arrived at his house, he went into an adjoining room and brought out a wolf-skin, and said, "Brother Woodruff, I want you to help me tan this." So I pulled off my coat, went to work and helped him, and felt honored in so doing. He was going with the brethren of Zion's camp, and he wanted this wolf-skin to put upon his wagon seat, as he had no buffalo robe.

This was my first acquaintance with the Prophet Joseph. And from that day until the present I never saw a moment when I had any doubt with regard to this work. I have felt to rejoice exceedingly in what I saw of Brother Joseph, for in his public and private career he carried with him the Spirit of the Almighty, and he manifested a greatness of soul which I had never seen in any other man.

The evening after I arrived in Kirtland several of the brethren came in and talked with Brother Joseph, and asked what they should do, for they had not means to bear their expenses from there to Missouri. Brother Joseph said, "I am going to have some money soon."

The next morning he received a letter containing a hundred and fifty dollars.

On Sunday, he called a priesthood meeting. The elders all gathered in a little cabin. There I first heard Joseph Smith speak publicly. He called upon the elders to bear testimony of the gospel of Christ. He then arose and said, "Brethren, I am very much edified and interested in listening to your testimony. But I want to tell you that you know no more concerning the result of this work and what lies before you as the elders of Israel, and before this people, than a parcel of little children."

He told them this work would fill the whole earth, and that all nations would have to hear the proclamation of the gospel. He further said: "This work will fill the Rocky Mountains with tens of thousands of Latter-day Saints, and there will be joined with them the Lamanites who dwell in those mountains who will receive the gospel of Christ at the mouth of the elders of Israel, and they will be united with the Church and the kingdom of God, and bring forth much good."

I have heard the Prophet Joseph pray when the power of God rested upon him, and all who heard him felt it; and I have seen his prayers answered in a marvelous manner, almost immediately. Governor Reynolds, of Missouri, on one occasion employed men to try and kidnap Joseph, and they almost accomplished their designs. Thereafter, the governor continued to harass him with writs, and was determined to destroy Joseph. The Prophet and the Twelve went before God in prayer. Joseph asked the Lord to deliver him from the power of that man. In about forty-eight hours from that time, word reached Joseph that Reynolds had blown his brains out.

There is another instance. A certain man took a stand against Joseph and endeavored to bring persecution on him. Joseph went to God and laid the matter before Him, asking to be delivered out of the hands and power of that wicked man. Joseph knew the voice of the Spirit when it spoke to him. After offering up his prayer, the whispering of the still small voice came to him saying, "Wait with patience."

The next day that man was taken sick with cholera, and died in a few hours.

While I was living in a cabin in an old barracks at Nauvoo, we experienced a day of God's power with the Prophet Joseph. It was a very sickly time and Joseph had given up his home to the sick, and was living in a tent pitched in his dooryard. The large number of Saints who had been driven out of Missouri were flocking in, but had no homes and were living in wagons, in tents, and on the ground. Many were sick through the exposure they were subjected to. Brother Joseph had waited on the sick until he was worn out and nearly sick himself.

On the morning of the 22nd of July, 1839, he arose reflecting upon the situation of the Saints of God in their persecutions and afflictions. He called upon the Lord in prayer, and the power of God rested mightily upon him. And as Jesus healed all the sick around Him in His day, so Joseph, the Prophet of God, healed all around on this occasion. He healed all in his house and dooryard, then, in company with Sidney Rigdon and several of the Twelve, he went through among the sick lying on the bank of the river, and he commanded them in a loud voice, in the name of Jesus Christ, to come up and be made whole, and they were all healed.

When he healed all that were sick on the east side of the river, they crossed the Mississippi River to Montrose, where we were. The first house they went into was President Brigham Young's. He was sick on his bed at the time. The Prophet went into his house and healed him, and they all came out together. As they were passing by my door, Brother Joseph said, "Brother Woodruff, follow me."

These were the only words spoken by any of the company from the time they left Brother Brigham's house till we crossed the public square and entered Brother Elijah Fordham's house. Brother Fordham had been dying for an hour, and we expected each minute would be his last.

I felt the power of God that was overwhelming His prophet. When we entered the house, Brother Joseph walked up to Brother

Fordham and took him by the right hand; in his left hand he held his hat.

He saw that Brother Fordham's eyes were glazed, and that he was speechless and unconscious.

After taking hold of his hand, the Prophet looked down into the dying man's face and said, "Brother Fordham, do you not know me?"

At first he made no reply; but we could all see the effect of the Spirit of God resting upon him.

Joseph again said, "Elijah, do you not know me?"

With a low whisper, Brother Fordham answered, "Yes."

The Prophet then said, "Have you not faith to be healed?"

The answer, which was a little plainer than before, was, "I am afraid it is too late. If you had come sooner, I think I might have been."

He had the appearance of a man waking from sleep. It was the sleep of death.

Joseph then said, "Do you believe that Jesus is the Christ?"

"I do, Brother Joseph," was the response.

Then the Prophet of God spoke with a loud voice, as in the majesty of the Godhead, "Elijah, I command you, in the name of Jesus of Nazareth, to arise and be made whole!"

The words of the Prophet were not like the words of man, but like the voice of God. It seemed to me that the house shook from its foundation. Elijah Fordham leaped from his bed like a man raised from the dead. A healthy color came to his face, and life was manifested in every act. His feet were done up in Indian-meal poultices. He kicked them off his feet, scattered the contents, then called for his clothes and put them on. He asked for a bowl of bread and milk and ate it. Then he put on his hat and followed us into the street to visit others who were sick.

As soon as we left Brother Fordham's house, we went into the house of Joseph B. Noble, who was very low and dangerously sick. When we entered the house, Brother Joseph took him by the hand, and commanded him, in the name of Jesus Christ, to arise and be made whole. He did arise and was immediately healed.

While this was going on, the wicked mob in the place, led by one Kilburn, had become alarmed, and followed us into Brother Noble's house. Before they arrived there, Brother Joseph had called upon Brother Fordham to offer prayer. While he was praying, the mob entered, with all the evil spirits accompanying them. As soon as they entered, Brother Fordham, who was praying, fainted and sank to the floor.

When Joseph saw the mob in the house, he arose and had the room cleared of both that class of men and their attendant devils. Then Brother Fordham immediately revived and finished his prayer.

This shows what power evil spirits have upon the tabernacles of men. The Saints are only saved from the devil by the power of God.

This case of Brother Noble's was the last one of healing upon that day. It was the greatest day for the manifestation of the power of God through the gift of healing since the organization of the Church.

When we left Brother Noble, the Prophet Joseph went with those who accompanied him from the other side of the bank of the river, to return home. While waiting for the ferryboat, a man of the world, knowing of the miracles which had been performed, came to him and asked him if he would not go and heal his twin children, about five months old, who were both lying sick nigh unto death. They were some two miles from Montrose.

The Prophet said he could not go, but after pausing some time, he said he would send some one to heal them. He then turned to me and said, "You go with the man and heal his children."

He took a red silk handkerchief out of his pocket and gave it to me, and told me to wipe their faces with the handkerchief when I administered to them, and they should be healed. He also said unto me, "As long as you will keep that handkerchief, it shall remain a league between you and me."

I went with the man, and did as the Prophet commanded me, and the children were healed.

I have possession of the handkerchief unto this day.

It has been my faith and belief from the time that I was made acquainted with the gospel that no greater prophet than Joseph

Smith ever lived on the face of the earth, save Jesus Christ. He was raised to stand at the head of this great dispensation—the greatest of all dispensations God has ever given to man.

Millennial Star, LIII (October 5, 1891), pp. 627-628; LIV (September 19, 1892), p. 605; *Journal of Discourses,* VII pp. 100-101; Woodruff, *Leaves From My Journal,* pp. 62-65.

Edward Stevenson

I first saw Joseph Smith at Pontiac, Michigan, in 1834, when he visited the Pontiac Branch. The meetings were crowded. The Prophet stood at a table for a pulpit. Before he got through, he was in the midst of the congregation with uplifted hand. His countenance seemed to assume a heavenly whiteness. He testified with great power concerning the visit of the Father and the Son, and the conversation he had with them. Never before did I feel such power. Though only a small percentage of those who saw and heard him accepted the restored gospel, there was not one who dared to dispute it. Many were heard to say, "Well, if Mormonism is true, it will stand; if not true, it will fall."

A prediction made by the Prophet was afterwards literally fulfilled. Joseph said, "If you will obey the gospel with honest hearts, I promise you in the name of the Lord that the gifts as promised by our Savior will follow you, and by this you may prove me to be a true servant of God."

I both saw and heard the gifts follow those who believed and obeyed the gospel.

During the Prophet's visit, he came to our house. My heart swelled with love as I selected and presented him with some of our choice apples. While looking over our copy of a large English Book of Martyrs, he expressed sympathy for the Christian martyrs and a hope for their salvation. He asked to borrow the book, promising to return it when he should meet us again in Missouri. On returning it he said, "I have, by the aid of the Urim and Thummim [Seer Stone?], seen those martyrs. They were honest, devoted followers of Christ, according to the light they possessed. They will be saved."

The Prophet also looked over our large Bible and remarked that much of the Apocrypha was true, but it required the Spirit of God to select the truth out of those writings.

Finally, in speaking of the latter-day work, he said, "There are thousands of good people in England and those old countries who are waiting for the fulness of the gospel, and it will not be long before they will flock to Zion, for Ephraim dwells largely in those parts."

I have often seen the Prophet indulge in a game of checkers. He was cheerful—often wrestling with Sidney Rigdon. One time he had his pants torn badly, but had a good laugh over it. In Missouri, when mob forces oppressed the Saints, we were encamped in Adam-ondi-Ahman, mostly around campfires without tents. One night the snow fell four or five inches. The Prophet, seeing our forlorn condition, called on us to form into two parties —Lyman Wight at the head of one line and he (Joseph) heading the other line—to have a sham battle. The weapons were snowballs. We set to with a will full of glee and fun.

I stood with Joseph Smith and others when he pointed out the sacred spot of Adam's altar. Turning to the lovely valley below us, in a large bend of Grand River, he said, "Here is the real valley where Father Adam called his posterity together and blessed them."

He also stated that the Garden of Eden was in Jackson County—the Center Place of Zion where a great temple will be reared.

Twelve days after the Prophet escaped from Missouri, a General Conference of the Church was held at Quincy, Illinois. His soul was filled with emotion, and it seemed as though he could not utter his feelings, only with a flood of tears. He looked calm, however, and a halo of brightness hovered about him. He was of a tender heart, as well as of a stern and firm disposition when occasion required it. I have known the Prophet to weep with tender affection, and have seen him with his sword drawn, as a military officer, when he was mighty as well as powerful.

After the Prophet had looked over the congregation, he said, "To look over this congregation of Latter-day Saints who have been driven from their homes and are still in good faith, without homes, as pilgrims in a strange land, and to realize that my life has been spared to behold your faces again seemed to be so great a pleasure that words were only a vague expression of my soul's gratitude."

I have heard the Prophet say that he did not claim perfection, but possessed human weaknesses. He said, "When I speak as a man it is Joseph only that speaks. But when the Lord speaks through me, it is no more Joseph Smith who speaks; but it is God, and let all Israel hear."

Joseph Smith, Wilford Woodruff and Willard Richards saw a light in the heavens, in the southwest quarter of the sky, and a broad sword, from half past seven to nine o'clock. The Prophet said, "As sure as there is a God who sits enthroned in the heavens, and as sure as he ever spoke by me, so sure will there be a speedy and bloody war; and the broad sword seen this evening is a sure sign thereof."

We very often went to Nauvoo to meetings. I have never heard or seen a man so filled with inspiration as the Prophet. He was full of light. I began to believe that he possessed an infinity of knowledge. I looked upon him as upon no other man. I have often heard him speak under divine influence, and I have felt as though I have been lifted in spirit beyond mortality, and that I was looking upon a simile of God, and at times I found myself in tears of joy. Others have I seen in the same condition, and at times even those not members of our church.

The Prophet gave rich instructions relative to preaching the gospel by the Spirit and power of the Holy Ghost. He also explained several passages of scripture. He taught that the Lord's prayer should state, "Leave us not in temptation"—not, "Lead us not into temptation." (Matthew 6:13.) John's revelation on Patmos should read, "Blessed are the dead which die in the Lord, . . . and they shall continue in their work"—not, "and their works do follow them." (Revelation 14:13.) The epistle to the Hebrew saints should say, "Therefore *not* leaving the principles of the doctrine of Christ, let us go unto perfection"—not, "Therefore leaving the principles of the doctrine of Christ." He said that the plural term "baptisms" in this passage had reference to baptism for the living, baptism for the dead, and rebaptism. (Hebrews 6:1-2.)

I loved to hear the Prophet teach us. On one occasion he said, "Oh! how I would delight to bring before you things you never thought of, but poverty and the cares of the world prevent. But I am glad I have the privilege of communicating to you some things which, if grasped closely, will be a help to you when earthquakes bellow, the clouds gather, the lightnings flash, and the storms are ready to burst upon you like peals of thunder. Lay hold upon these things, and let not your knees or joints tremble, and your hearts faint."

He was cheerful and comforting. He said, "I shall not be sacrificed until my time comes; then I shall be offered freely."

I heard the Prophet state, while preaching on a stand erected on the east side of the Temple, that he now saw the time he had long desired to see. "Now I am a *free man*," he declared. "There are men now prepared to carry out the work of the kingdom of God here on earth, and it will roll on forever. Thank God I have lived to see this day."

I never saw him so full of power. It thrilled through my whole system.

> "Autobiography of Edward Stevenson," Typewritten manuscript, Church Historian's Library, Salt Lake City, Utah, pp. 7-9, 33-36, 57-58, 65-68, 78, 96.

Benjamin F. Johnson

I feel in every degree incompetent to the task of recounting what I have witnessed in the life and character of our great Prophet, who stood in the presence of both the Father and the Son and personally conversed with them both; being often visited by holy angels, while continually receiving by revelation the word of the Lord to His people. And yet he was of like passion with his brethren and associates.

As a son, he was nobility itself, in love and honor of his parents; as a brother he was loving and true, even unto death; as a husband and father, his devotion to wives and children stopped only at idolatry. His life's greatest motto, after "God and His Kingdom," was that of "wives, children and friends." On one Sunday morning while sitting with him in the Mansion dining room, in private converse, two of Emma's children came to him as just from their mother, all so nice, bright and sweet. Calling them to my attention, he said,"Benjamin, look at these children. How could I help loving their mother?"

Joseph, the Prophet, as a friend was faithful, long suffering, noble and true to that degree that the erring who did love him were reminded that the rod of a friend was better than the kiss of an enemy, while others who "sopped in his dish" but bore not reproof became his enemies and, like Law, Marks, Foster, Higbee and others who hated him, conspired to his death.

As a companion, socially, he was highly endowed—was kind, generous, and mirth loving. For amusements, he would sometimes wrestle a friend, or others; would test strength with others by sitting upon the floor with feet together and stick grasped between them. But he never found his match. Jokes, rebuses, matching couplets in rhymes, etc., were not uncommon. But to call for the singing of one or more of his favorite songs was more frequent. Of those, "Wives, Children and Friends," "Battle of River Russen," "Soldier's Tear," "Soldier's Dream," and "Last Rose of Summer" were most common. And yet, although so social and even convivial at times, he would allow no arrogance or undue liberties.

While with him in such fraternal, social and sometimes convivial moods, we could not then so fully realize the greatness and majesty of his calling, which, since his martyrdom, has continued to magnify in our view, as the glories of this last dispensation were more fully unfolded to our comprehension.

In 1833, I went to Kirtland, Ohio, where were gathered many converts to the new revelation. Though the Prophet was hardly more than a boy in appearance, I soon learned that he was a man indeed in wisdom and council; and although younger than he, I had great opportunity to scrutinize his life and habits. Such were the social and religious elements of his unselfish nature that those who knew him best loved him most; and to me, who became associated with him personally in his family, who became his confidential friend, his financial agent, his trusted companion and nurse in his sickness—to me, he was the embodiment and perfection of all that I could comprehend in perfect manhood.

But as he was the most loved by those who knew him best, so he was the most hated by those who did not and would not know him. For as in the case of the Great Nazarene, who was no one "but the carpenter's son," so he was of poor parentage and uneducated, and therefore was despised by the rich and the learned who, with all classes, sought by false witnesses and otherwise to entangle him in lawsuits and to incite mob violence, and for no real cause but that he professed a new revelation from heaven.

In the summer of 1833, a mob drove the Saints from Jackson County. Zion's Camp was prepared to start, in which I desired to accompany the brethren. But the Prophet deemed it best for me not to go, owing to the opposition of my father, and as I had not yet received my baptism. I was assured by the Prophet Joseph that no loss should come to me for waiting, for although not fully a member I had partaken of every hope, desire, and spiritual influence with which those around me were animated.

Previous to the dedication of the Temple, on the 27th of March, 1836, all who had labored upon it were called together, and in the public congregation received their blessings under the hands of the First Presidency. I felt a great joy in these prophetic words that filled and thrilled me. Yet all the time I was thinking that these blessings would only be for those who had labored with their hands upon the Temple. As I had not myself worked upon it, not being strong enough for such labor, I felt that I would not receive any blessing and it grieved me exceedingly. On the last day of blessings, I was standing by the door in the crowded congregation. How I did yearn for a blessing! As the last blessing was given, the Prophet earnestly looked towards the door where I was standing and said to his brother Hyrum, "Go and see if there is not one more yet to be blessed."

Brother Hyrum came to the door and put his hand upon my shoulder, and asked me if I had not worked upon the Temple.

I said, "No sir," but it seemed like passing a sentence upon my fondest hopes.

He then asked if I had done nothing towards it.

I then thought of a new gun I had earned and given as a donation, and of the brick I had helped to make. I said, "I did give often."

"I thought there was a blessing for you," he said; and he almost carried me to the stand.

The Prophet blessed me with a confirmation of all his father had sealed upon me in my patriarchal blessing, and many more also. I felt then that the Lord had respect for my great desire.

In 1839, after the Prophet escaped from Missouri and arrived at Nauvoo, I was with him. The people had flocked in from the terrible exposures of the past, and nearly everyone was sick with intermittent or other fevers, of which many died. The Prophet, too, had a violent sickness. As Emma was in no degree able to care for him, it wholly devolved upon me. Both day and night through a period of a little less than two weeks I was hardly absent from his room. Almost his only food was gruel, and about the only treatment he would accept was a flush of the colon with warm water, perhaps tinctured slightly with capsicum of myrrh, or a little soda and salt, both of which were prepared and administered by me in the room he occupied. If any sleep came to me, it was while lying upon his bed or sitting in my chair.

At this time, with so much sickness and death, a great fear began to prevail, with a desire in some to abandon Nauvoo, and with this feeling President Rigdon was greatly exercised, making grave complaints. The Prophet now arose in great power, like a lion, or as a giant refreshed with wine, shook off his own sickness, went to Brother Rigdon, rebuked his fearful and complaining spirit, and told him to repent or a scourge from the Lord awaited him. Those being sick he commanded to be healed, which they were. He then called for a skiff and crossed the river to Montrose, where he found Elijah Fordham, drawing apparently his last breath. By his command, life returned and he arose and was at once made whole. The Prophet then visited Brother Joseph B. Noble and other places, full of the power of God, healing the sick.

Soon after the Prophet's recovery, I too came apparently nigh unto death through a violent attack of the fever, through which my comfort was kindly looked after by the Prophet.

About the middle of October, a letter came to say that my dear mother and young sister were apparently near to death, in Springfield, Illinois, and were anxious for my return. In my anxiety to see my mother again, I procured quinine, which was just becoming known as an antidote for fever, and taking it in large quantities, my fever soon abated. Under its tonic influence, I fancied I had become well, and in great joy and hope hastened preparations to start for the home of my mother and kindred in Springfield. My horse was in the yard ready to mount, but I wished to take leave of the Prophet with the hope of receiving his blessing. I had but one ten-dollar bill left, and I thought that at least I would pay a tithing. So, going to the Prophet, I told him I was ready to leave, and giving him the bill, I said, "As this is all I have left, I want to pay a tithe of it."

He saw I was weak in body and that my heart was sad, so, thinking to cheer and arouse me, when putting the nine dollars in my hand, he playfully knocked my hand upward, scattering the money all over the room.

My heart was full of tears, and my emotion must have vent, so forgetting all but the feeling that we were boy companions playing together, I sprang at and grappled him, so as to teach him a lesson. But the lesson was all to me, for on making the one grand effort to throw him, I found myself in strength no more than a bullrush as compared with him, and as my strength was fictitious and my real recovery but an illusion, I collapsed and fainted in his arms. He placed me in repose, and did all necessary for my restoration and comfort. He then gathered up the scattered money.

After a period of delay, weak, trembling and desolate, yet determined to start, I led my horse to the outer gate. As I was passing through, with the bridle on my arm, his hand detained me. Placing his hands upon my head, he seemed to pour out his soul in blessing me. He told the Lord I had been faithful to care for others, but I was now worn and sick, and that on my journey I would need His care, and he asked that a guardian angel might go with me from that day and stay with me through all my life.

O! how often I have seen through life the footprints of that angel, and knew that his hand had drawn me back from death.

Living in one of the Prophet's homes was Father G. W. Harris, who had married the widow of William Morgan. She had two children, Lucinda and Thomas. Lucinda, then sixteen years of age, appeared to be very lovable, both in purity and beauty, and being often companions naturally drew us together in feeling. The Prophet, seeing our partiality for each other, told me to make her my wife, seeming to enjoin it upon me. I at once moved to that object, and we soon pledged our vows to each other.

Having later left Nauvoo on a mission, I returned in the Spring of 1842 and saw the Prophet, who cordially welcomed me with renewed blessing. I conversed with him upon business matters. He said that he wished me to remain in Ramus, Illinois, as it was then called, and act as trustee or agent for the Church property at that place.

The Prophet often came to Ramus, but after my arrival he lodged in no house but mine. I was proud of his partiality and took great delight in his society and friendship. When with us there was no lack of amusement, for with jokes, games, etc., he was always ready to provoke merriment, one phase of which was matching couplets in rhyme, by which we were at times in rivalry; and his fraternal feeling in great degree did away with the disparity of age or greatness of his calling.

Sometimes when at my house I asked him questions relating to the past, present and future. Some of his answers are now recorded in the Doctrine and Covenants.

In talking with my mother after the revelation on plural marriage was given, Joseph Smith told her that when the Lord required him to move in plural marriage his first thought was to come and ask her for some of her daughters; and I can now understand that the period alluded to was at Kirtland, where she had three unmarried daughters at home, two of whom died there.

As I have alluded to the law of plural marriage, I will relate the time and manner in which it was taught to me. About the first of April, 1843, the Prophet, with some of the Twelve and others, came to Macedonia to hold a meeting, which was to convene in a large cabinet shop owned by Brother Joseph E. and myself. As usual, he put up at my house.

Early on Sunday morning he said, "Come Brother Bennie, let us have a walk."

I took his arm, and he led the way into a by-place in the edge of the woods surrounded by tall brush and trees. Through the swale ran a small spring brook, across which a tree was fallen and was clean of its bark. On this we sat down, and the Prophet began to tell me that the Lord had revealed to him that plural or patriarchal marriage was according to His law; and that the Lord had not only revealed it to him but had commanded him to obey it; that he was required to take other wives; and that he wanted my Sister Almira for one of them, and wished me to see and talk to her upon the subject.

If a thunderbolt had fallen at my feet, I could hardly have been more shocked or amazed. He saw the struggle in my mind and went on to explain. But the shock was too great for me to comprehend anything, and in almost an agony of feeling I looked him squarely in the eye and said, while my heart gushed up before him, "Brother Joseph, this is all new to me. It may all be true—you know, but I do not. To my education it is all wrong. But I am going, with the help of the Lord, to do just what you say, with this promise to you—that if ever I know you do this to degrade my sister I will kill you, as the Lord lives."

He looked at me, oh, so calmly, and said, "Brother Benjamin, you will never see that day, but you shall see the day you will know it is true, and you will fulfill the law and greatly rejoice in it." And he said, "At this morning's meeting, I will preach you a sermon that no one but you will understand. And furthermore, I will promise you that when you open your mouth to your sister, it shall be filled."

At the meeting he read the Parable of the Talents, and showed plainly that to him that hath shall be given more, and from him that had but one should be taken that he seemed to have, and given to him who had ten. This, so far as I could understand, might relate to families, but to me there was a horror in the idea of speaking to my sister upon such a subject, the thought of which made me sick.

But I had promised, and it must be done. I did not remember his words and have faith that light would come. I only thought, "How dark it all looks to me. But I must do it."

And so I told my sister I wished to see her in a room by herself. I stood before her trembling, but I opened my mouth and my heart opened to the light of the Lord. My tongue was loosened, and I was filled with the Holy Ghost. I preached a sermon that forever converted me and her also to the principle, even though her heart was not yet won by the Prophet. And so I had great joy after my tribulation.

He had asked me to bring my sister to the city, which I soon did. His brother, Hyrum, said to me, "Now, Brother Benjamin, you know that Brother Joseph would not sanction this if it was not from the Lord. The Lord revealed this to Brother Joseph long ago, and he put it off until the angel of the Lord came to him with a drawn sword and told him that he would be slain if he did not go forth and fulfill the law."

He told my sister to have no fears, and he there and then sealed my sister, Almira, to the Prophet.

One evening the Prophet called me and my wife to come and sit down, for he wished to marry us according to the law of the Lord. I thought it a joke, and said I should not marry my wife again unless she courted *me,* for I did it all the first time. He chided my levity, told me he was in earnest, and so it proved, for we stood up and were sealed by the Holy Spirit of Promise.

This occurrence is referred to in the life of Joseph Smith as "Spending the evening in giving counsel to Brother Johnson and wife."

The Prophet's "teaching of love" was not to work upon the sympathies and sensibilities of the people, rather it was his great example and self-sacrifice, and his showing us that while all the world was against us, our only hope was in our union, and that union was only possible as the fruit of our love for each other. In teaching us the "Fatherhood of God, and the brotherhood of man," we could begin to see why we should "love God supremely, and our brothers as ourselves."

He taught us that God was the great head of human procreation, was really and truly the father of both our spirits and our bodies; that we were but parts of a great whole, mutually and equally dependent upon each other, according to conditions. And in our love of God we show, as do the members of our bodies, a greater love and protection for our head.

You will not forget that the march in science has in many things reversed the world's thought, changed its "modus" and almost its face, and in fact, exploded the dogmas of outside theology. The keys to all this knowledge were first committed to the Prophet Joseph, as a part of the gospel, for the world's benefit, for all of which he was derided. He was the first to teach in this age "substantialism," the eternity of matter, that no part or particle of the great universe could become annihilated or destroyed; that light and life and spirit were one; that all light and heat are the "glory of God," which is His power, that fills the "immensity of space," and is the life of all things, and permeates with latent life, and heat, every particle of which all worlds are composed; that light or spirit, and gross matter, are the two first great primary principles of the universe, or of being; that they are self-existent, co-existent, indestructible, and eternal, and from these two elements both our spirits and our bodies were formulated.

He taught that all systems or worlds were in revolution, the lesser around the greater. He taught that all the animal kingdoms would be resurrected, and made us understand that they would remain in the dominion of those who, with creative power, reach out for dominion, through the power of eternal lives. He taught us that the Saints would fill the great West, and through Mexico and Central and South America we would do a great work for the redemption of the remnant of Jacob. And he taught us relating to the kingdom of God as it would become organized upon the earth through "all nations learning war no more" and all adopting the God-given Constitution of the United States as a palladium of liberty and equal rights.

I was present when the Prophet gave his last charge to the Quorum of the Twelve Apostles. It was in Nauvoo early in 1844, in the meeting of a council of the Prophet's most trusted friends, including the Twelve, but not all of the constituted authorities of the Church. The Prophet stood before that association, and with great feeling and animation he graphically reviewed his life of persecution, labor and sacrifice for the Church and the kingdom of God, both of which he declared were now organized upon the earth, the burden of which had become too great for him longer to carry, that he was weary and tired with the weight he had so long borne. He then said, with great vehemence: "And in the name of the Lord, I now shake from my shoulders the responsibility of bearing off the kingdom of God to all the world, and here and now I place that responsibility, with all the keys, powers and privileges pertaining thereto, upon the shoulders of you, the Twelve Apostles, in connection with this council; and if you will accept this, to do it, God shall bless you mightily and shall open your way; and if you do it not, you will be damned. I am henceforth free from the blood of this generation and of all men."

Shaking his skirt with great vehemence, he raised himself from the floor, while the Spirit that accompanied his words thrilled every heart.

At his last visit to us at Ramus, he preached with great animation to a large congregation and blessed nineteen children. He then turned to me and said, "Benjamin, I am tired, let us go home."

My home being only a block distant, we soon reached it, and entering we found a warm fire with a large chair in front, and my wife sitting near with her babe, our eldest, upon her lap. Approaching her, I said, "Now, Melissa, see what we have lost by not going to meeting. Brother Joseph has blessed all the children in the place but ours, and it is left out in the cold."

But the Prophet at once said, "You shall lose nothing." He then proceeded to bless our first born.

Then with a deep-drawn breath, as a sigh of weariness, he sank down heavily in his chair, and said, "Oh! I am so tired—so tired that I often feel to long for my day of rest. For what has there been in this life but tribulation for me? From a boy I have been persecuted by my enemies, and now even my friends are beginning to join with them, to hate and persecute me! Why should I not wish for my time of rest?"

His words and tone thrilled and shocked me, and like an arrow pierced my hopes that he would long remain with us. I said, as with a heart full of tears, "Oh! Joseph, what could we, as a people, do without you and what would become of the great latter-day work if you should leave us?"

He was touched by my emotions, and in reply he said, "Benjamin, I would not be far away from you, and if on the other side of the veil I would still be working with you, and with a power greatly increased, to roll on this kingdom."

Early on June 28, 1844, I heard of the assassination of Joseph and Hyrum. To attempt to delineate the feelings of woe and unutterable sorrow that swelled every heart too full for tears, I need not attempt. I stood up, dazed with grief, could groan but could not weep. The fountain of tears was dry! "Oh God! what will thy orphan Church and people now do!" was the only feeling or thought that now burst out in groans.

I did not go to see their mutilated bodies. I had no wish to look into their grave; I knew they were not there, and the words of Brother Joseph began to come back to me: "I could do so much more for my friends if I were on the other side of the veil." These words, "my friends"—oh, how glad I was that he was my friend! These thoughts gradually gained the empire in my heart, and I began to realize that in his martyrdom there was a great and eternal purpose in the heavens.

The journal of Benjamin F. Johnson, Church Historian's Library, Salt Lake City, Utah; "An Interesting Letter," from Patriarch Benjamin F. Johnson to George S. Gibbs, 1903; Benjamin F. Johnson file, Church Historian's Library, Salt Lake City, Utah.

Samuel Miles

My recollections and acquaintance with the Prophet Joseph are those of a boy from the age of eight to eighteen, when he was martyred.

His kind manner and gentle words when I first met him in company with my father, and he took me by the hand; his noble deportment when before the people; his easy, jovial appearance when engaged in the sports which were common in the days of Nauvoo; his firm dislike of that which was degrading—all these combined to give me a very favorable opinion of this noble man.

My father's farm, two miles south of Far West, Missouri, on the rich prairie and bottoms of a branch of Log Creek, produced phenomenal growths of vegetables, etc. Among other things a mammoth musk-melon was being developed. Father said, "We will give this to the Prophet."

I watched over it with great care, and we had much satisfaction when it was ripe in presenting it to Joseph and receiving his thanks.

When times of trouble came on in Missouri, I have seen the Prophet mustering in the ranks, his rifle on his shoulder, encouraging the Saints by his example as well as by his cheering words.

On his first visit to Nauvoo, traveling from Quincy, he stayed over night in the little town of Lima, where several families of the Saints had found shelter. I recollect how joyful we all were to greet the Prophet and the brethren who accompanied him. In the morning, we all came out to bid them Godspeed on their journey to find a location for the Saints. Joseph's spirited black horse, when he attempted to mount him, made a start, wheeling partly around, but the Prophet with a sudden spring gained the saddle minus his tall black hat, containing, as was customary in those days, his papers, etc. There being at the time a light wind, hat and papers went flying around. But we were not long in getting them together and restoring them to their owner.

The Juvenile Instructor, XXVII (March 15, 1892), pp. 173-174.

Jesse N. Smith

I first saw the Prophet in Kirtland, though I was then but a child. Afterwards I met him at Nauvoo. The Prophet was incomparably the most God-like man I ever saw. I know that by nature he was incapable of lying and deceitfulness, possessing the greatest kindness and nobility of character. I felt when in his presence that he could read me through and through. I know he was all that he claimed to be.

In 1843, for a short time, I attended a school kept by a Miss Mitchell, in Hyrum Smith's brick office. Passing the Prophet's house one morning, he called me to him and asked what book I read in at my school. I replied, "The Book of Mormon."

He seemed pleased, and taking me into the house he gave me a copy of the Book of Mormon to read at school, a gift greatly prized by me.

The Juvenile Instructor, XXVII (January 1, 1892), pp. 23-24.

Sariah A. Workman

The Prophet used to come to the home of my father, Joel H. Johnson, before I can remember. He was a great lover of children and made a great impression upon me from my earliest recollection. But what I remember best is that I always felt a divine influence whenever I was in his presence. The Holy Ghost testified to me then, though I was only twelve years of age at the time of his martyrdom, and that testimony has still remained with me, that he is a prophet of the true and living God.

Young Woman's Journal, XVII (December, 1906), p. 542.

Susan E. J. Martineau

The Prophet frequently came to our house and sometimes stayed overnight. He partook of a Christmas dinner at my father's; and standing at the head of the table, the Prophet carved the turkey. Fearing that his clothing might accidentally be soiled, my step-mother tied a long apron upon him. He laughed and said it was well, for he did not know what might happen to him. My brother Seth and I were in the room, admiring, in our childish way, him whom we thought the greatest man on earth.

When I was but a child, I had a positive testimony that Joseph was a prophet of God, and as I looked at him he seemed to me like a heavenly being.

Young Woman's Journal, XVII (December 1906), pp. 541-542.

Henry William Bigler

The first Sunday after I reached Far West, I went to meeting with the hopes of hearing the Prophet. How disappointed I was when he called to the stand a beardless boy (Erastus Snow). But I soon found there was preach in him. When he finished, the Prophet got up and complimented the young man, but said: "I will correct the idea in regard to the little stone rolling forth, as foretold in Daniel, chapter 2. This is not so. It is stationary, like a grind stone, and revolves. (He made a motion with his hands showing how it turned.) When the Elders go abroad to preach the gospel, and the people become believers in the Book of Mormon and are baptized, they are added to the little stone. Thus, they are gathered around it so that it grows larger and larger until it begins to pinch the toes of the image, and finally breaks it into pieces to be carried away like the chaff of a summer's threshing, while the stone will keep growing until its fills the whole earth."

Speaking about praying to our Father in heaven, I once heard Joseph Smith remark, "Be plain and simple, and ask for what you want, just like you would go to a neighbor and say, I want to borrow your horse to go to the mill."

I heard him say to some Elders going on missions, "Make short prayers and short sermons, and let mysteries alone. Preach nothing but repentance and baptism for the remission of sins, for that was all John the Baptist preached."

"Life Sketch of Henry William Bigler," Church Historian's Library, Salt Lake City, Utah; *The Juvenile Instructor,* XXVII, (March 1, 1892), pp. 151-152.

John W. Hess

In the autumn of 1838, Joseph the Prophet and others came to my father's house near the Richmond Landing and stayed there thirteen days. Father was the only Mormon in that part of the country.

At that time Joseph was studying Greek and Latin. When he got tired studying, he would go and play with the children in their games about the house, to give himself exercise. Then he would go back to his studies. I was a boy then about fourteen years old. He used to take me up on his knee and caress me as he would a little child. I relate this to show the kindness and simplicity of his nature. I never saw another man like Joseph. There was something heavenly and angelic in his looks that I never witnessed in the countenance of any other person. During his short stay, I became very much attached to him, and learned to love him more dearly than any other person I ever met, my father and mother not excepted.

The next time I saw the Prophet was at the Richmond court house, in chains, after the surrender of the city of Far West. I used to walk six miles every day to see him during his stay in the Richmond jail. Although a boy of about fourteen years, I became convinced beyond doubt that he was a prophet of God, and that testimony has never left me.

The Juvenile Instructor, XXVII, (May 15, 1892), pp. 302-303.

David Osborn

The first time I saw Joseph Smith was at Far West, in 1837. He and others were seated on a wagon box. There was a large congregation. Joseph said, "You have heard many reports about me. Some perhaps are true and others not true. I know what I have done and I know what I have not done. You may hug up to yourselves the Bible, but, except through faith in it you get revelation for yourself, the Bible will profit you but little. The Book of Mormon is true, just what it purports to be, and for this testimony I expect to give an account in the day of judgment. If I obtain the glory which I have in view, I expect to wade through much tribulation."

In closing his remarks, he said, "The Savior declared the time was coming when secret or hidden things should be revealed on the house tops. Well, I have revealed to you a few things, if not on the house top, on the wagon top."

On another occasion he preached and chastised the rich, or those who had money, for buying land at government price and selling it in small lots to their poor brethren at a high price. He said the Lord was not pleased with their conduct. "You say I am a prophet. Well, then, I will prophesy, and when you go home write it down and remember it. You think you have been badly treated by your enemies; but if you don't do better than you are now doing, I prophesy that the state of Missouri will not hold you. Your sufferings have hardly commenced."

About eighteen months after this we all left the state.

I have many times put a piece of corn bread in my pocket and walked to the city of Nauvoo, 4½ miles, to hear Joseph and others preach, and felt that I was well paid for my pains. It was a perfect feast to me.

The Juvenile Instructor, XXVII (March 15, 1892), p. 173; Diary of David Osborn, Brigham Young University Library, p. 13.

Mosiah L. Hancock

We went with Joseph Smith to Missouri, and it was there on the road to Far West that I learned to love the noble course of the Prophet.

I asked Father, "Who made the father of our God?"

Brother Joseph answered, "Brother Levi, it is just as natural for God to have a father as it is for you or me to have one."

It was the disposition of the Prophet Joseph when he saw little children in the mud to take them up in his arms and wash the mud from their bare feet with his handkerchief. And oh how kind he was to the old folks, as well as to little children. He always had a smile for his friends, and was always cheerful.

The mobocrats in Missouri tried to make it appear that the Mormons were disloyal to the government. None but the most ignorant ever said that of the Saints. They were from Eastern or Puritan stock, and the songs of liberty and freedom were on every tongue. The mobocrats were known to say that the law could not reach the Saints, but that powder and ball could! During the Fourth of July celebration, lightning struck the liberty-pole at Far West, Missouri, and made it a mass of splinters. Brother Joseph said, "There goes the liberty of the people."

The summer of 1841 I played my first game of ball with the Prophet. We took turns knocking and chasing the ball, and when the game was over the Prophet said, "Brethren, hitch up your teams."

We did, and we all drove to the woods. I drove our one-horse wagon, standing on the front bolster, and Brother Joseph and Father rode on the hounds behind. There were thirty-nine teams in the group and we gathered wood until our wagons were loaded. When our wagon was loaded, Brother Joseph offered to pull sticks with anyone who wanted to compete with him—and he pulled them all up one at a time. Afterwards the Prophet sent the wagons out to different places where people needed help; and he told them to cut the wood for the Saints who needed it. Everybody loved to do as the Prophet said, and even though we were sickly, and death was all around us, folks smiled and tried to cheer everyone up.

I saw many remarkable cases of healing under the hands of the Prophet while we were at Nauvoo.

Well do I remember the Prophet's speech from a frame in front of his mansion—where he said, "Brethren, I now roll this work onto the shoulders of the Twelve; and they shall bear and send this gospel to every nation under heaven."

He asked the members of the Legion if they were not all his boys, and they shouted "Yes!"

I stood on the rail of the fence in front of the Mansion. The Prophet said, "Brethren, the Lord Almighty has this day revealed to me something I never comprehended before! That is—I have friends who have at a respectful distance been ready to ward off the blows of the adversary (he brought his hand down on my father's head as he was acting as bodyguard to the Prophet), while others have pretended to be my friends, have crept into my bosom, and have become vipers—my most deadly enemies. I wish you to be obedient to these true men as you have promised. ARE YOU WILLING TO DIE FOR ME?"

"Yes!" was the shout.

"You have said you are willing to die for me—." Then he drew his sword and cried, "I WILL DIE FOR YOU! If this people cannot have their rights, my blood shall run upon the ground like water."

I saw the Prophet and the rest when they departed from Nauvoo for the last time; and I went out to meet their martyred bodies when they were brought from Carthage with Apostle John Taylor, who was himself so badly wounded that he could not stir. Many of the Saints went out to meet them, and their hearts were full of sorrow. I went to see those noble martyrs after they were laid out in the Mansion.

After the people had gone home, my father took me again into the Mansion and told me to place one hand on Joseph's breast and to raise my other arm and swear with hand uplifted that I would never make a compromise with any of the sons of hell, which vow I took with a determination to fulfill to the very letter. I took the same vow with Hyrum.

> Autobiography of Mosiah L. Hancock, Brigham Young University Library, pp. 2-3, 9-10, 21, 22, 24, 25, 27-30.

Orange L. Wight

We moved to Daviess County, Missouri, and made our principal settlement at Adam-ondi-Ahman. The Prophet Joseph told us that it was the place where Adam offered his holy sacrifices. The altar was not far from our house.

Adam-ondi-Ahman was visited a number of times by the Prophet Joseph Smith, and I became acquainted with him. Being now fourteen years old, I could comprehend and appreciate all, or nearly all, he would say. He was very kind and sociable with both young and old. We often bathed in the limpid waters of the Grand River. Although but a boy, I was invited to bathe with them. At one time we had a jolly time. There was Joseph the Prophet, my father Lyman Wight, Sidney Rigdon, and several others.

Mother and I made several trips to the Liberty Jail, in Clay County, Missouri. Most of the trips were made with sisters whose husbands were in prison with my father and the Prophet. While in the prison with the Prophet, I got better acquainted with him and could appreciate his divine mission.

Later in Quincy, Illinois, I had further opportunities to become better acquainted with the Prophet Joseph, and had an increase of my faith in his holy mission, being at an age when I could judge and see more perfectly that he was an inspired prophet of God.

In the fall of 1839, we moved to Nauvoo and stopped in the house with the Prophet Joseph for several weeks.

After I returned to Nauvoo in 1843, Joseph asked me a great many questions about my mission. I told the Prophet that a man by the name of Brank was coming to Nauvoo. He looked troubled for a moment, and said he had trouble enough with that man. Brank was an apostate. Then his countenance changed to one of inspiration, and he said, "Orange, he will not come."

He never did come. That was a prophecy which, my having seen the Prophet and heard his words, I can never forget. It was proof to me that he was inspired.

> Letter written by Orange L. Wight to Joseph I. Earl and Harriet M. Earl, Bunkerville, Nevada, May 4, 1903, typewritten copy in the Brigham Young University Library, pp. 3-9.

Anson Call

In the month of September, 1838, I received a visit from Joseph, Hyrum, and Sidney Rigdon at the Three Forks of the Grand River, near Adam-ondi-Ahman, in Missouri. Joseph stated that he had come on a special errand. It was on the Sabbath, and the brethren were congregated at my house to meet with a number of Missourians. After the meeting, he slipped into the cornfield with about twelve of the brethren. He stated that we must leave, for there were going to be difficulties. We inquired from what source. He said it was not for him to say. The message he had received was for us to leave and go to Far West, or Adam-ondi-Ahman.

We unanimously agreed to do so. We then inquired whether it was necessary for us to go forthwith, or whether we could stay and save our crops and sell our farms. He said we need not sell our farms, and he presumed we should have time to get away. But how much time he knew not. These leaders then left us, after the dinner.

We were very anxious to save our crops and we concluded we would do so if we could. It was agreed by the brethren that I should travel through Daviess, Caldwell and Ray Counties, and see if there was any stir among the people. I accordingly started the next day and discovered no excitement among the people. We therefore concluded we could give ourselves sufficient time to secure our crops.

After doing so, we decided we could go bee hunting. After seven days' hunt, we still found that all was peace. Since we had done so well, we decided to take another hunt.

But on our return we found the whole country in arms, between us and Adam-ondi-Ahman and Far West. Cornelius Gilliam had a company of mobbers placed to prevent the Mormons from going to and from either place. They told us that if we stayed we should not be harmed, but that if we attempted to go away it would be death.

About the middle of May, 1839, after the Saints had been driven out of Missouri, I was one day traveling to Warsaw, Illinois, when to my great surprise I met Brothers Joseph and Hyrum. I asked him when and how he had made his escape from Missouri.

He said, "I am in a great hurry, for my enemies are pursuing me. I will say in short that the prayers of the brethren brought me here."

He then inquired of me where I lived. He said, "In about a week I will be at your house; then I will relate the whole matter to you."

He passed on in great haste. I was filled with great joy to see our prophet in the enjoyment of liberty.

He came to my house about the appointed time, had his dinner and spent the principal part of the afternoon in conversation on the circumstances of his escape from Missouri.

On the 14th of July, 1843, with quite a number of his brethren, the Prophet crossed the Mississippi River to the town of Montrose, to be present at the installment of the Masonic Lodge of the "Rising Sun." A block schoolhouse had been prepared with shade in front, under which was a barrel of ice water.

Joseph, as he was tasting the cold water, warned the brethren not to be too free with it. With the tumbler still in his hand, he prophesied that the Saints would yet go to the Rocky Mountains. Said he, "This water tastes much like that of the crystal streams that are running from the snow-capped mountains."

I had before seen him in a vision, and now saw his countenance change to white; not the deadly white of a bloodless face, but a living, brilliant white. He seemed absorbed in gazing at something at a great distance, and said, "I am gazing upon the valleys of those mountains."

This was followed by a vivid description of the scenery of these mountains, as I have since become acquainted with it. Pointing to Shadrach Roundy and others, he said, "There are some men here who shall do a great work in that land."

Pointing to me, he said, "There is Anson. He shall go and shall assist in building up cities from one end of the country to the other, and you (rather extending the idea to all those he had spoken of) shall perform as great a work as has been done by man, so that the nations of the earth shall be astonished, and many of them will be gathered in that land and assist in building cities and temples, and Israel shall be made to rejoice."

It is impossible to represent in words the grandeur of Joseph's appearance, his beautiful descriptions of this land, and his wonderful prophetic utterances as they emanated from the glorious inspirations that overshadowed him. There was a force and power in his exclamations of which the following is but a faint echo: "Oh the beauty of those snow-capped mountains! The cool refreshing streams that are running down through those mountain gorges!"

Then looking in another direction, as if there was a change of locality: "Oh the scenes that this people will pass through! The dead that will lie between here and there."

Then turning in another direction as if the scene had again changed: "Oh the apostasy that will take place before my brethren reach that land! But the priesthood shall prevail over its enemies, triumph over the devil and be established upon the earth, never more to be thrown down!"

He then charged us with great force and power to be faithful to those things that had been and should be committed to our charge, with the promise of all the blessings that the priesthood could bestow: "Remember these things and treasure them up. Amen."

Autobiography of Anson Call, Brigham Young University Library, pp. 6-7, 18-20. Edward W. Tullidge, *History of Northern Utah and Southern Idaho: Biographical Supplement,* pp. 271-272.

Alexander McRae

During our imprisonment in Liberty Jail we had many visitors, both friends and enemies. Among the latter, many were angry with Brother Joseph and accused him of killing a son, a brother, or some relative of theirs, at what was called the Crooked River Battle. This looked rather strange to me, that so many should claim a son, or a brother killed there, when they reported only one man killed.

After we had been there some time and had tried every means we could to obtain our liberty by the law, without effect (except Sidney Rigdon who was bailed out), and also having heard from a reliable source that "the Mormon prisoners would have to be condemned or the character of the state would have to go down," we came to the conclusion that we would try other means to effect it.

Accordingly, on the 7th day of February, 1839, after counseling together on the subject, we concluded to try to go that evening when the jailor came with our supper. But before deciding fully, and to make it more sure, Brother Hyrum asked Brother Joseph to inquire of the Lord as to the propriety of the move.

He did so, and received answer to this effect—that if we were all agreed, we could go clear that evening; and if we would ask, we should have a testimony for ourselves.

I immediately asked, and had no more than asked until I received as clear a testimony as ever I did of anything in my life that it was true. Brother Hyrum Smith and Caleb Baldwin bore testimony to the same. But Lyman Wight said we might go if we chose, but he would not.

After talking with him for some time, he said if we would wait until the next day, he would go with us.

Without thinking we had no promise of success on any other day than the one above stated, we agreed to wait.

When night came, the jailor came alone with our supper, threw the door wide open, put our supper on the table, and went to the back part of the room where a pile of books lay, took up a book and went to reading, leaving us between him and the door, thereby giving us every chance to go if we had been ready. As the next day was agreed upon, we made no attempt to go that evening.

When the next evening came, the case was very different. The jailor brought a double guard with him, and with them six of our brethren, to wit, Erastus Snow, William D. Huntington, Cyrus Daniels, David Holeman, Alanson Ripley and Watson Barlow. I was afterwards informed that they were sent by the Church. The jailor seemed to be badly scared. He had the door locked and everything made secure. It looked like a bad chance to get away, but we were determined to try it. So when the jailor started out, we started too. Brother Hyrum took hold of the door and the rest followed. But before we were able to render him the assistance he needed, the jailor and guard succeeded in closing the door, shutting the brethren in with us, except Cyrus Daniels, who was on the outside.

The scene that followed defies description. I should judge from the number that all the town and many from the country gathered around the jail, and every mode of torture and death that their imagination could fancy was proposed for us. But they were so divided among themselves that they could not carry out any of their plans.

During this time, some of our brethren spoke of our being in great danger; and I confess I felt that we were. But Brother Joseph told them not to fear, that not a hair of their heads should be hurt, and that they would not lose any of their things, even to a bridle, saddle, or blanket; that everything should be restored to them; they had offered their lives for us and the gospel; that it was necessary the Church should offer a sacrifice, and the Lord accepted the offering.

The brethren who had come to visit the prisoners had to undergo a trial, but the excitement was so great that they (the officers) dared not take them out until it abated a little. While they were waiting for their trial, some of the brethren employed lawyers to defend them. Brother Erastus Snow asked Brother Joseph whether he had better employ a lawyer or not. Brother Joseph told him to plead his own case.

"But," said Brother Snow, "I do not understand law."

Brother Joseph asked him if he did not understand justice.

He said he thought he did.

"Well," said Brother Joseph, "go and plead for justice as hard as you can, and quote Blackstone and other authors now and then, and they will take it all for law."

He did as he was told, and the result was as Joseph had said it would be. When he got through his plea, the lawyers flocked around him and asked him where he had studied law, and said they had never heard a better plea. When the trial was over, Brother Snow was discharged, and all the rest were held to bail, and were allowed to bail each other by Brother Snow going bail with them. They got everything that was taken from them. Nothing was lost, although no two articles were in one place.

Sometime during our stay in Liberty Jail an attempt was made to destroy us by poison, and it was only by much faith and prayer that the effect was overcome.

We never suffered ourselves to go into any important measure without asking Brother Joseph to inquire of the Lord in relation to it. Such was our confidence in him as a prophet that when he said, "Thus saith the Lord," we were confident it would be as he said. The more we tried it, the more confidence we had, for we never found his word to fail in a single instance.

A short time before we were to go to Daviess County for trial, word came to us that either General Atchison or Doniphan would raise a military force and go with us to protect us from the wrath of that people. The matter was discussed by the brethren (except Brother Joseph), and they naturally enough concluded it would be best. Although I had nothing to say, I concurred with them in my feelings.

Brother Hyrum asked Brother Joseph what he thought of it. Brother Joseph hung his head a few moments and seemed in a deep study, then raised up and said, "Brother Hyrum, it will not do. We must trust in the Lord. If we take a guard with us we shall be destroyed."

This was very unexpected to us, but Brother Hyrum remarked, "If you say it in the name of the Lord, we will rely on it."

Said Brother Joseph, "In the name of the Lord, if we take a guard with us, we will be destroyed, but if we put our trust in the Lord we shall be safe, and no harm shall befall us, and we shall be better treated than we have ever been since we have been prisoners."

This settled the question, and all seemed satisfied. It was decided that we should have no extra guard, only such as they chose for our safe keeping.

When we arrived at the place where the court was held, I began to think he was mistaken for once, for the people rushed upon us *en masse* crying, "Kill them: - - - - - - - - them, kill them."

I could see no chance for escape, unless we could fight our way through. And we had nothing to do it with.

At this, Brother Joseph, at whom all seemed to rush, rose up and said, "We are in your hands; if we are guilty, we refuse not to be punished by the law."

Hearing these words, two of the most bitter mobocrats in the country—one by the name of William Peniston and the other Kinney, or McKinney—got up on benches and began to speak to the people, saying, "Yes, gentlemen, these men are in our hands; let us not use violence, but let the law have its course. The law will condemn them, and they will be punished by it. We do not want the disgrace of taking the law into our own hands."

In a very few minutes they were quieted, and they seemed now as friendly as they had a few minutes before been enraged. From that time until we got away they could not put a guard over us who would not become so friendly that they dared not trust him, and the guard was very frequently changed. We were seated at the first table with the judge, lawyers, etc., and had the best the country afforded, with feather beds to sleep on—a privilege we had not before enjoyed in all our imprisonment.

On one occasion while we were there, the above-named William Peniston, partly in joke and partly in earnest, threw out a rather hard insinuation against some of the brethren. This touched Joseph's feelings and he retorted a good deal in the same way, only with such power that the earth seemed to tremble under his feet: "Your heart is as black as your whiskers," which were as black as any crow.

He seemed to quake under it and left the room.

The guards, who had become friendly, were alarmed for our safety and exclaimed, "O, Mr. Smith, do not talk so. You will bring trouble upon yourself and companions."

Brother Joseph replied, "Do not be alarmed; I know what I am about."

He always took up for the brethren, when their characters were assailed, sooner than for himself, no matter how unpopular it was to speak in their favor.

History of the Church, III, pp. 256-259.

Peter Hardeman Burnett

Joseph Smith was much more than an ordinary man. He possessed the most indomitable perseverance, was a good judge of men, and deemed himself born to command, and he did command. His views were so strange and striking, and his manner was so earnest and apparently so candid that you could not but be interested. There was a kind, familiar look about him that pleased you. He was very courteous in discussion, readily admitting that he did not intend to controvert, and would not oppose you abruptly, but had due deference to your feelings. He had the capacity for discussing a subject in different aspects and for proposing many original views, even of ordinary matters. His illustrations were his own.

He had great influence over others. As an evidence of this I will state that after he had been taken a prisoner in Missouri, I saw him out among the crowd conversing freely with everyone and seeming to be perfectly at ease. In the short space of five days he had managed so to mollify his enemies that he could go unprotected among them without the slightest danger.

Among the Mormons he had much greater influence than Sidney Rigdon. The latter was a man of superior education, an eloquent speaker, of fine appearance and dignified manners; but he did not possess the native intellect of Smith, and lacked his determined will.

Joseph Smith was a very stout, athletic man, and was a skillful wrestler. This was known to the men of Daviess County, and some of them proposed to Smith that he should wrestle with one of their own men. He at first courteously objected, alleging substantially that though he was once in the habit of wrestling, he was now a minister of the gospel and did not wish to do anything contrary to his duty as such, and that he hoped they would excuse him upon that ground.

They replied that they did not desire to do anything contrary to his calling; that they would not bet anything; that it was nothing but a friendly trial of skill and manhood, for the satisfaction of others, and to pass away the time pleasantly; and that they hoped he would, under all the circumstances, comply with their request.

He consented. They selected the best wrestler among them, and Smith threw him several times in succession, to the great amusement of the spectators.

Peter Hardeman Burnett, *An Old California Pioneer* (Oakland, 1946), pp. 40-41.

George Miller

In the early part of November, 1838, the wolves being unusually destructive to my sheep, I resolved to take most of them into the adjoining state of Missouri (I was then living in McDonough County, Illinois) and sell them.

While I was ferrying my sheep over the Mississippi, at Quincy, Illinois, I met a young man who had been in the town to get armed and equipped to enter the "Mormon War," as he pleased to call it. This declaration of the ignorant young man was indeed news to me.

By the time I got home, the Mormons expelled from Missouri began to cross the Mississippi River in a poor and distressed condition.

During the winter, I found my health very much declining. I had concluded to rent my farm and move into the village. I had 300 acres tillable land, between 5,000 and 8,000 bushels of grain that I had no market for, a large quantity of bacon and lard, about 250 head of hogs, about 100 head of cattle, together with sheep and poultry, and fourteen well-selected horses, well suited for the saddle or harness; also three yearling colts.

The encumbrance of this property was greatly in the way of my resolution to move to the village. I resolved to seek out some poor Mormon families, and establish them as farmers on my homestead, as I was well supplied with house room.

I had a friend in Quincy who had in one of his houses the families of Joseph Smith, Sen., Samuel H. Smith, Don Carlos Smith, Jenkins Salsbury, and a Brother Henry Hoit. He said they were all destitute and he thought gentlemen, and would suit my purpose.

I waited on the venerable patriarch and those under his roof. He frankly said that his sons would take charge of my farm and effects, and praised God that I had been sent in answer to his prayers.

I arrived home and the Brothers Smith came as was agreed upon. I told them to inform all the destitute Mormons to come and get provisions, and they could be had without money or price.

About this time news reached us that the Prophet Joseph Smith had escaped from prison, and arrived in Illinois, and was making an effort to buy the village of Commerce. I had great anxiety to see him, but Don Carlos informed me that as soon as a place was fixed for the gathering of the Saints, Joseph would be at my place to pay them a visit.

One bright morning I prevailed on my wife to ride on horseback to visit our tenants on the farm. On our return home, I perceived that a carriage containing a number of persons was meeting us. As we neared it, the appearance of a large man sitting in front driving seemed to be familiar to me, as if I had always known him. Suddenly the thought burst on my mind that it was none other than the Prophet Joseph Smith.

My whole frame was in a tremor with the occurrence of the thought, and my heart seemed as if it were coming up into my mouth.

Getting in speaking distance, he suddenly reined up his horses as making ready to speak. I was much agitated as the words came from his mouth: "Sir, can you tell me the way to the farm of a Mr. Miller, living somewhere in the direction I am going?"

Instead of answering him directly, my reply was, "I presume, sir, that you are Joseph Smith, Jr., the Mormon Prophet?"

"I am, sir," he said, adding, "I also presume that you are the Mr. Miller whose farm I inquired for?"

"I am, sir," I replied.

He then introduced me to his wife and family.

I solicited him to preach. He excused himself as not feeling like sermonizing, having just escaped from prison; that he felt like a bird uncaged and was more disposed to reconnoiter the country and visit his friends and people.

Upon my urging the matter, he suddenly turned to me, saying that he did think of some one of the elders preaching for me, but he was now resolved on doing it himself; that it had been whispered that a Samaritan had bound up the wounds of his bleeding friends, adding that he would do the best he could in the way of preaching. Accordingly the time and place was fixed upon, and I went to notify the people of the appointment of the Mormon Prophet to preach.

The appointed time arrived. The house and dooryard were filled with people, apparently anxious to hear more for the purpose of fault finding than seeking after truth. He took for his text the chapter in the writings of Luke where a certain man fell among thieves when journeying from Jerusalem to Jericho, and was taken and ministered to by the Samaritan.

He took an extensive latitude while treating on this text, and took up a long time. Notwithstanding it was a rainy day, those outside of the house stood in the rain sheltered by umbrellas until the service was over. I had no remaining doubts left in regard to the truth of the Prophet Joseph, and the doctrine of the gospel as taught by the Latter-day Saints. Shortly thereafter I was baptized by Elder John Taylor, and here a new era of my life was fully ushered in.

> *Correspondence of Bishop George Miller with the*
> *Northern Islander,* pp. 1-6.

Wandle Mace

My eyes rested upon the great Prophet of the last days for the first time in 1839. I was introduced to him and his brother, and shook hands with them. Their sister—the wife of brother McClary —hurried to and fro, pressing them to partake of refreshments, at the same time telling them how anxious they had been, and how fearful they were lest the mob would take their lives. Joseph said to her, "You were much troubled about us, but you did not know the promises of God to us."

On the landing at the top of some stairs at the back of a house the Prophet addressed the people. This is the first time I heard him preach, and I shall never forget his words. In the course of his remarks he said, "Yes," said the angel, "your name shall go out for good and for evil."

He was a fine looking man, tall and well proportioned, strong and active, with a light complexion, blue eyes, and light hair, and very little beard. He had a free and easy manner, not the least affectation, yet he was bold and independent, and very interesting and eloquent in speech.

Almost as soon as the father and mother of the Prophet set their feet upon the hospitable shore of Illinois, I became acquainted with them. I frequently visited them and listened with intense interest as they related the history of the rise of the Church.

With tears they could not withhold, they narrated the story of the persecution of their boy Joseph when the angel first visited him and informed him of the great things the Lord was about to bring to pass. Since that time it had been one continual scene of persecution.

In these conversations, Mother Smith related much of their family history. She said their family must have presented a peculiar appearance to a stranger, as they were seated around the room, father, mother, brothers, and sisters, all listening with the greatest interest to Joseph, as he taught them the pure principles of the gospel as revealed to him by angels, and the glorious visions he beheld, as he saw the Father and the Son descend to earth.

She said: "During the day our sons would endeavor to get through their work as early as possible, and say, 'Mother, have supper early, so we can have a long evening to listen to Joseph.' Sometimes Joseph would describe the appearance of the Nephites, their mode of dress and warfare, their implements of husbandry, etc., and many things he had seen in vision. Truly ours was a happy family, although persecuted by preachers, who declared there was no more vision, the canon of scripture was full, and no more revelation was needed."

But Joseph had seen a vision and must declare it.

Oh, how many hours I have spent with these good old folks. They were as honest and true as it was possible for mortals to be; and they exemplify the words of the apostle who said, "All who will live godly in Christ Jesus, shall suffer persecution."

Meetings in Nauvoo were held in a Jack Oak Grove, in the open air, and here I listened to the words of inspiration as they fell from the lips of the Prophet. Who could listen to these words of inspiration and honestly say Joseph Smith is an impostor? No one, not even his bitter enemies. I have listened to the Prophet Joseph in public, and in private, in sunshine and shower—as many others have done; and I do know that no man could explain the scriptures—throw them wide open to view, so plain that none could misunderstand their meaning—except he had been taught of God.

I have felt ashamed myself sometimes, having studied the scriptures so much [before joining the Church, he memorized the New Testament], that I had not seen that which was so plain when he touched them. He, as it were, turned the key, and the door of knowledge sprang wide open, disclosing precious principles, both new and old. I have many times been pondering upon a subject, and seemed to come to a standstill, not knowing how to gain further information relating to it, when upon going to meeting on the Sabbath, the key would be touched by Joseph and the subject would be so plain I wondered why I had not seen it before.

One day Joseph rode up to the Temple grounds, as we stood together talking after our day's work, and called out, "Boys, has Bonaparte any friends in the French Army?" Of course we were all attention to know his meaning. He then told us that Orrin Porter Rockwell had been thrown in jail, in Missouri, and that for the sum of two hundred dollars his mother could obtain his release. Joseph said he had not sufficient money himself, so he wanted the brethren to assist him. All present responded heartily.

Joseph dismounted from his horse and engaged in a friendly wrestle with some of the "boys," as he called us. He often tried to get me to wrestle with him. I never could. I was a strong man. Often when we met and shook hands, he would pull me to him for a wrestle and say, slapping my shoulder with his hand, "If you are not a strong man there is no use of putting a man upright."

I have been with him at times when approached by a long-faced religious stranger, who seemed to think that it was almost a sin to smile, and that the Prophet should be as sedate and as cheerless as himself. The Prophet would challenge someone present for a wrestle—to the utter astonishment of the religious stranger, who would be almost shocked at the mention of a wrestle, but would extol Jacob, who seemed to be an accomplished wrestler and also a great favorite with God.

Such was Joseph, the great Prophet of the last days. As he often joined us on the Temple grounds, we were sure of a rare treat if we could get him to talk to us. Some one present, being in a hurry to hear him, would say, "Brother Joseph talk to us."

He would say: "What do you want to talk about? Start something."

Soon a conversation would bring out some question for Joseph to answer. Then I would lean back and listen. Ah, what pleasure this gave me! He would unravel the scriptures and explain doctrine as no other man could. What had been mystery he made so plain it was no longer mystery.

He fed us deliciously with spiritual food. His discourses were becoming better every time he addressed the Saints, and we anticipated a continuance of these things.

I have both seen and heard him when filled with the Holy Ghost prophesy in the name of the Most High God, and I have lived to see many of those prophesies fulfilled, and some are now being fulfilled, and all will be in the due time of the Lord. I have heard him rebuke the wicked for their misdeeds until they would fear and trembled before him. I have seen him lay hands on the sick, and heard him rebuke disease, and in an instant raise from beds of sickness some who to all human appearance were past recovery, and this by the power of God which was in him. Indeed, he was a prophet of the living God.

Journal of Wandle Mace, Brigham Young University Library, pp. 36-37, 45-47, 92-93, 100-102, 129, 299-300.

William G. Nelson

In the summer of 1836 the Prophet stopped overnight with my father in Missouri. This was the first time I had ever seen him. Some time after this we moved to Nauvoo, where I saw the Prophet quite often. Father and he were personal friends, and he came to our home many times and talked with Father in the presence of the family.

One day he rode up to the gate and called to my mother, "Where is Brother Nelson today?"

Mother told him he was on the Island cutting wood.

"I should like to have seen him. Is your family well?"

Mother answered that one of the boys was sick with chills and fever.

"Tell Brother Nelson that the boy will get well, and you will not have any more sickness in your family as long as you live in Nauvoo," the Prophet said.

This prophecy was literally fulfilled.

I have heard the Prophet speak in public on many occasions. In one meeting I heard him say: "I will give you a key that will never rust—if you will stay with the majority of the Twelve Apostles, and the records of the Church, you will never be led astray."

Young Woman's Journal, XVII (December 1906), pp. 542-543.

Mercy R. Thompson

A small company of friends gathered to witness the ceremony of my marriage to Robert B. Thompson, at Kirtland. The Prophet performed the ceremony. After the ceremony, we listened to the words of instruction and counsel which fell from the inspired lips of Joseph Smith, each word carrying to our hearts deeper and stronger convictions that we were listening to a mighty prophet of God. And yet there was not the slightest appearance of ostentation or conscious power on his part. He was as free and sociable as though we had all been his own brothers and sisters, or members of one family. He was as unassuming as a child.

In Nauvoo, I became more intimately acquainted with the Prophet, in consequence of my husband being employed as his secretary, and to whom the Prophet became very much attached, so much so that one day he jocosely said to me, "Sister Thompson, you must not feel bad towards me for keeping your husband away from you so much, for I am married to him."

They truly loved each other with fervent brotherly affection.

I have seen the Prophet under a great variety of circumstances. I have seen him as if carried away by the power of God beyond all mortal conception, when speaking to the Saints in their public gatherings; and in less public places I have heard him explaining to the brethren and sisters the glorious principles of the gospel as no man could, except by prophetic power.

I have seen him in the lyceum and heard him reprove the brethren for giving way to too much excitement and warmth in debate, and have listened to his clear and masterly explanations of deep and difficult questions.

To him all things seemed simple and easy to be understood, and thus he could make them plain to others as no other man could that I ever heard.

In a social gathering of the Saints at the bowery near the site of the Temple, I saw him rejoicing with the people, perfectly sociable and without reserve, occasionally uttering jokes for their amusement and moving upon the same plane with the humblest and poorest of his friends. To him there were no strangers.

Still he had enemies, and they were always bitter, who, wolf-like toward the lamb, hated him not so much as they thirsted for his blood, because their deeds were evil and their natures and their appetites had fallen to crave for violence and delight in vengeance.

I received my endowments by the directions of the Prophet Joseph, his wife Emma officiating in my case. In his instructions to me at that time, he said, "This will bring you out of darkness into marvelous light."

I saw him by the bedside of Emma, his wife, in sickness, exhibiting all the solicitude and sympathy possible for the tenderest of hearts and the most affectionate of natures to feel. And by the deathbed of my beloved companion, I saw him stand in sorrow, reluctantly submitting to the decree of Providence, while the tears of love and sympathy freely flowed.

This indeed was a time of sorrow, but I can never forget the tender sympathy and brotherly kindness he ever showed toward me and my fatherless child. When riding with him and his wife Emma in their carriage, I have known him to alight and gather prairie flowers for my little girl.

At another time—a time never to be forgotten—I was present at a meeting when Joseph knelt down with the small congregation surrounding him, when every sentence he uttered seemed to convey to my mind, and to the minds of others present, the impression that this was our last meeting together—and so it was.

It seemed to me that there was nothing forgotten or omitted by him, at that time, which pertained either to himself or the Church generally.

A few days after this, he called at his brother Hyrum's to take leave of the family previous to their crossing the Mississippi River, intending to go west to the Rocky Mountains to seek out, if possible, a place of peace and safety for the Saints. His parting words to my sister Mary, as she wept at their going, were these: "Sister Mary, don't feel bad. The Lord will take care of you, and He will deliver us, but I do not know how."

The two brothers then started to cross the river, not knowing whether they would ever see their homes again or not. But on account of the feelings expressed by some of the brethren, who should have been their truest friends, and by their urgent request, sent after them, they returned to Nauvoo the following day. Although I did not know that the brothers had returned home to be taken as "lambs to the slaughter," my feelings were indescribable, and the very air seemed burdened with sorrowful forebodings.

The Juvenile Instructor, XXVII, (July 1, 1892), pp. 398-400.

Christopher Merkley

After the Prophet Joseph came out of prison in Missouri, he called a conference at Quincy, Illinois. While the people were gathering, I was standing near the Prophet when a brother approached him and dunned him for money. The Prophet asked him where he thought he could have money, as he had just gotten out of prison. The man, however, still importuned him. The debt was not the Prophet's, but another brother's who had bought land from this man in Missouri. The Prophet had endorsed for the man who bought.

The Prophet told him that under the circumstances he thought he ought not to demand any pay. But the man was very obdurate, and insisted on having it.

Brother Joseph finally told him he had just five dollars in his pocket. If four dollars would do him any good, he could have them. These the man accepted.

Brother Joseph took five silver dollars out of his pocket and gave him four of them, returning one to his own pocket.

While I was walking around with the Prophet, a man came and told him a sister wanted to see him. Brother Joseph went to see her. I followed him. The sister was sick, and her friends had written to her from the East telling her if she would come back they would take care of her. She asked him what she should do.

Brother Joseph asked her what she would rather do.

She said she would rather stay with the Saints, if she was not too burdensome.

He said, "Then stay, sister, and God bless you."

He put his hand in his pocket and gave her his last dollar. He then instructed the brethren not to let her suffer.

At the close of the conference the Prophet Joseph went to Commerce. On his way he stopped at Lima to take dinner. I met him there and asked him if he would like a little money.

He said, "Yes, Brother Merkley. I am now on a journey of fifty miles, and I have not a dime in my pocket."

I gave him a sovereign.

He took me by the hand and blessed me, and said, "Brother Merkley, may you never want."

I never have.

Biography of Christopher Merkley, pp. 9-11.

Bathsheba W. Smith

The Prophet was a handsome man—splendid looking, a large man, tall and fair. He had a very nice complexion. His eyes were blue, and his hair a golden brown, and very pretty.

My first impressions were that he was an extraordinary man, a man of great penetration; was different from any other man I ever saw; had the most heavenly countenance; was genial, affable and kind; and looked the soul of honor and integrity.

I know him to be what he professed to be—a true prophet of God, and the Lord through him restored the everlasting gospel and every ordinance and endowment that will lead us into the celestial kingdom.

I have heard the Prophet Joseph preach many times. I have heard him prophesy, and I never knew but that everything came to pass that he said.

I heard him preach baptism for the dead; saw him baptizing for the dead in the Mississippi River. I heard him say, "Peradventure, the Ten Tribes were not on this globe, but a portion of this earth had cleaved off with them and went flying into space, and when the time comes, when the 'earth reels to and fro like a drunken man and the stars fall from heaven,' it will join on again."

I heard him preach that the ancient order of Abraham should be restored. He counseled the sisters not to trouble themselves in consequence of plural marriage, that all would be right, and the result would be for their glory and exaltation.

In Nauvoo, at his home, while playing with my baby boy, he said that children were the "honor, glory, and royal diadem of women."

Once when speaking in one of our general fast meetings, he said that we did not know how to pray to have our prayers answered. But when I and my husband had our endowments, in February, 1844, Joseph Smith presiding, he taught us the true order of prayer. I met many times with Brother Joseph and others who had received their endowments, in company with my husband, in an upper room dedicated for that purpose, and prayed with them repeatedly in those meetings.

I was present when William Law, Joseph Smith's counselor, was dropped from that Quorum by each one present voting yes or no in his turn. He was the first member that was dropped who had received his endowments. One member hesitated to vote, which called for earnest remarks from the Prophet Joseph. He showed clearly that it would be doing a serious wrong to retain him longer. After this explanation the vote was unanimous.

Joseph Smith attended one of our Relief Society meetings in the lodge room. He opened the meeting by prayer. His voice trembled very much, after which he addressed us and said, "According to my prayer, I will not be with you long to teach and instruct you, and the world will not be troubled with me much longer."

I used to go very often to Brother Joseph's house, though not much before I was married. Once at dinner, I knew he was looking at me, but I did not feel afraid bcause I knew I had always been good and obedient and had all the faith possible in him and Mormonism. So I just let him look at me. Pretty soon he said to my sister-in-law, "George hit the right stick when he got her."

And I have proved it, for my husband (George A. Smith) and I have lived happily together—like lovers.

The Prophet said we would come to the Rocky Mountains, and he had a company of young men selected to hunt a location for a home for the Saints. I heard of it when we were in Illinois, and I remember an old lady coming in and talking to Mother about what Joseph, the Prophet, had said, that we would be in the Rocky Mountains sometime. I said I would like the time to come soon. I would like to get away from our enemies. She gave me a right good scolding, saying it was terrible to think of going to the Rocky Mountains.

I have seen very many good men, but they had not the gift and blessing Joseph had. He was truly a prophet of God.

The Juvenile Instructor, XXVII (June 1, 1892), pp. 344-345; *Young Woman's Journal*, XVI (December, 1905), pp. 549-550; "Reminiscences of Bathsheba W. Smith," Church Historian's Library, Salt Lake City, Utah, pp. 5-11.

Sarah Ann Gregory Hales

I first saw the Prophet when I was about sixteen, at Nauvoo. While we lived there I was stricken with ague and my parents called the Prophet in to administer to me. He did so and said, "Brother Gregory, your daughter will die here. Bring her up to our house until she is well. Emma will be glad to have her come."

I improved from then on.

I heard the Prophet speak many times and can bear testimony that he was a true prophet of the Lord, and that this is the true and everlasting gospel.

Young Woman's Journal, XIX (December, 1908), p. 672.

Benjamin Brown

Having moved to Nauvoo, my family, with myself, were taken sick, and I lay so for two or three weeks. I was so far gone that I was quite senseless, and all thought I was dying. One day Joseph Smith was passing by my door and was called in, and, as I was afterwards informed, laid his hands upon me and commanded me to rise and walk in the name of the Lord. The first thing I knew was that I found myself walking on the floor, perfectly well, and within ten minutes afterwards I was out of the house visiting my daughter, whom I had not seen for nearly a month. I felt so full of joy and happiness that I was greatly surprised that every one else was not as full of praise as myself. This was the second time that I had been healed instantly by the power of God, through His servants. This man, Joseph Smith, was the one that the world says was an impostor, and a false prophet; the world denies that he ever performed any miracles, or, if any are too well attested to be denied, it attributes them to the power of the imagination over the body. Was it the power of imagination that cured me, when I did not even hear Joseph's voice, or know that any operation on my behalf was going on, until I found myself well?

During a period of about seven years I had frequent opportunities of continuing my acquaintance with Joseph Smith, seeing him nearly every day. From my actual knowledge, I can testify to the purity and uprightness of his life, and I know that he was a man of God. I had every opportunity to acquire this information, for, when escaping from his enemies, he has lived sometimes for a week at a time in my residence.

Testimonies for the Truth: A Record of Manifestations of the Power of God, Miraculous and Providential, Witnessed in the Travels and Experiences of Benjamin Brown (Liverpool, 1853), p. 19.

Rachel Ridgeway Grant

The first time I saw the Prophet Joseph Smith was in New Jersey, before I joined the Church. He preached there that night, but I was prejudiced at the time. I just went to hear him mostly out of curiosity.

The Baptist minister warned me. He said if I did not stop going, I must give up my place in the Baptist Church; and then I went right along. I commenced to read the *Voice of Warning* and the Book of Mormon. I read nearly all night in the Book of Mormon, and felt that it was true, and then I got the spirit of gathering and went to Nauvoo.

The Prophet was not at home very much. His life was so often sought that he had to be hid up. After he had been in hiding and had came out, he was always jolly and happy. He would play with the people, and he was always cheerful and happy whenever he would come out. He was different in that respect from Brother Hyrum, who was more sedate, more serious. I thought at the time Hyrum seemed more like a prophet than Joseph did. You see, there was a great deal of sectarianism about me. Once when a schoolmate wanted me to go with her to hear the Mormons, I went Saturday, but did not want to go on Sunday at all. But I thought it would be impolite not to do as she wished, so I went. When I came home, I went right up stairs and asked the Lord to forgive me for going to hear them on Sunday.

I was many times at the Prophet's house, but not so many times when I saw him. We used to have parties there.

I guess you have seen the picture where Brother Joseph was preaching to the Indians. I was there at that time. The Indians were all kneeling down on the grass in front of the Mansion, and if you have seen that picture, that just describes the way everything was, though it is a miserable picture of the Prophet. He was a fine, noble looking man, always so neat. There are some of the pictures that do not look a particle like him. When he was preaching you could feel the power and influence.

I know Joseph Smith was a prophet, and I have lived to see many of his sayings fulfilled.

Young Woman's Journal, XVI, (December, 1905), pp. 550-551.

Margarette McIntire Burgess

One morning when the Prophet called at our house, I had a very sore throat. It was much swollen and gave me great pain. He took me up in his lap and administered to me, and I was healed. I had no more pain nor soreness.

Another time my older brother and I were going to school, near the building which was known as Joseph's store. It had been raining the previous day, causing the ground to be very muddy, especially along that street. My brother Wallace and I both got fast in the mud and could not get out, and of course, childlike, we began to cry, for we thought we would have to stay there. But looking up, I beheld the loving friend of children, the Prophet Joseph, coming to us. He soon had us on higher and drier ground. Then he stooped down and cleaned the mud from our little, heavy-laden shoes, took his handkerchief from his pocket and wiped our tear-stained faces. He spoke kind and cheering words to us, and sent us on our way to school rejoicing. Was it any wonder that I loved that great, good and noble man of God? As I grew older I felt to honor and love him, for his mission to earth in restoring the gospel of our Lord and Savior Jesus Christ.

Joseph's wife, Sister Emma, lost a young babe. My mother having twin baby girls, the Prophet came to see if she would let him have one of them. Of course it was rather against her feelings, but she finally consented for him to take one of them, providing he would bring it home each night. This he did punctually himself, and also came after it each morning. One evening he did not come with it at the usual time, and mother went down to the Mansion to see what was the matter, and there sat the Prophet with the baby wrapped up in a little silk quilt. He was trotting it on his knee, and singing to it to get it quiet before starting out, as it had been fretting. The child soon became quiet when my mother took it, and the Prophet came up home with her.

Next morning when he came after the baby, mother handed him Sarah, the other baby. They looked so much alike that strangers could not tell them apart. But as mother passed him the other baby, he shook his head and said, "This is not my little Mary."

Then she took Mary from the cradle and gave her to him, and he smilingly carried her home with him. The baby Mary had a very mild disposition, while Sarah was quite cross and fretful, and by this my mother could distinguish them one from the other, though generally people could not tell them apart. But the Prophet soon knew which was the borrowed baby.

After his wife became better in health he did not take our baby any more, but often came in to caress her and play with her. When, after a time, the little one died, he grieved as if he had lost one of his own. I remember seeing him embrace the little cold form and say, "Mary, oh my dear little Mary!"

> *The Juvenile Instructor,* XXVII (January 1, 1892), pp. 66-67; "Stories from the Notebook of Martha Cox, Grandmother of Fern Cox Anderson," Church Historian's Library, Salt Lake City, Utah; Lee C. LaFayette, "Recollections of Joseph Smith," Church Historian's Library, Salt Lake City, Utah.

William Huntington

About the month of August, 1856, William D. Huntington and I [Levi Curtis] went into Hobble Creek Canyon to get a log suitable for making drums. After we started for home, our conversation turned upon the experiences of the past, when the life and labors of the Prophet Joseph were touched upon. This subject aroused into more than usual earnestness the mind and conversation of my associate.

He said that in Nauvoo he lived in the family of and worked for Joseph Smith at the time the Prophet had such a wonderful time with the sick. He said he had been sick some weeks and kept getting weaker, until he became so helpless that he could not move. Finally he got so low he could not speak, but had perfect consciousness of all that was passing in the room. He saw friends come to the bedside, look at him a moment, commence weeping, then turn away.

He further stated that he presently felt easy, and found that he was in the upper part of the room near the ceiling, and could see the body he had occupied lying on the bed, with weeping friends standing around.

About this time he saw Joseph Smith and two other brethren come into the room. Joseph turned to his wife Emma and asked her to get him a dish of clean water. This she did; and the Prophet with the two brethren washed their hands and carefully wiped them. Then they stepped to the bed and laid their hands upon the head of his body, which at that time looked loathesome to him, and as the three stretched out their hands to place them upon the head, he by some means became aware that he must go back into that body, and started to do so. The process of getting in he could not remember; but when Joseph said "Amen," he heard and could see and feel with his body. The feeling for a moment was most excruciating, as though his body was pierced in every part with some sharp instruments.

As soon as the brethren had taken their hands from his head he raised up in bed, sitting erect, and in another moment turned his legs off the bed.

At this juncture Joseph asked him if he had not better be careful, for he was very weak. He replied, "I never felt better in my life," almost immediately adding, "I want my pants."

His pants were found and given to him, which he drew on, Joseph assisting him, although he thought he needed no help. Then he signified his intention to sit in a chair at or near the fireplace. Joseph took hold of his arm to help him along safely, but William declared his ability to walk alone, notwithstanding the continued help.

Throughout the room, astonishment had taken the place of weeping. Every looker-on was ready to weep for joy; but none were able or felt inclined to talk.

Presently William said he wanted something to eat. Joseph asked him what he would like, and he replied that he wanted a dish of bread and milk.

Emma immediately brought what he called for. Every hand was anxious to supply the wants of a man who, a few moments before, was dead, really and truly dead! Brother Huntington ate the bowl of bread and milk with as good a relish as any he ever ate.

In a short time all felt more familiar, and conversation upon the scene that transpired followed. William related his experience, and the friends theirs.

Joseph listened to the conversation and in his turn remarked that they had just witnessed as great a miracle as Jesus did while on the earth. They had seen the dead brought to life.

At the close of his narrative to me, William Huntington remarked, "Now I have told you the truth, and here I am a live man, sitting by the side of you on this log, and I testify that Joseph Smith was a prophet of God."

The Juvenile Instructor, XXVII (June 15, 1892), pp. 385-386.

Sarah M. Kimball

I went with my husband, Hiram Kimball, to his home in Nauvoo, Illinois, three weeks after my marriage. When my eldest son was three days old, the Church was in need of help to assist in raising the Temple walls. I belonged to The Church of Jesus Christ of Latter-day Saints, but my husband was not yet a member. I wished to help on the Temple, but did not like to ask my husband (who owned considerable property) to help for my sake.

My husband came to my bedside, and as he was admiring our three-day-old darling, I said, "What is the boy worth?"

He replied, "Oh, I don't know; he is worth a great deal."

I said, "Is he worth a thousand dollars?"

The reply was, "Yes, more than that if he lives and does well."

I said, "Half of him is mine, is it not?"

"Yes, I suppose so."

"Then I have something to help on the Temple."

Pleasantly, "You have?"

"Yes, and I am thinking of turning my share right in as tithing."

"Well, I'll think about that."

Soon after the above conversation, Mr. Kimball met the Prophet and said, "Sarah has got a little the advantage of me this time. She proposes to turn out the boy as church property."

President Smith seemed pleased with the joke, and said, "I accept all such donations, and from this day the boy shall stand recorded, *church property.*"

Then turning to Willard Richards, his secretary, he said, "Make a record of this; and you are my witness."

Joseph Smith then said, "Major (Mr. Kimball was major in the Nauvoo Legion), you now have the privilege of paying $500 and retaining possession, or receiving $500 and giving possession."

Mr. Kimball asked if city property was good currency.

President Smith replied that it was.

"Then," said Mr. Kimball, "how will that block north of the Temple suit?"

President Smith replied, "It is just what we want."

The deed was soon made out and transferred in due form.

President Smith said to me, "You have consecrated your first born son. For this you are blessed of the Lord. I bless you in the name of the Lord God of Abraham, of Isaac and of Jacob. And I seal upon you all the blessings that pertain to the faithful."

In the summer of 1843, a Miss Cooke was seamstress for me. The subject of combining our efforts for assisting the Temple hands came up in conversation. She desired to help, but had no means to furnish. I told her I would furnish material if she would make some shirts for the workmen. It was then suggested that some of our neighbors might wish to combine means and efforts with ours, and we decided to invite a few to come and consult with us on the subject of forming a Ladies' Society. The neighboring sisters met in my parlor and decided to organize. I was delegated to call on Sister Eliza R. Snow and ask her to write a constitution and by-laws, and submit them to President Smith prior to our next meeting. When she read them to him, he replied that the constitution and by-laws were the best he had ever seen.

"But," he said, "this is not what you want. Tell the sisters their offering is accepted of the Lord, and he has something better for them than a written constitution. I invite them all to meet with me and a few of the brethren next Thursday afternoon, and I will organize the women under the priesthood after the pattern of the priesthood."

He further said, "The Church was never perfectly organized until the women were thus organized."

He wished to have Sister Emma Smith elected to preside in fulfillment of the revelation which called her an elect lady.

Woman's Exponent, XII (September 1, 1883), p. 51.

William Farrington Cahoon

My impression, after hearing Joseph bear his testimony of what he had seen, was that he was a prophet of the Most High God. I have seen the sick healed under his administrations in many instances. I have seen cripples healed immediately, and leap for joy after being administered to. I was present, and well remember when Elijah Fordham was healed at Montrose, Iowa.

I was called and ordained to act as a teacher to visit the families of the Saints. I got along very well till I found that I was obliged to call and pay a visit to the Prophet. Being young, only about seventeen years of age, I felt my weakness in visiting the Prophet and his family in the capacity of a teacher. I almost felt like shrinking from duty. Finally I went to his door and knocked, and in a minute the Prophet came to the door. I stood there trembling, and said to him, "Brother Joseph, I have come to visit you in the capacity of a teacher, if it is convenient for you."

He said, "Brother William, come right in, I am glad to see you; sit down in that chair there and I will go and call my family in."

They soon came in and took seats. He then said, "Brother William, I submit myself and family into your hands."

He then took his seat. "Now Brother William," said he, "ask all the questions you feel like."

By this time all my fears and trembling had ceased, and I said, "Brother Joseph, are you trying to live your religion?"

He answered, "Yes."

I then said, "Do you pray in your family?"

He said, "Yes."

"Do you teach your family the principles of the gospel?"

He replied, "Yes, I am trying to do it."

"Do you ask a blessing on your food?"

He answered, "Yes."

"Are you trying to live in peace and harmony with all your family?"

He said that he was.

I then turned to Sister Emma, his wife, and said, "Sister Emma, are you trying to live your religion? Do you teach your children to obey their parents? Do you try to teach them to pray?"

To all these questions she answered, "Yes, I am trying to do so."

I then turned to Joseph and said, "I am now through with my questions as a teacher; and now if you have any instructions to give, I shall be happy to receive them."

He said, "God bless you, Brother William; and if you are humble and faithful, you shall have power to settle all difficulties that may come before you in the capacity of a teacher."

As a teacher, I then left my parting blessing upon him and his family and took my departure.

The Juvenile Instructor, XXVII (August 15, 1892), pp. 492-493.

Howard Coray

On the 3rd or 4th day of April, 1840, I set out with a few others for Nauvoo, for the purpose of attending conference, and to gratify a curiosity that I had to see the Prophet. Joseph Wood introduced me to Brother Joseph. The Prophet, after looking at me for a little and asking me some questions, wished to know if I would come to Nauvoo and clerk for him. I engaged at once to do so; and in a couple of weeks I was on hand to go to work.

The first thing he gave me to do was to copy a large pile of letters into a record. This labor was performed in his kitchen, our having no other place at that time to do such business.

While thus engaged, I had many very precious opportunities. Great and small, almost every day, were calling on him—some for one thing, and some for another; politicians and preachers of different persuasions, some with the view of testing the depth of his knowledge and, if possible, confounding him and putting him to shame. Well, what did I discover but that he was equal to every occasion, and perfect master of the situation. He possessed the power to make everybody realize his superiority, which they evinced in an unmistakable manner. I could clearly see that Joseph was the captain, no matter whose company he was in. Knowing the meagerness of his education, I was truly gratified at seeing his great ease, even in the company of the most scientific minds, and the ready, off-hand manner in which he would answer their questions. I heard him say that God had given him the key of knowledge by which he could trace any subject through all its ramifications.

I had heard it remarked that Joseph Smith was Sidney Rigdon's cat's-paw. Soon after President Rigdon returned from the East, he came to see Joseph, and the thought went through my mind: "Now I will see who the cat's-paw is."

Well, I did see. After passing the usual compliments, Rigdon said to Joseph: "When I was preaching in Philadelphia, after I had finished my discourse a man stepped up to me and desired me to explain something in John's Revelation (mentioning at the same time what it was). I could not do it. How is it Joseph?"

Joseph cited him at once a passage in Ezekiel and something in some other book of the Old Testament, saying that they explained all about it.

I thought to myself, "That doesn't look much like Joseph was a cat's-paw."

Stephen A. Douglas called to see him and ask him some questions. One thing he desired to know was how Joseph managed to govern a people so diverse, coming from so many different countries with their peculiar manners and customs.

"Well," Joseph said, "I simply teach them the truth, and they govern themselves."

Among other great men who called to see him was Cyrus Walker, a lawyer of much note. He tried to sound the Prophet, and see how deep he was. Well, it was with Walker as it had been with all the others. He soon got enough, found Joseph too deep for his lead and line, and gave up the enterprise. Thus it was in every instance that came under my observation. How could we expect it to be otherwise—for any man who had never peered into heaven and seen heavenly things to be a match for one who had had a half a score or more heavenly messengers for teachers.

I continued the work of copying his letters until I finished. He then desired me to write up the church history, saying that he would furnish all the material. I declined, telling him that I did not feel myself competent; but finally, having more confidence in him that I had in myself, I engaged in the business of a historian. He placed in my hands some items and scraps of history to arrange chronologically and fix up as best I could. We had now moved into his new office—a two-story building where it was arranged to do the office work in the upper story.

John C. Bennett was occupying a portion of the room, engaged in writing the Nauvoo Charter. Joseph dictated much of the charter. I could overhear the instruction he gave Bennett, and I know it was gotten up mainly as Joseph required.

One morning I went as usual into the office to go to work. I found Joseph sitting on one side of a table and Robert B. Thompson on the opposite side, and the understanding I got was that they were hunting in the manuscript of the new translation of the Bible for something on priesthood which Joseph wished to present or have read to the people the next conference. Well, they could not find what they wanted, and Joseph said to Thompson, "Put the manuscript to one side and take some paper, and I will tell you what to write."

Brother Thompson took some foolscap paper that was at his elbow and made himself ready for the business. I was seated probably six or eight feet on Joseph's left side, so that I could look almost squarely into the side of his eye. The Spirit of God descended upon him, and a measure of it upon me, insomuch that I could fully realize that God, or the Holy Ghost, was talking through him. I never, neither before or since, have felt as I did on that occasion.

In June, 1841, I met with an accident. The Prophet and I, after looking at his horses and admiring them across the road from his house, started thither. The Prophet at the same time put his arm over my shoulder. When we had reached about the middle of the road, he stopped and remarked, "Brother Coray, I wish you were a little larger. I would like to have some fun with you."

I replied, "Perhaps you can as it is"—not realizing what I was saying. The fact that Joseph was a man of over 200 lb., while I was scarcely 130 lb., made it not a little ridiculous for me to think of engaging with him in anything like a scuffle.

However, as soon as I made this reply, he began to trip me. He took some kind of a lock on my right leg, from which I was unable to extricate it, and throwing me around broke it some three inches above the ankle joint.

He immediately carried me into the house, pulled off my boot, and found at once that my leg was decidedly broken; then got some splinters and bandaged it. A number of times that day he came in to see me, endeavoring to console me as much as possible.

The next day when he happened in to see me after a little conversation, I said: "Brother Joseph, when Jacob wrestled with the angel and was lamed by him, the angel blessed him. Now I think I am also entitled to a blessing."

To that he replied, "I am not the Patriarch, but my father is, and when you get up and around, I'll have him bless you."

He said no more for a minute or so. Then, looking very earnestly at me, he declared, "Brother Coray, you will soon find a companion, one that will be suited to your condition, and whom you will be satisfied with. She will cling to you like the cords of death; and you will have a good many children."

In nine days after my leg was broken I was able to get up and hobble about the house by the aid of a crutch, and in two weeks thereafter I was about recovered—so much so that I went to meeting on foot, a distance of a mile. I considered this no less than a case of miraculous healing.

Some three or four weeks after getting my leg broke, and while at meeting, the blessing of the Prophet came into my mind, VIZ: that I should soon find a companion. So I thought I would take a look at the congregation, that possibly the fair one promised me might be present. After looking awhile at the audience, my eyes settled upon a young lady sitting in a one-horse buggy. She was an entire stranger to me. I concluded to approach near enough to her to scan her features well, and thus be able to decide in my own mind whether her looks would satisfy my taste.

She had dark brown eyes, very bright and penetrating (at least they penetrated me), and I said to myself, "She will do."

The fact is, I was decidedly struck. After the dismissal of the meeting, instead of going for my dinner, I remained on the ground and commenced promenading about to see what I could see. I had not gone far before I came square in front of the lovely miss, walking arm in arm with a Mrs. Harris with whom I was well acquainted. They stopped and Mrs. Harris said, "Brother Coray, I have the honor of introducing you to Miss Martha Knowlton, from Bear Creek."

I, of course, bowed as politely as I knew how, and she curtsied, and we then fell into somewhat familiar conversation. I discovered at once that she was ready, offhand, and inclined to be witty; also, that her mind took a wider range than was common for young ladies of her age.

This interview, though short, was indeed very enjoyable; it closed with the hope that she might be the one whom the Lord had picked for me. And thus it proved to be.

I let Brother Joseph into the secret—showed him a letter that I had written designed for her. He seemed to take uncommon interest in the matter. He took pains to see her and talk with her about me, telling her that I was just the one for her. A few letters passed between us. I visited her at her home, proposed, was accepted; and, on the 6th day of February, 1841, we were married at her father's house, Brother Robert B. Thompson performing the ceremony.

I will say in this connection that what the Prophet said in regard to the companion which I should soon find has been fully verified. A more intelligent, self-sacrificing, and devoted wife and mother few men have been blessed with. She became well acquainted with the Prophet; and, as such, greatly venerated him. I have frequently heard her say that he himself was the greatest miracle to her she had ever seen, and that she valued her acquaintance with him above almost everything else.

> Journal of Howard Coray, Brigham Young University Library, pp. 7-13; Howard Coray Folder, Church Historian's Library, Salt Lake City, Utah.

Lucy Walker Kimball

In the spring of 1841, Father took his family to Nauvoo. My brother, who had been staying with the Prophet, met us with an invitation to dinner, which we gladly accepted. We were introduced to the Prophet and his wife Emma, the dear children, who in after years I learned to love as my own brothers, and Julia, an adopted daughter, as my sister.

During the summer, Mother was taken with chills and fever. One after another of the children were also attacked with the same disease until all were in a helpless condition. Mother was invited to spend a few days at the Prophet's house, the Prophet's family thinking a change would benefit her. But she could not be content away from her afflicted family. She lingered until January, 1842, then passed away.

Calling her children around her bed, she bore a faithful testimony that Joseph Smith was a prophet of God, and that through him the gospel of the Son of God had been restored in its fulness. She then closed her eyes, and her sweet spirit passed away, leaving a beautiful smile on her dear face. We were in the depths of despair. Ten motherless children! The youngest was not yet two years old. What were we to do?

The Prophet came to our rescue. He said, "If you remain here, Brother Walker, you will soon follow your wife. You must have a change of scene, a change of climate. You have just such a family as I could love. My house shall be their home. I will adopt them as my own. For the present I would advise you to sell your effects, place the little one with some kind friends, and the four eldest shall come to my house and be received and treated as my own children, and if I find the others are not content or not treated right, I will bring them home and keep them until you return."

I wrung my hands in the agony of despair at the thought of our being broken up as a family, and being separated from my loved ones. "But," said the Prophet, "my home shall be your home, eternally yours."

My father sought to comfort us by saying two years would soon pass away, then we might be together again. Soon after he left, my sister Lydia (aged eight years and eleven months) was attacked with brain fever. We had visited her several times and found that all that was done did not relieve her sufferings. When we told the Prophet how very sick she was, he told the boys to put a bed in the carriage and he went with them. He told the family that they must excuse him, but he was under the greatest obligation to look after their welfare and had come to take her to his own house where he could see to her himself. Everything that could be done was done, but she was to join her dear mother in the spirit world, and we were left more lonely than before.

Our own father and mother could scarcely have done more or manifested greater solicitude for her recovery than did the Prophet and his wife Emma. They watched with us by her bedside; and when all was over, they accompanied us to her last resting place beside her mother.

One after another was brought to the Prophet's home, until all the younger members of the family were there except the baby. My brother William married Olive Hovey Farr, in the fall of 1843. They boarded at the Mansion six months, then went to housekeeping and took the children with them.

The Prophet and his wife introduced us as their sons and daughters. Every privilege was accorded us in the home. He often referred to my brother Lorin as "his Edwin." He was his trusted friend; arm in arm they walked and conversed freely on various subjects. He was with him when he was arrested at Dixon, by Wilson and Reynolds, who were determined to take him down the river into Missouri, but were foiled in this attempt.

They were forced to take him through the state by way of Nauvoo. Lorin hurried on home, brought the Prophet's favorite horse Charley, and met him on foot, weary and covered with dust. The Prophet warmly embraced him, mounted his horse, and rode into Nauvoo. As they drew near the city the people turned out en masse to greet him.

At the time he crossed the river and was making arrangements to go beyond the Rocky Mountains, he said, "I have the promise of life for five years if I listen to the voice of the Spirit."

But when Emma and some of his brethren besought him to return, he said, "If my life is worth nothing to you it is worth nothing to me."

He well knew that he must sacrifice his life for the principles God had revealed through him. Death had no terrors for him although life was dear. I have often heard him say he expected to seal his testimony with his blood. He anticipated great joy in meeting his parents and friends beyond the grave. He believed that as soon as the spirit left the body we were shaking hands with and greeting our friends.

The Prophet Joseph Smith often referred to the feelings that should exist between husbands and wives, that they, his wives, should be his bosom companions, the nearest and dearest objects on earth in every sense of the word. He said men should beware how they treat their wives, that they were given them for a holy purpose, that the myriads of spirits waiting for tabernacles might have pure and healthy bodies. He also said many would awake on the morning of the resurrection sadly disappointed; for they, by transgression, would have neither wives nor children, for they surely would be taken from them and given to those who should prove themselves worthy. Again he said, a woman would have her choice; this was a privilege that could not be denied her.

President Joseph Smith taught me the principle of plural marriage, which, after much serious thought and prayer for many months, I became convinced was a principle revealed from heaven. On the first day of May, 1843, I consented to become the Prophet's wife, and was sealed to him for time and all eternity, at his own house, by Elder William Clayton.

Woman's Exponent, XXXIX, (November, 1910), pp. 33-34; (January, 1911), p. 43.

William Moore Allred

I was present one time when Joseph said that if he should tell all the Lord had revealed to him, some would seek his life. Said he, "Even as good a man as old Father Cole here (pointing back to him as he sat on the stand) would do so."

I have played ball with him many times. But it was quite a stumbling block to some. After some had found fault about it, he was preaching one day and told a story about a certain prophet who was sitting under the shade of a tree amusing himself in some way. A hunter came along and reproved him. The prophet asked the hunter if he always kept his bow strung up. "Oh, no," said he.

"Why not?"

"Because it would lose its elasticity."

Said the prophet: "It is just so with my mind. I do not want it strung up all the time."

Reminiscences and Diary of William Moore Allred, Church Historian's Library, Salt Lake City, Utah.

Joseph Taylor, Sr.

When I first saw Joseph Smith I believed he was one of God's noblemen; and as I grew older I became thoroughly convinced that he was a true prophet of God.

In February, 1841, my brother was in jail, in the hands of the Missourians, about two hundred miles from home, and my dear widowed mother was very much concerned about his safety. On one occasion she was crying and fretting about him. When I saw her in trouble, I asked what was the matter.

She replied that she was afraid the Missourians would kill her dear son, and she would never see him again.

I was strongly impressed to go to the Prophet Joseph and ask him if my brother would ever come home. She was very desirous for me to do so.

The Prophet Joseph lived about three miles from our house. When I reached there, Sister Emma Smith said that he and his son Joseph had just gone up the river near Nauvoo to shoot ducks. I rode up to them, and the Prophet inquired about Mother's welfare.

I told him that Mother was very sad and downhearted about the safety of her son, and she had requested me to come and ask him as a man of God whether my brother would ever return home.

He rested on his gun, and bent his head for a moment as if in prayer or deep reflection. Then, with a beautiful beaming countenance, full of smiles, he looked up and told me to go and tell Mother that her son would return in safety inside of a week. True to the word of the Prophet, he got home in six days after this occurrence. This was a great comfort to Mother, for her son had been absent about six months.

The Juvenile Instructor, XXVII (April 1, 1892), pp. 202-203.

James Leech

After arriving in Nauvoo from England, we were five or six weeks looking for employment. Finally, I said to my brother-in-law, "Let us go and see the Prophet. I feel that he will give us something to do."

He considered a short time, then consented to go. We found the Prophet in a little store selling a lady some goods. This was the first time I had had an opportunity to be near him and get a good look at him. I felt there was a superior spirit in him. He was different from anyone I had ever met before; and I said in my heart, he is truly a prophet of the Most High God.

Because I was not a member of the Church, I wanted Henry to ask him for work, but he did not do so. So I had to. I said, "Mr. Smith, if you please, have you any employment you could give us, so we can get some provisions?"

He viewed us with a cheerful countenance, and with kindness said, "Well, boys, what can you do?"

We told him what our employment was before we left our native land.

Said he, "Can you make a ditch?"

I replied that we would do the best we could.

"That's right boys." Picking up a tape line, he said, "Come along with me."

He took us a few rods from the store, gave me a ring to hold, and stretched all the tape from the reel, and marked a line for us to work by.

"Now, boys," said he, "can you make a ditch three feet wide and two and a half feet deep along this line?"

We said we would do our best, and he left us. We went to work, and when it was finished I went and told him it was done.

He came and looked at it and said, "Boys, if I had done it myself, it could not have been done better. Now come with me."

He led the way back to his store, and told us to pick the best ham or piece of pork for ourselves. Being rather bashful, I said we would rather he would give us some. So he picked two of the largest and best pieces of meat and a sack of flour for each of us, and asked us if that would do. We told him we would be willing to do more work for it. But he said, "If you are satisfied, boys, I am."

We thanked him kindly and went on our way home rejoicing in the kindheartedness of the Prophet of our God.

In November of the same year, I was baptized into the Church, and from that time until the martyrdom of our Prophet,

I often had the privilege of seeing his noble face lit up by the Spirit and power of God, as he taught the Saints the principles of eternal life.

The Juvenile Instructor, XXVII (March 1, 1892), pp. 152-153.

Jesse W. Crosby

The Prophet had great ability as a financier; and had his enemies left him, he would have become one of the wealthiest men in America. Everything his hand touched seemed to prosper. His fields were always in good condition and yielded well. When people came to see him—and he had many visitors—their teams were fed the best of hay and his barn was full. No other orchard had as fine fruit as did his. If an inferior cow was by any means shoved on him, it would be but a short time before she became a first-class milker. Many men sought his advice when in financial difficulty, and none failed to profit by it if they followed the counsel he gave.

A period of great prosperity for him would seem to induce a raid upon him. One trial after another would be launched upon him, until he would be left penniless and perhaps in debt.

On one of these occasions when the Prophet had been absent from home for some time, I went to his home to see if I might render some assistance. When I made the purpose of my visit known, the Prophet's wife burst into tears and said that if the persecution would cease they could live as well as any other family in the land. They could even have the luxuries of life.

The Prophet was strong and active, and could build more rods of good fence in one day than most men could in two, and he always left his fence clear of everything that might gather fire, such as underbrush, loose limbs, and tall strong weeds. He was orderly. His woodyard was an example of order. Logs were neatly piled and all trash cleared away. If he did not finish the log on which he was chopping, the remnant was laid back on the pile and not left on the ground for a stumbling block. The chips he made he picked up himself into a basket and put them in a wooden box which stood in the woodyard, or carried them into the house to be burned.

During a period of financial depression for the Prophet, the ax was stolen from his woodyard, and I contrived to loan him my ax because of the unfailing habit of the Prophet to always sharpen the ax he had been using before it left his hand. People in that section burned hard wood, and to keep the ax in good shape required much time and energy.

I went one day to the Prophet with a sister. She had a charge to make against one of the brethren for scandal. When her complaint had been heard the Prophet asked her if she was quite sure that what the brother had said of her was utterly untrue.

She was quite sure that it was.

He then told her to think no more about it, for it could not harm her. If untrue it could not live, but the truth will survive. Still she felt that she should have some redress.

Then he offered her his method of dealing with such cases for himself. When an enemy had told a scandalous story about him, which had often been done, before he rendered judgment he paused and let his mind run back to the time and place and setting of the story to see if he had not by some unguarded word or act laid the block on which the story was built. If he found that he had done so, he said that in his heart he then forgave his enemy, and felt thankful that he had received warning of a weakness that he had not known he possessed.

Then he said to the sister that he would have her to do the same: search her memory thoroughly and see if she had not herself unconsciously laid the foundation for the scandal that annoyed her.

The sister thought deeply for a few moments and then confessed that she believed that she had.

Then the Prophet told her that in her heart she could forgive that brother who had risked his own good name and her friendship to give her this clearer view of herself.

The sister thanked her advisor and went away in peace.

With some other brethren, I once went to the Prophet and asked him to give us his opinion on a certain public question. The request was refused. He told us he did not enjoy the right vouchsafed to every American citizen—that of free speech. He said that when he ventured to give his private opinion on any subject of importance, his words were often garbled and their meaning twisted, and then given out as the word of the Lord because they came from him.

One day when the Prophet carried to my house a sack of flour he had borrowed, my wife remarked that he had returned more than he had received. He answered that it should be so; that anything borrowed should be returned always with interest to the lender. "Thus," he said, "the borrower, if he be honest, is a slave to the lender."

Some of the home habits of the Prophet—such as building kitchen fires, carrying out ashes, carrying in wood and water, assisting in the care of the children, etc.—were not in accord with my idea of a great man's self-respect. The above incident of the Prophet carrying the sack of flour gave me the opportunity to give him some corrective advice which I had desired to do for a long time. I reminded him of every phase of his greatness and called to his mind the multitude of tasks he performed that were too menial for such as he; to fetch and carry flour was too great a humiliation. "Too terrible a humiliation," I repeated, "for you who are the head, and you should not do it."

The Prophet listened quietly to all I had to say, then made his answer in these words: "If there be humiliation in a man's house, who but the head of that house should or could bear that humiliation?"

Sister Crosby was a very hardworking woman, taking much more responsibility in her home than most women take. Thinking to give the Prophet some light on home management, I said to him, "Brother Joseph, my wife does much more hard work than does your wife."

Brother Joseph replied by telling me that if a man cannot learn in this life to appreciate a wife and do his duty by her, in properly taking care of her, he need not expect to be given one in the hereafter.

His words shut my mouth as tight as a clam. I took them as terrible reproof. After that I tried to do better by the good wife I had and tried to lighten her labors.

"Stories from the Notebook of Martha Cox, Grandmother of Fern Cox Anderson," Church Historian's Library, Salt Lake City, Utah; Lee C. LaFayette, "Recollections of Joseph Smith," Church Historian's Library, Salt Lake City, Utah.

John Lyman Smith

In my early years I used to eat often at the table with Joseph the Prophet. At one time he was called to dinner. I was at play in the room with his son Joseph when he called us to him, and we stood one on each side of him. After he had looked over the table he said, "Lord, we thank Thee for this johnny cake, and ask Thee to send us something better. Amen."

The cornbread was cut and I received a piece from his hand. Before the bread was all eaten, a man came to the door and asked if the Prophet Joseph was at home.

Joseph replied he was, whereupon the visitor said, "I have brought you some flour and a ham."

Joseph arose and took the gift, and blessed the man in the name of the Lord. Turning to his wife, Emma, he said, "I knew the Lord would answer my prayer."

From this time to his death I always revered and honored him, and when but a boy of ten or twelve years have often said to him that I was ready to die for him.

When I was playing in the yard of the Mansion, in Nauvoo, with Joseph and Frederick, two of the Prophet's sons, a gentleman drove to the gate and asked if Joseph Smith was at home. The Prophet came forward, and the gentlemen drove his horse up to a tie post and left the lines lying loose.

When he was about half way to the house, Joseph said, "Mr., I think you would do well to tie your horse; he might get a scare and run away and break your carriage."

The gentleman replied, "I have driven that horse for some years and never tie him. I am a doctor and cannot afford to tie up at every place I call.

Joseph repeated, "You had better tie, all the same. Your horse might get a scare and run away."

The doctor replied, "No fear."

Joseph seemed quite uneasy, and got up several times from his chair on the porch. Suddenly the horse started up the street and struck a wheel against a post and scattered the pieces for a block or more. The doctor sprang to his feet, and looking after the horse, cried out to Joseph, "I'll be d - - - - d if you ain't a prophet!"

The Juvenile Instructor, XXVII (March 15, 1892), pp. 172-173.

Henrietta Cox

In the spring of 1841, my parents started for Nauvoo with some other Saints. They camped for a few days on the bank of the Mississippi until they could find homes.

The Prophet visited them, and a meeting was held in a log house. When the Prophet came into the room, he shook hands with all, old and young. I cannot remember much that was said that day in the meeting, as I was so very young, but one incident of the day's proceedings fastened itself so firmly upon my mind that I have never forgotten it.

Brother Joseph was sitting with his head bent low, as if in deep thought, and had not spoken for a few minutes, when one of the elders present began to chide him for being bowed in spirit, saying, "Brother Joseph, why don't you hold your head up and talk to us like a man?"

Brother Joseph presently answered the elder by calling his attention to a field of ripening grain, saying that many heads of grain in that field bent low with their weight of valuable store, while others containing no grain to be garnered stood very straight.

Proof of the correctness of his words was given shortly after, for the elder to whom they were addressed soon after apostatized and went back East.

The Juvenile Instructor, XXVII (April 1, 1892), p. 203.

William Holmes Walker

My father sent me to Nauvoo on some business with the Prophet. I arrived at his house just as his family was singing, before the accustomed evening prayer. His wife, Emma, was leading the singing. I thought I had never heard such sweet, heavenly music before. I was equally interested in the prayer offered by the Prophet. Much pleased with my visit, and my business accomplished satisfactorily, I returned home in a few days.

Later, I returned to Joseph Smith's and entered his employ, and was a member of his family, taking an interest in his domestic affairs, remaining three years without asking compensation. I went into the hayfield with him and assisted in mowing grass with a scythe many a day, putting in ten hours of good hard work. Very few, if any, were his superior in that kind of work. The more extensive my acquaintance and experience became with him, the more my confidence in him increased.

On one occasion when he was mayor of the city of Nauvoo, it became his duty to fine a Negro for violating the city ordinance with regard to selling liquor. The Negro pleaded for mercy, saying that his object in doing so was to raise money to send for his family. The mayor would not shrink from his duty, and he fined him $75.00, but told him that if he would not be guilty of doing so again he would make him a present of a horse to assist him, which he accepted.

The Urim and Thummim [the Seer Stone?] were once placed in my charge for a time, and many other important trusts were confided to me, which I am happy to say were held sacred to myself.

The Prophet had a great many callers, not merely those of his own faith. True and well-tried friends, and those from different parts of the earth, came to make a permanent home in Nauvoo and were anxious to see him; but strangers from all parts of the country, traveling up and down the river, almost invariably made it a point to call and see "The Prophet," as they called him.

On one occasion a man by the name of Joseph Jackson called. Not finding Joseph at home, I heard him say to Mrs. Smith, "You tell the Prophet that the wickedest man on earth called to see him."

Future developments proved that he told the truth for once.

It was quite a common occurrence in those days for officers to suddenly appear with an arrest for "Old Joe Smith," on some flimsy, trumped-up charge. One day in the summer of 1842, I was sitting at the dinner table with the Prophet, when, without a word being spoken by any person present, he arose suddenly from the table and went out of the room. No sooner had he closed the door than an officer entered by another door. Joseph walked some twenty rods across the block in a path leading to the brick store, in full view of another officer. Then he disappeared, without being discovered by either.

On another occasion some officers came into the city and put up at the hotel, just above his residence. Joseph gave me directions to take his horse "Joe Dunkin" (named after Governor Dunkin) and put on his military bridle, saddle, and portmanteaus (the articles cost $100.00) and ride up Main Street to the upper landing, cross on the ferry boat to Montrose, from there to Keokuk. From that the report started that I had taken the horse to "Joe" Smith, and he had gone on west. Meantime I returned to Nauvoo with the horse, but no one knew that the horse had returned, neither friend or foe.

An incident shows the contempt he had for any person of questionable character. In regard to his private life, as to purity, honesty, virtue, charity, benevolence, liberality, refined and sensitive feelings, and nobility of character, his superior did not exist on earth.

Not long after the Mansion was open as a hotel, a stranger came and registered. Just before supper he insulted one of the hired girls. The Prophet heard of it after the stranger had retired. The next morning he met him as he came down from his room and said, "Sir, I understand that you insulted one of the employees of this house last evening."

The stranger began to make all kinds of apologies, but nothing would answer the purpose. The Prophet told the stranger to get his baggage and to get, in a tone of voice that almost made his hair stand straight on his head. The man offered to pay his bill.

"I want you to get. I want none of your money, or any other man's of your stamp."

Upon that, the stranger struck a lively exit.

In the spring of 1844, President Smith thought it wise, considering that his life was in danger in Nauvoo, to go west with his family and select friends. His wife and some others thought that if they left the city would be laid in ashes, and the people destroyed. They were so zealous they said they would stay and die with them. However, Joseph Smith and his brother started west. Delegation after delegation was sent to him, to prevail on him to return and give himself up.

Sunday morning, three days before the martyrdom, I was in front of the Mansion with Emma. Looking up the street, she exclaimed, "There is lawyer Wood. I am glad. Joseph will have confidence in him and will come back."

Wood had been sent by Governor Ford with a pledge for the Prophet's safety, and fair trial. In answer to the argument for Joseph to give himself up, the Prophet said, "If my life is of no value to my people, it is of no value to me."

Sure enough, about sunset June 23, he and his brother Hyrum returned to the Mansion. I was at the time sitting alone in the private parlor. Joseph was so overcome with grief he could hardly speak at first. As soon as he could control his feelings, he said he was going to give himself up for trial.

Diary of William Holmes Walker, Brigham Young University Library, pp. 3, 7-14.

Andrew Workman

I first saw the Prophet Joseph in May, 1842. He was with about a dozen others on the stand in a meeting. I knew him as soon as I saw him.

A few days after this I was at Joseph's house. Several men were sitting on the fence. Joseph came out and spoke to us all. A man came and said that a poor brother who lived out some distance from town had had his house burned down the night before. Nearly all of the men said they felt sorry for the man. Joseph put his hand in his pocket, took out five dollars and said: "I feel sorry for this brother to the amount of five dollars. How much do you all feel sorry?"

The Juvenile Instructor, XXVII (October 15, 1892), p. 641.

Lucy M. Smith

I first met the Prophet Joseph Smith when I landed at the ferry in Nauvoo. The first words he said were, "I guess you are all Latter-day Saints here, by the singing I heard when the boat landed."

He shook hands with each one in the company, and then took his sister's (Lucy Milican) seven-month-old boy in his arms and sat down and wept for joy, as his sister was thought to be in a decline when she left home the year before with her husband. She was the picture of health, and this gave the Prophet double joy in meeting her with her son.

I heard the Prophet preach twice, once at his Mansion and once at the bowery. He spoke on the plurality of gods. He said, "There are lords many and gods many, but to us there is but one God. There are gods to other planets. We read in the Bible, 'Father, Son and Holy Ghost, these three are one.' It should read, 'These three agree.'"

He remarked that he would like to speak to the people two hours, but the rain made such a noise on the umbrellas (it was raining at the time) it would be useless. "But," said he, "I have brought the Laws' and Fosters' prophecy to the ground, as they predicted I should never speak from this stand again; but I have."

He then said, "Brethren and sisters, love one another; love one another and be merciful to your enemies."

He repeated these words in a very emphatic tone of voice, with a loud, "Amen."

Within a few days he went to Carthage; and on the evening of the 27th of June, such a barking and howling of dogs and bellowing of cattle all over the city of Nauvoo I never heard before nor since. I was at Brother David Smith's house. I knelt down and tried to pray for the Prophet, but I was struck speechless, and knew not the cause till next morning. Of course the awful deed was already accomplished, when the Spirit refused to give me utterance to pray the evening before. The next day the bodies were brought to the Mansion. Thousands of men, women and children were weeping all around.

The little children were very much attached to the Prophet, for he used to play with them as one of their equals. Indeed, he was loved best by those who were the most acquainted with him. His daughter, Julia, told me that her papa talked to her before he left, and told her to be a good girl; and he particularly enjoined it upon her to never mistreat any of her playmates, and then he should be happy to meet her again.

"Oh," said she, "how bad I should feel if I thought I should not be prepared to meet my dear papa!"

My two brothers, Freeborn and David Smith, came to Nauvoo in the fall of 1842. They were very much attached to the Prophet Joseph Smith. My brother David was passing his store one day and he said the man of God ran out, took him by the hand and said, "God bless you, Brother Smith."

He said it made him feel so good to have the Prophet of God take so much pains to come out to shake his hand and bless him, he felt it through his whole system.

The Juvenile Instructor, XXVII (August 1, 1892), pp. 470-471.

Eunice Billings Snow

I went to school with the Prophet Joseph's children. There was an adopted daughter in the family named Murdock, generally called Julia Smith. She was a constant companion of mine, and for that reason I often visited the Prophet's home.

During the persecution of the Prophet, especially when he was in hiding, he would sometimes be allowed to visit his family for an evening, and would request my father and mother to come to sing for him. They would take me with them, and when Joseph found that I could sing a part alone he requested them to bring me. We would sing his favorite hymns: "When Joseph His Brethren Beheld," "Redeemer of Israel," "The Spirit of God," and several others. He would become so inspired with the spirit of the music that he would clap his hands and shout hosanna to the Lord.

He would have me sit close to him, and laying his hands on my head would say, "My little sister, you will be able to sing the songs of Zion as long as you desire."

He also blessed me on different occasions.

I was always very much affected by the Spirit which he manifested. At first I did not know what it was, but my mother told me it was the power which Joseph possessed.

My mother sometimes did knitting for Emma Hale, and one time when I took some work home I was ushered directly into Emma's bedroom, when some person jumped behind the door. Emma called to him, it being the Prophet, and said, "Do not be afraid, it is Mrs. Billings' young daughter."

It was the time of a raid. When Joseph appeared from behind the door, he put his hand on my head and remarked, "God bless you, you won't tell where I am, will you?"

I replied, "No, sir, I will not."

I would have suffered any punishment before I would have told where he was. It made me feel so strange at the time when he put his hand on my head, and again I asked my mother why it was, and she said it was the power which he possessed.

Some of the most impressive moments of my life were when I saw the Nauvoo Legion on parade with the Prophet (then General Joseph Smith) with his wife, Emma Hale Smith, on horseback at the head of the troops. It was indeed an imposing sight. He so fair, and she so dark, in their beautiful riding-habits. He in full military suit, and she with her habit trimmed with gold buttons, a neat cap on her head, with a black plume in it, while the Prophet wore a red plume in his, and a red sash across his breast. His coat was black, while his white pants had red stripes on the outside seams. He also wore a sword at his side. His favorite riding-horse was named Charlie, a big black steed.

I remember hearing the Prophet the last time he spoke in Nauvoo. He said, "I go like a lamb to the slaughter," referring to the great shadow, which seemed even then to hover over his life and to foreshadow his impending doom.

On the last day which he spent in Nauvoo, he passed our house with his brother Hyrum, both riding. My mother and I were standing in the dooryard, and as he passed he bowed with uplifted hat to my mother. Hyrum seemed like one in a dream, sad and despondent, taking no notice of anyone. They were on their way to the Carthage jail, and it was the last time I saw the Prophet alive. Shortly after this, my father came home and told my mother that the Prophet and his brother had been murdered, whereupon my mother exclaimed, "How can it be possible? Will the Lord allow anything like that?"

Immediately she sank back in her chair and fainted. When she came to herself, my father lamented the fact with her.

Lucy Mack Smith, Emma Hale Smith, my mother and I, together viewed the bodies, and I shall never forget the impression made upon me when the Prophet's mother saw the bodies of her dead sons. Falling on her knees and clasping her hands, she cried out, "O God, why were my noble sons permitted to be martyred?"

Then controlling herself with a mighty effort, she said, "Thy will, not mine, O Lord, be done."

Woman's Exponent XXXIX (August, 1910), p. 14; (September 1910), p. 22.

James Palmer

When the Sabbath day came, the Saints assembled in a grove near the Temple where was erected a stand or platform for the speakers. The Prophet did not always address the meetings, but when he did all ears were opened and the most profound silence was observed, and those that spoke in his presence, no matter on what subject, allowed themselves to be corrected if needed, which he did in a kind and Christianlike manner.

It did not take long to win my most profound regard and esteem for this man of God. He could make the gospel so plain to the understanding that you would think you had always known it, whereas you had only just been taught it. While preaching, he had the appearance of one that was heaven-born, who had been sent from the heavenly worlds on a divine mission. He was a man of fine form and stature, measuring over six feet in height. He was of light complexion. His hair was of a flaxen color. He wore no whiskers. His chin was a little tipped; his nose was long and straight; his mouth was narrow, and his upper lip rather long and a little inclined to be thick. He had a large full chest and intelligent eyes, and fine legs. Altogether he presented a very formidable appearance, being a man of gentlemanly bearing. The kindness he manifested in all the walks of life caused him to be beloved by the little boys and girls, who often sought his company, as well as by the many thousands of his people who looked upon him with pride as their leader and director in the great latter-day work.

There were great threats of mob violence by the anti-Mormons who lived in adjoining counties. They wished to drive us from the state because we outnumbered them at the ballot box. On election days, we could elect our county officers. They despised us also because of our religion. They would muster and parade and call it a wolf hunt. Some of our brethren were shot at while quietly at home inside their own houses. At this time, the Prophet proclaimed a day of fasting and prayer through all the wards of the city, praying Almighty God to turn away the anger of our enemies and allow us to live in peace. At the same time he advised us to prepare to protect ourselves if they came upon us.

The Prophet had to hide, for some among us were his avowed enemies. However, he wrote to the Church from time to time, instructing on the ordinance of baptism for the dead and other important matters.

In a public meeting of the Saints near the Temple he said that he had accomplished that which the world could never rob him of. The Church of Christ was established, never more to be cast down or overcome, or given to another people. Said he, "I did translate the Book of Mormon by the gift and power of God, and it is before the world; and all the powers of earth and hell can never rob me of the honor of it."

On another occasion, he spoke of the angel coming forth as recorded in the revelation of Saint John on the Isle of Patmos, which reads: "I saw another angel fly in the midst of heaven, having the everlasting gospel to preach to them that dwell on the earth, and to every nation, and kindred, and tongue, and people, saying with a loud voice, Fear God, and give glory to him; for the hour of his judgment is come." (Revelation 14:6-7.)

The Prophet said this was the angel that appeared unto him and commissioned him to preach the gospel. His was a divine mission that God would honor, and he wished the Saints to understand this, and to be firm and know most assuredly that this was so. Yes, verily so.

This was a testimony that I was glad to hear. It was given in such a kind manner, and with such force and power, that it seemed to me no man could disbelieve such a powerful statement as he made that day, and the Spirit of God seemed to carry his words deep into the hearts of the people. It might be consistently said that all present believed him, for they manifested by signs unmistakable, throughout the entire congregation, that such was the fact.

I was in attendance at a public meeting held in a grove when the Prophet delivered a lengthy discourse on the dreadful war that would be brought about between the Northern and Southern States. He predicted in what state it would commence, and the condition of the contending armies: that many of the slain would not get a decent burial, but would rot upon the ground, and the wolves and turkey buzzards would eat their flesh by thousands. There was a large audience present. I was minus a seat, so I moved quietly to the back of the stand which the Prophet occupied, and there I discovered Theodore Turley pacing to and fro, and strongly contemplating upon the Prophet's discourse as it was then pealing forth from the stand. Said I to him, "What think you of this?"

"Oh," said he, "this is dreadful, and it will all come to pass just as sure as we are here this day."

James Palmer, "Reminiscence and Journal," original handwritten manuscript in Church Historian's Library, Salt Lake City, Utah, pp. 69, 73-76.

Emmeline Blanche Wells

I journeyed from my home in Massachusetts to Nauvoo, Illinois, with a company of Latter-day Saints. Among them was the late Jacob Gates and his wife. Sister Gates talked a great deal about the Prophet Joseph, and when she saw that I was specially interested in him, she promised me that she would introduce me to him on our arrival in Nauvoo.

As we neared our destination, the Elders were full of enthusiasm at the thought of seeing the Prophet again. But not once in all the conversation did I hear a description of his personal appearance. I had not formed any idea of him, except of his wonderful power.

At last the boat reached the upper landing, and a crowd of people came to the bank of the river. As we stepped ashore, I could see one person who towered above the others; in fact, I did not see distinctly any others. His majestic bearing, so entirely different from anyone I had ever seen (and I had seen many superior men), was more than a surprise. It was as if I beheld a vision; I seemed to be lifted off my feet, to be as it were walking in the air, and paying no heed whatever to those around me. I made my way through the crowd. Then I saw this man whom I had noticed, because of his lofty appearance, shaking hands with all the people, men, women and children. Before I was aware of it he came to me, and when he took my hand, I was simply electrified —thrilled through and through to the tips of my fingers, and every part of my body, as if some magic elixir had given me new life and vitality. I am sure that for a few minutes I was not conscious of motion. I think I stood still. I did not want to speak, or be spoken to. I was overwhelmed with indefinable emotion.

Sister Gates came to me and said, "I'll introduce you to the Prophet Joseph now. He is here."

I replied, "I don't want to be introduced to him."

She was astonished, and said curtly, "Why, you told me how desirous you were of meeting him."

I answered, "Yes, but I've seen him and he spoke to me."

"But he didn't know who you were."

I replied, "I know that, but it doesn't matter."

Sister Gates walked away without another word of explanation. I was in reality too full for utterance. I think had I been formally presented to the Prophet, I should have fallen down at his feet. The one thought that filled my soul was, I have seen the Prophet of God. He has taken me by the hand. This testimony has never left me in all the "perils by the way." For many years, I felt it too sacred an experience even to mention.

I heard him preach all his last sermons and frequently met him and shook hands with him. I always felt in my inmost soul that he was indeed a man unlike all others.

In the Prophet, I recognized the great spiritual power that brought joy and comfort to the Saints; and withal he had that strong comradeship that made such a bond of brotherliness with those who were his companions in civil and military life, and in which he reached men's souls, and appealed most forcibly to their friendship and loyalty.

He possessed, too, the innate refinement that one finds in the born poet, or in the most highly cultivated intellectual and poetical nature. This extraordinary temperament and force combined is something of a miracle and can scarcely be accounted for except as a "heavenly mystery" of the "higher sort."

He was beyond my comprehension. The power of God rested upon him to such a degree that on many occasions he seemed transfigured. His expression was mild and almost childlike in repose; and when addressing the people, who loved him it seemed to adoration, the glory of his countenance was beyond description. At other times, the great power of his manner, more than of his voice (which was sublimely eloquent to me), seemed to shake the place on which we stood and penetrate the inmost soul of his hearers, and I am sure that then they would have laid down their lives to defend him. I always listened spellbound to his every utterance—the chosen of God in this last dispensation.

Young Woman's Journal, XVI, (December 1905), pp. 554-556.

"Aunt" Jane James

Yes, indeed. I guess I did know the Prophet Joseph. That lovely hand! He used to put it out to me. Never passed me without shaking hands with me, wherever he was. Oh, he was the finest man I ever saw on earth. I did not get much of a chance to talk with him. He'd always smile, always just like he did to his children. He used to be just like I was his child.

I think about Brother Joseph and Sister Emma and how good they was to me. When I went there I only had two things on me, no shoes nor stockings, wore them all out on the road. They was looking for us, because I wrote them a letter. There was eight of us: my mother and two sisters and a brother and sister-in-law, and we had two children, one they had to carry all the way there, and we traveled a thousand miles.

Sister Emma, she come to the door first, and she says, "Walk in, come in all of you."

She went upstairs, and down he comes and goes into the sitting room and told the girls that they had there that he wanted to have the room this evening, for we have got company come.

I knew it was Brother Joseph, because I had seen him in a dream. He went and brought Dr. Bernhisel down and Sister Emma, and introduced him to every one of us, and said, "Now, I want you to tell me about some of your hard trials. I want to hear of some of those hard trials."

And we told him. He slapped his hands. "Dr. Bernhisel," he said, "what do you think of that?"

He said, "I think if I had had it to do I should not have come; would not have had faith enough."

Brother Joseph kept our folks a whole week until they got homes, and I was left. He came in every morning to see us and shake hands and know how we all were. One morning, before he came in, I had been up to the landing and found all my clothes were gone. Well, I sat there crying. He came in and looked around.

"Why, where's all the folks?"

"Why, Brother," I says, "they have all got themselves places. But I hain't got any place," and I burst out a-crying.

"We won't have tears here," he says.

"But," I says, "I have got no home."

"Well, you've got a home here," he says. "Have you seen Sister Emma this morning?"

"No, sir," I says.

So he started out and went upstairs and brought Sister Emma down and says, "Here's a girl who says she's got no home. Don't you think she's got a home here?"

And she says, "If she wants to stay here."

And he says, "Do you want to stay here?"

"Yes, sir," says I.

"Well, now," he says, "Sister Emma, you just talk to her and see how she is."

We had come afoot, a thousand miles. We lay in bushes, and in barns and outdoors, and traveled until there was a frost just like a snow, and we had to walk on that frost. I could not tell you, but I wanted to go to Brother Joseph.

I did not talk much to him, but every time he saw me he would say, "God bless you," and pat me on the shoulder.

To Sister Emma, he said, "Go and clothe her up, go down to the store and clothe her up."

Sister Emma did. She got me clothes by the bolt. I had everything.

Brother Joseph was tall, over six feet; he was a fine, big, noble, beautiful man! He had blue eyes and light hair, and very fine white skin.

When he was killed, I liked to a died myself. If it had not been for the teachers, I felt so bad. I could have died, just laid down and died. I was sick abed, and the teachers told me, "You don't want to die because he did. He died for us, and now we all want to live and do all the good we can."

Things came to pass what he prophesied about our colored race being freed. Things that he said has come to pass. I did not hear that, but I knew of it.

After I saw him plain, I was certain he was a prophet because I knew it. I was willing to come and gather, and when he came in with Dr. Bernhisel I knew him. Did not have to tell me because I knew him. I knew him when I saw him back in old Connecticut in a vision, saw him plain and knew he was a prophet.

This is the gospel of Jesus Christ, and there will never be any other on earth. It has come to stay.

Young Woman's Journal, XVI (December 1905), pp. 551-553.

William Taylor

My first acquaintance with the Prophet Joseph Smith began on my nineteenth birthday, when he appeared at my father's house in the woods, accompanied by my brother, John Taylor, S. Roundy, and J. D. Parker, about the middle of the night, September 2, 1842. Late in the night the Prophet had gone to my brother John's house in Nauvoo and said to him, "I want you to go with me to your father's."

My brother said, "But I can't go, Brother Joseph; I am sick in bed!"

The Prophet replied, "I'll come in and help you dress, and you'll find no inconvenience from going out."

So Brother John got up, dressed and started out with him, and by the time they reached our home, none of us could tell that he had been the least sick.

The four stayed at our house a few days and then the Prophet sent the other three back to Nauvoo to see if anything was going wrong at that place. During their absence the Prophet and I spent most of our time during the day in the woods, near our house on the Henderson bottom, walking around, shooting squirrels sometimes, or doing anything we could to amuse ourselves. I was the Prophet's only companion in these tramps through the woods, and I have often thought it strange, that though there were many people in that part of the country, we never met anyone when we were out.

During the stay of Brother Joseph at my father's, Brother William Clayton came to see him, and recorded the revelations which the Prophet had at this time. They were some of the grandest that ever were given to him. (D&C 127, 128.)

I do not remember exactly how long the Prophet remained at our home, but it seems to me it was about two weeks, but in this short period, owing to the nature of the circumstances surrounding us, I had more real close association with him than I would have had in a lifetime under different conditions.

It is impossible for me to express my feelings in regard to this period of my life. I have never known the same joy and satisfaction in the companionship of any other person, man or woman, that I felt with him, the man who had conversed with the Almighty. He was always the most companionable and lovable of men—cheerful and jovial! Sometimes in our return home in the evening after we had been tramping around in the woods, he would call out, "Here, Mother, come David and Jonathan."

Much has been said of his geniality and personal magnetism. I was witness of this—people, old or young, loved him and trusted him instinctively.

I said to him once, "Brother Joseph, don't you get frightened when all those hounding wolves are after you?"

And he answered, "No, I am not afraid; the Lord said he would protect me, and I have full confidence in His word."

I knew the danger that whatever happened to him would happen to me, but I felt no more fear than I now feel. There was something superior to thoughts of personal safety. Life or death was a matter of indifference to me while I was the companion of the Lord's anointed!

He said to me often, "I'll never forsake you, William," and I knew he wouldn't.

He seemed to be just as familiar with the spirit world, and as well acquainted with the other side, as he was with this world.

Never in all my life have I seen anything more beautiful than the striking example of brotherly love and devotion felt for each other by Joseph and Hyrum. I witnessed this many times. No matter how often, or when or where they met, it was always with the same expression of supreme joy. It could not have been otherwise, when both were filled to overflowing with the gift and power of the Holy Ghost! It was kindred spirits meeting!

Young Woman's Journal, XVII, (December 1906), pp. 547-548.

William E. Jones

It would be impossible for me to describe my impressions when I first saw Joseph Smith. I have many times listened to his inspired words; and I never shall forget the words he spoke on the first Sunday after I came to Nauvoo. The Temple was built a few feet above the ground. While preaching he pointed towards it and said, "The Lord has commanded us to build that Temple. We want to build it, but we have not the means. There are people in this city who have the means, but they will not let us have them. What shall we do with such people? I say damn them!"

Then he sat down. On the following day several persons came forward with their means, and this averted the curse which would doubtless otherwise have followed them.

The Juvenile Instructor, XXVII (January 15, 1892), pp. 65-66.

James P. Terry

My first recollection of the Prophet Joseph Smith was in 1842 or 1843. I knew him well from that time on until his death. Once when he was speaking, a flock of wild geese flew over. When all eyes were turned to them, the Prophet said, "If you think more of the quacking of a flock of geese than of my preaching, all right," and sat down. If my memory serves me right, the meeting was dismissed immediately.

I knew him in life; I saw him in death. Though but a boy, I seemed to have as great a love and affection for him as any person I ever saw; and I testify in the fear of heaven that he was a true prophet.

The Juvenile Instructor, XXVIII (May 15, 1893), pp. 331-332.

Angus M. Cannon

The time I was most impressed by the Prophet Joseph Smith's expressions was on his return from Dixon, when two men from Missouri had endeavored to kidnap him. He mounted the well-curb, east of his residence, holding on by the uprights with one hand, while he swung his hat with the other and proclaimed aloud with a voice that thrilled my entire being. He called to the multitude congregated to bid him welcome: "I am thankful to the God of Israel who has delivered me out of the hands of the Missourians once more."

His words so affected many of the people that they wept tears of joy.

He was one of the grandest samples of manhood that I ever saw walk or ride at the head of a legion of men. As he addressed the Saints, his words sometimes so affected me that I would rise upon my feet in the agitation that would take hold of my mind.

I remember Brother Joseph as he addressed an assembly of the Saints in the spring of 1844, under some large oak trees in a hollow south of the Temple. He was discoursing upon the fact that God, in establishing His Church, had provided that only one man was authorized to receive revelations for the Church. It was on this occasion that I heard the Prophet declare he had received the Melchizedek Priesthood under the administration of Peter, James and John.

Young Woman's Journal, XVII (December, 1906), pp. 546-547.

Joseph Lee Robinson

When we arrived at Nauvoo, my brother Ebenezer had a house for us not very far from the residence of Joseph Smith.

The Prophet's voice was like the thunders of heaven, yet his language was meek and his instructions edified much. There was a power and majesty that attended his words and preaching that we never beheld in any man before. He truly had been educated pertaining to the kingdom of God. He was highly charged with the Holy Ghost, which was his constant companion.

I will mention several of his sayings: "There is not one key or one power to be bestowed on this church to lead the people into the celestial kingdom but I have given you, shown you and talked it over with you; the kingdom is set up and you have the perfect pattern and you can go and build up the kingdom, go in at the celestial gate, taking your train with you."

Instructions to the Quorum of the Twelve before his death: "Though we or an angel from heaven preach any other gospel or introduce any order of things other than those things which ye have received and are authorized to receive from the First Presidency, let him be accursed."

Again, I heard the Prophet say, "If I should reveal the things that God has revealed to me, there are some on this stand that would cut my throat or take my heart's blood."

I once asked the Prophet what my tithing was. He said, "Your tithing is one-tenth of what you have when you commence to pay tithing, and after that one-tenth of your increase annually."

The Lord gave us a beautiful daughter. But she became afflicted and had fits, and it seemed we could not stop them. We had heard the Prophet Joseph say that if any member of a family was sick and the head of the family would fast three days, the sick should get better. Knowing him to be a true prophet of God, we believed what he said.

My wife proposed to fast. I replied, "If you think you can stand it nursing a child, I certainly will try it."

I was afflicted with rheumatism in my back and hips, so I had this also to fast and pray for.

The first day was the hardest day for me. The second day came and no eating, but plenty of work. The third day we ate no dinner until supper time. We felt satisfied that our three days' fast was completed. We ate our supper, but as yet there had been no change with the fits on the child or with my lameness. We retired to our bed to rest after saying our prayers as usual, and as the Lord liveth those fits upon our child stopped, and my lameness went entirely away. We received this as a signal favor and a great blessing from the hand of God.

A pioneer company was organized to search out a land of promise for the Latter-day Saints in the West. The Prophet Joseph had been very anxious to get this people into the Rocky Mountains. He said at one time he wanted temples built all over the Rocky Mountains.

Prior to the death of our Prophet, he spoke at length upon the salvation and importance of this government, and mighty and once happy nation, deploring the situation that it was in at the present time, proposing many important improvements in the management and policy of the rulers and lawmaking departments, to save the nation from ruin and utter destruction.

The Journal of Joseph Lee Robinson, pp. 10-13, 16, 19, 30.

Jane Snyder Richards

Joseph Smith was one of the most engaging personalities it has ever been my good fortune to meet. As Prophet he seemed to understand, and was able to foretell the future with a marked degree of accuracy and nearly as much readiness as the ordinary individual could relate the happenings of the past. As Seer and Revelator he was fearless and outspoken, yet humble, never considering that he was more than the mouthpiece through whom God spoke. As the leader of his people, he was ever active and progressive but always modest and considerate of them and their trying circumstances. Socially he was an ideal of affability and always approachable to the humblest of his acquaintances.

On one occasion when his enemies were threatening him with violence, he was told that quite a number of little children were gathered together praying for his safety. He replied: "Then I need have no fear; I am safe."

It was the common custom for men, women and children alike to flock to the road side and salute him as he passed along.

Young Woman's Journal, XVI (December 1905), p. 550.

Mary Ann Winters

In April, 1843, when our family returned from England to Nauvoo with my stepfather, Parley P. Pratt, Brother Joseph came to the landing to meet the company. He shook hands with our family, took my two little brothers on his knees, and said, "Well, well, Brother Parley, you have come home, bringing your sheaves with you."

The tears rolled down his cheeks. Brother Pratt answered, "Why Brother Joseph, if you feel so bad about our coming, I guess we will have to go back again."

Then a smile went all around. Brother Joseph arose and said, "Come, bring your folks right up to my house."

In August, 1843, there was an excursion down the river to Quincy, Illinois. The mayor of that city had invited the Prophet and some of the leading citizens of Nauvoo to be his guests for the day, and he was at the landing to receive his visitors. Brother Joseph was the after-dinner entertainer. He talked, and the others listened with the greatest attention, and were loath to have him depart.

As we were going home on the little boat, Brother Joseph sat on the upper deck with the company gathered around him listening to his wonderful words. My father sat opposite him, so near that their knees almost touched. I, a little girl, being tired and sleepy, my Pa took me in his arms to rest. Brother Joseph stopped speaking, stooped and took my feet on his knees. When I would have drawn them away, he said, "No, let me hold them; you will rest better."

I stood close by the Prophet while he was preaching to the Indians in the grove by the Temple. The Holy Spirit lighted up his countenance till it glowed like a halo around him, and his words penetrated the hearts of all who heard him. The Indians looked as solemn as eternity.

I saw him on parade at the head of the Nauvoo Legion, looking noble and grand as a leader could do. His commanding presence could be discerned above all others, and all eyes were centered on him, as he rode back and forth giving the commands of his office.

I was at a meeting in the grove on Mulholland Street when Brother Joseph asked the children to bring their Testaments and hymn books and meet there the next Sabbath to have Sunday School. He said, "I don't know as I will be here. I will if I can, but Brother Stephen Goddard will be here and take charge of you. Won't you Brother Goddard?"

I attended two Sabbaths, when those awful days of June, 1844, came and terminated our gathering for that purpose.

Young Woman's Journal, XVI (December 1905), pp. 557-558.

Mary C. Westover

I was very small when we lived in Nauvoo, but I always attended the meetings. The most striking thing I remember was a prophecy Joseph Smith made, which I saw fulfilled immediately. I was at the funeral service of King Follett, in the Nauvoo Grove. A heavy thunderstorm arose. The people became frightened and started to go home. But the Prophet arose and told the multitude that if they would remain still and pray in their hearts the storm would not molest them in their services.

They did as they were bidden, and the storm divided over the grove. I well remember how it was storming on all sides of the grove, yet it was calm around us as if there was no sign of a storm so near by.

I thought as I sat there that the Lord was speaking through Joseph.

Young Woman's Journal, XVII (December 1906), p. 545.

Mary Alice Cannon Lambert

I first saw Joseph Smith in the Spring of 1843. When the boat reached the landing at Nauvoo, several of the leading brethren were there to meet the company. Among them was the Prophet Joseph Smith. I knew him the instant my eyes rested upon him, and at that moment I received my testimony that he was a prophet of God, for I never had such a feeling for mortal man as then thrilled my being. He was not pointed out to me. I knew him from all the other men; and though I was only fourteen, I knew that I saw a prophet of God.

Many times I heard him preach. The love the Saints had for him was inexpressible. They would willingly have laid down their lives for him. If he was to talk, every task would be laid aside that they might listen to his words.

He was not an ordinary man. Saints and sinners alike felt and recognized a power and influence which he carried with him. It was impossible to meet him and not be impressed by the strength of his personality and influence.

In May, 1844, he went to the stone shops where the men were working on the Nauvoo Temple and blessed each man by the power of his priesthood. Brother Lambert (whom I afterward married) he gathered right in his arms and blessed, and it was ever his testimony that he was thrilled from head to foot by that blessing.

I well remember the night of the Prophet's death. The spirit of unrest was upon all, man and animal, in the city of Nauvoo. My father was on guard. No one in the house had slept, the dogs were noisy, and even the chickens were awake.

About 3 o'clock the news of the martyrdom was brought to us, and we realized what had kept us awake. And oh, the mourning in the land! The grief felt was beyond expression—men, women and children, we were all stunned by the blow.

Young Woman's Journal XVI (December 1905), p. 554.

John F. Bellows

The morning after we arrived in Nauvoo we went to Joseph's Mansion to have an interview with the Prophet. He met us at the door smiling. He put out his hand and shook hands with my father first, then grasped my hand, inviting us to come in. I cannot describe the feelings I had when he grasped my hand. I thought he was the best and noblest man my eyes ever beheld. He led us into the sitting room, where we conversed for over an hour. Joseph and my father did most of the talking. Now and then he would ask me a few questions, and he paid considerable attention to me.

While we were in the Prophet's house, a knock was heard at the door. Joseph opened the door, and there stood two well-dressed men with tall, black stovepipe hats on. One of the men asked if Mr. Smith was in. Joseph said, "Yes, sir, I am the man."

There was silence for a moment, and then Joseph spoke up and said, "Gentlemen, I know what is in your hearts, but you do not know what is in mine; and I know who you are. You are officers from Missouri to arrest me. Wait a minute till I get my hat and I will go with you."

He turned around and made a polite bow and said, "Brother Bellows, please excuse me; call in again."

At this, Father and I followed Joseph out of the door. Joseph and the officers took the lead, and Father and I went on behind until we reached the gate. Here Joseph grasped the two men, one with each arm. This aroused my curiosity. I wanted to see the end, so I followed behind. Joseph led them to where some men were at work on the Nauvoo House. He led them around, and showing them the different rooms explained to them the design of the building. Presently they went inside out of my sight. I stayed there a short time and then returned to my stopping place. I had not been there more than thirty or forty minutes when the news was all over town that the officers from Missouri had come for Joseph and that they could not find him. How he got away from the officers I never learned.

My acquaintance with Joseph the Prophet was of short duration, only a little over a year; but in that short time I saw much of his doings and can say I never saw anything but what was noble and godlike.

The Juvenile Instructor, XXVII, (October 15, 1892), pp. 641-642.

Edwin Rushton
(Related by his son)

After sailing from England, our immigrant company reached Nauvoo, April 13, 1843. Father was very anxious to find the members of his family already established there, and hurried towards the town in search of them. He had gone only a short distance when he met a man riding a beautiful black horse. The man accosted him, saying, "Hey, Bub, is that a company of Mormons just landed?"

In much surprise, Father answered, "Yes sir."

"Are you a Mormon?" the stranger continued.

"Yes, sir," Father again answered.

"What do you know about old Joe Smith?" the stranger asked.

"I know that Joseph Smith is a prophet of God," said Father.

"I suppose you are looking for an old man with a long, gray beard. What would you think if I told you I was Joseph Smith?" the man continued.

"If you are Joseph Smith," said Father, "I know you are a prophet of God."

In a gentle voice, the man explained, "I am Joseph Smith. I came to meet those people, dressed as I am in rough clothes and speaking in this manner, to see if their faith is strong enough to stand the things they must meet. If not, they should turn back right now."

This was Father's introduction to the Prophet.

Father's acquaintance with and admiration for the Prophet grew rapidly, and there developed an intimate friendship between them. The Rushton family often serenaded the Prophet.

After the martyrdom, Father was one of four who took part in the second burial of the Prophet, to preserve the body from the hands of ruthless, designing men. Joseph Smith had prepared a burial vault for the Smith family, and when persecution became alarming he came to Father and requested him, in the event the Prophet was killed, to see that the remains of the Smith family were put into this vault.

When Joseph Smith was on his way to Carthage for the last time, Father was standing near by when Joseph said to his wife, "Emma, can you train my sons to walk in their father's footsteps?"

She answered, "Oh, Joseph, you are coming back."

Father says Joseph asked the same question three times, and that Emma gave the same answer each time. The Prophet then rode away to Carthage and his death.

> Edwin Rushton, Pioneer Journals, (no place or date of publication), pp. 2, 3, 5-6.

Sarah M. Pomeroy

My father moved from New York to Nauvoo in the spring of 1843. I was then in my ninth year. The day after our arrival I was out in the yard when a gentleman rode up and inquired for my father, Thomas Colborn. Of course I did not know who it was, but there was something so noble and dignified in his appearance that it struck me forcibly.

My father soon came out and cordially shook him by the hand, and called him Brother Joseph. I knew then it was the Prophet.

It was quite an exciting time just then. The Prophet had been falsely accused of an attempt to murder Governor Boggs of Missouri. Porter Rockwell, a firm friend of Joseph, had been kidnapped and taken to Missouri as an accomplice, and was about to have his trial. Joseph requested my father to lend him a hundred dollars to pay the lawyer who defended Porter Rockwell, and father freely counted out the money.

"This shall be returned within three days, if I am alive," said the Prophet, and departed.

My aunt, Father's sister, was quite wrathful. "Don't you know, Thomas," said she, "you will never see a cent of that money again. Here are your family without a home, and you throw your money away."

"Don't worry, Katie," Father replied, "if he cannot pay it, he is welcome to it."

This conversation was held before us children, and I thought seriously about it. Would he pay it, or would he not? But I had strong faith that he would.

The day came when it was to be paid—a cold, wet, rainy day. The day passed. Night came—9 o'clock, 10 o'clock, and we all retired for the night. Shortly after there was a knock at the door. Father arose and went to it, and there in the driving rain stood the Prophet Joseph.

"Here, Brother Thomas, is the money." A light was struck, and he counted out the hundred dollars in gold.

He said, "Brother Thomas, I have been trying all day to raise this sum, for my honor was at stake. God bless you."

My aunt had nothing to say. She afterwards left the Church.

Young Woman's Journal, XVII (December, 1906), pp. 538-539.

Charles Lambert

The day after I arrived at Nauvoo from England, as I had some business with the Prophet Joseph, I had an interview with him. I felt good.

I was present when the Prophet preached his last sermon, from a frame building put up to the square and a place floored over for him to stand on. It was powerful. There was a tall man standing behind me sobbing and crying. When I turned around to look at him, he said he would never fight against the Mormons; no, never. He was a stranger to me.

The Prophet used to hold meetings in a log house of his, sometimes twice a week. At one of these, he said he wished he had a people to whom he could reveal what the Lord had shown him. Said he, "But one thing I will say, there are thousands of spirits that have been waiting to come forth in this day and generation. Their proper channel is through the priesthood. A way has to be provided. The time has come, and they have got to come anyway."

Thus he left me in a fix.

Some time after this William Clayton told me that if I would come down into the basement of the Temple he wanted to show me something, and that I might bring Stephen Hales with me. Brother William Clayton read us the revelation on plural marriage. This explained the above.

I think it was on or about the 6th of May, 1844, the Prophet Joseph came up to the Temple and clasping his arms around me, lifted me off my feet, then said, "The Lord bless thee, and I bless thee, and I bless thee in the name of the Lord Jesus Christ."

It went through my whole system like fire.

Then he turned to those around and said, "The Lord bless the whole of you, and peace be with you."

> Autobiography of Charles Lambert, Church Historian's Library, Salt Lake City, Utah, pp. 9-10, 15-17.

Emily D. Partridge Young

My soul is harrowed up when I let my mind revert back to those days of sorrow and persecution that followed the Prophet Joseph all his life. His troubles at home were more sad and harder to bear than all the trials that could be heaped upon him by outside enemies.

I was intimately acquainted with him for several years. More acquainted with his home life than with his public—or rather, his private life outside of his home. I have known him to come in with his head bowed. He would walk the floor back and forth, with his hands clasped behind him (a way he had of placing his hands when his mind was deeply troubled), his countenance showing that he was weighed down with some terrible burden. Many times my heart has ached for him. He did not often speak to his family of his outside troubles.

Joseph was a prophet of God, and a friend of man. His was a noble character. All who knew him can testify to that assertion. He was all that the word *gentleman* would imply—pure in heart, always striving for right, upholding innocence, and battling for the good of all.

> Statement by Emily D. Partridge Young, written June 27, 1897, Salt Lake City, Utah, Church Historian's Library, Salt Lake City, Utah.

Christopher Layton

We arrived at Nauvoo from Liverpool one very cold morning, April 12, 1843. There stood our Prophet on the banks of the river to welcome us. As he heartily grasped our hands, the fervently spoken words, "God bless you," sank deep into our hearts, giving us a feeling of peace such as we had never known before.

On the following day, the Prophet Joseph called to see us and blessed us.

Brother John Marriott and myself went in with some brethren, to build a house each. But as we thought we were not fairly dealt with, we drew out and told Joseph about it. After counseling and instructing us, he gave us each two and a half acres of land and said, "You shall live to see the day when you can buy out everyone who has oppressed you."

This prophecy has come true, as has all that noble man ever uttered concerning me.

Our Prophet was at this time passing through severe trials and persecutions, but he was unruffled in his calm dignity. His faith was so strong that he knew no fear, and at one time when he was told by his friends that the mob was after him, he calmly replied, "Do not be alarmed; I have no fear and shall not flee. I will find friends and the Missourians cannot slay me, I tell you in the name of Israel's God."

On the 16th of June, 1844, Brother Joseph preached to the assembled Saints in the grove east of the Temple (while the rain fell heavily), from the revelation of St. John. After the city had been declared under martial law, the Legion was drawn up in front of the Mansion House and the Prophet, standing upon the framework of a building opposite, addressed them. Drawing his sword, he declared, "I call God and angels to witness that this people shall have their legal rights or my blood shall be spilt upon the ground and my body consigned to the tomb, but if there is one drop of blood shed on this occasion, the sword shall never again be sheathed until Christ comes to reign over the earth. Peace shall be taken from the land which permits these crimes against the Saints to go unavenged."

Autobiography of Christopher Layton (Salt Lake City, 1911), pp. 5-11, 18-21.

Helen Mar Whitney

Joseph was noted for his child-like love and familiarity with children, and he never seemed to feel that he was losing any of his honor or dignity in doing so. If he heard the cry of a child, he would rush out of the house to see if it was harmed.

Near the first of June, 1843, the Prophet invited my father, Heber C. Kimball, to ride with him to give invitations to his friends to take a pleasure trip down to Quincy. I was invited to go along. As we drove up the river a steamer was landing, and a number of strange gentlemen came ashore who had quite a curiosity to see the Prophet. He got out, and in his warm and genial way gave each of them a cordial shake of the hand. As the carriage was about to start away, one of them requested the privilege of riding. After going a few rods he got out. He wished to say that he had ridden with Joseph Smith, whom they styled the "American Mahomet."

We had a most enjoyable trip to Quincy. But on our return trip a heavy thunder storm came up, and Judge Elias Higbee became very ill, so that we were obliged to stop over night at Keokuk. The cabin was small, and the Judge was so sick the majority stayed on deck all night, with umbrellas our only protection from the beating storm. The heat had been very excessive, and being thinly clad, many were made sick. I was among that number.

The Prophet, who was noted for his tender sympathies towards the afflicted, could not rest until he went around and informed himself of the condition of each one who had accompanied him to Quincy, and offered advice. Some he administered to.

The morning of the second day after our return, he called at our house. He recommended some medicine to be given me. His counsel was strictly adhered to, and the result was precisely as he had predicted.

Our city was occasionally visited by Lamanites, and a deputation of Pottawatamie chiefs came to the city to see Joseph Smith in June, 1843. The Prophet had an ox killed for them, and some horses were also prepared for them.

They remembered the kindness of Joseph and his people, and when driven from Nauvoo they made us welcome upon their land, where we were obliged to make our winter quarters.

We had struggles with evil spirits at Winter Quarters, which were something similar to what the Prophet Joseph Smith experienced in Far West, Missouri. He said the devil contended with him face to face, after he had afflicted his little child, claiming that he had the best right to a house which Joseph had purchased, it having been previously occupied by some wicked people. But the Prophet rebuked the devil in the name of the Lord, and he had to leave the house.

My father also had some contests with the evil spirits when young in years and inexperienced. The Prophet once requested him to relate those occurrences and the vision of evil spirits which he had in England on the opening of the gospel to that people. After doing so, he asked Joseph what all those things meant, fearing there might be something wrong in him. Joseph's answer was, "No, Brother Heber. At that time, when you were in England, you were nigh unto the Lord. There was only a veil between you and Him. When I heard of it, it gave me great joy, for I then knew the work of God had taken root in that land. It was this that caused the devil to make a struggle to kill you."

Joseph then said the nearer a person approached to the Lord, the greater power would be manifest by the devil to prevent the accomplishment of the purposes of God.

Helen Mar Whitney, "Scenes and Incidents in Nauvoo," *Woman's Exponent,* X (December 1, 1881), pp. 97-98; XI (September 15, 1882), p. 58; (October 1, 1882), p. 70; XII (January 1, 1883), p. 144; (March 1, 1883), p. 146; XIV (December 15, 1885), p. 106.

John M. Bernhisel

Having been a boarder in General Smith's family for more than nine months, with abundant opportunities to contemplate his character and observe his conduct, I have concluded to give you a few of my "impressions" of him. General Joseph Smith is naturally a man of strong mental powers, and is possessed of much energy and decision of character, great penetration, and a profound knowledge of human nature. He is a man of calm judgment, enlarged views, and is eminently distinguished by his love of justice. He is kind and obliging, generous and benevolent, sociable and cheerful, and is possessed of a mind of a contemplative and reflective character. He is honest, frank, fearless and independent, and as free from dissension as any now to be found.

But it is in the gentle charities of domestic life, as the tender and affectionate husband and parent, the warm and sympathizing friend, that the prominent traits of his character are revealed, and his heart is felt to be keenly alive to the kindest and softest emotions of which human nature is susceptible.

He is a true lover of his country and a bright and shining example of integrity and moral excellence in all the relations of life. As a religious teacher as well as a man, he is greatly beloved by this people.

Concerning his views on the pre-earth existence of spirits and the arrangements which were then made for sending spirits into this world, the Prophet said: "We were predestined to undergo a probation here, to serve an allotted time on this earth, in order to test our integrity and determine the fact of our faith, and our strength to overcome the wiles and devices of Lucifer, the great prince and power on this earth at the present day."

Joseph Smith also said: "In the future it will become a question of government on earth, and that of the priesthood, being the only perfect order, must necessarily prevail. Melchizedek, to whom Abraham paid his tithes, was a priest of this divine order, which was declared to be without beginning of days or end of years. In other words, that divine order became the word of God, and the revealed will of the Father to the inhabitants of the earth. If obeyed, peace, happiness and union would result, but if absolute obedience was not rendered, anarchy and confusion must necessarily follow. The object of Satan was to prevail over the frailties of mankind that they might continue in their disobedient course and follow his rule. We, being to a certain extent free agents, could select either path.

"In every previous dispensation, Lucifer had prevailed and driven the priesthood from the earth. But in this last dispensation the reign of the Son of God and His priesthood was firmly established, nevermore to depart; thus all the inhabitants of the world might partake of the gifts and blessings of God. Our integrity to our Father and His righteousness is the only plan whereby we can save ourselves and acquire 'eternal lives and progression,' which is the greatest blessing God can confer on his faithful sons."

"It is only a question of time," said the Prophet, "a few years, or a few hundred, perhaps, according to our reckoning; but time and space being without limit in the estimation of our Father, the course will be determined in accordance with the 'eternal fitness of things' through His will only. Lucifer's reign of anarchy prevails at present, and the nations are even now arming for the conflict which even they foresee must necessarily ensue. In the cruel desolation of war, men will be slain by hundreds, thousands, and perhaps millions. Their widows and orphans will be compelled to flee to Zion for safety, and it will become the bounden duty of the Elders of Israel to provide for their sustenance and welfare."

"Our present system," said the Prophet, "will eventually resolve itself into a 'united order' in which every member will work not purely for his individual aggrandizement, but with an earnest desire to promote the interests of the kingdom of God on the earth."

> Letter of John M. Bernhisel to Governor Thomas Ford, June 14, 1844, Church Historian's Library, Salt Lake City, Utah; Washington Franklin Anderson, "Reminiscences of John M. Bernhisel," typewritten manuscript, Church Historian's Library, Salt Lake City, pp. 1-4.

Andrew J. Stewart

Several families of Latter-day Saints from Missouri moved into our neighborhood in Fox River, Iowa, and I began to question them about "Mormonism." Later, two Elders came to my house asking to stay overnight. After several meetings, my wife and I were baptized, on February 18, 1844. Afterwards, the Elders explained that they had been sent by the Prophet to baptize me and my family, and to stay until this mission was accomplished. They then asked me to go to Nauvoo with them to see the Prophet.

After we spent five days in Nauvoo, mostly with the Prophet, he requested me to attend April Conference, be ordained a Seventy and take a mission.

Joseph presented my name to the conference and appointed me to go to New York with Brigham Young on a mission, to stir up the state of New York on politics, for Joseph Smith to be President of the United States.

I returned to Nauvoo, June 10, to find all the people excited over the destroying of the *Nauvoo Expositor*. I went immediately to the Prophet to learn how and where I was to join Brigham Young. The Prophet said he was glad I had come, but he wanted to change my mission, and take me with him to find a place for the Saints. "For," he said, "the Saints could not build up the Church in the States." They would have to go and find a place in the mountains, where they could find a place to live in peace, and in five years they would not be disturbed or driven away again. He said he had a company made up, but he wanted me, especially, as I had been west on the Indian Land to the Missouri River.

I had a very fine horse the Prophet wanted to buy, and he offered two hundred dollars for it. I told him I would not sell the horse but would make him a present of it. He then asked me if I had other horses to ride and pack, and if I could fit out myself for the trip proposed.

I told him I could, and I was glad to go instead of to New York.

During the time I stayed in the city, I called on the Prophet every day, and was introduced to some of the company who had agreed to go with him. I was surprised that we would have to go into the mountains, or wilderness, and leave that great city and the Temple that was being built. He was eager to get the Temple built and give endowments before we left.

The plan the Prophet proposed was this: I was to go home to Fox River, fifty-five miles west, on the road from Nauvoo to the mountains, take the horse I had given him, and get ready. He would cross over the Mississippi River with a few men, come to my place the first night, and the next night go on, for at that time it was only fifteen miles to the Indian Land boundary which was outside of the United States. He said he would start in about a week, and the company could come on later. This was on June 12, 1844.

I went home, taking the horse with me, and got ready for the trip to the mountains. Later, in the evening of June 22, Joseph and Hyrum Smith, and Willard Richards left Nauvoo and crossed the Mississippi River to find the place for the Saints. I heard that the Prophet had crossed the river for the mountains, and expected him every night until I heard that he was martyred.

Scraps from An Old Timer's Journal, written April 5, 1908, Church Historian's Library, Salt Lake City, Utah.

Gilbert Belnap

After arriving in Nauvoo, June 1, 1844, I went to the residence of the Prophet, where a friend had agreed to meet me. I was
introduced to the Prophet, whose mild and penetrating glance
denoted great depth of thought and extensive forethought. While
I was standing before his penetrating gaze, he seemed to read the
very recesses of my heart. A thousand thoughts passed through
my mind. I seemed to be transfigured before him. I gazed with
wonder at his person and listened with delight to the sound of
his voice. My very destiny seemed to be interwoven with his.

I loved his company. The sound of his voice was music to
my ears. His counsels were good, and his acts were exemplary
and worthy of imitation. His theological reasoning was of God.
In his domestic circle, he was mild and forbearing, but resolute,
and determined in the accomplishment of God's work. Although
opposed by the combined powers of earth, he gathered his thousands around him and planted a great city which was to be the
foundation of a mighty empire, and consecrated it to God as the
land of Zion. At the same time, he endured the most unparalleled
persecution of any man in the history of our country. With a
mind that disdained to confine itself to the old beaten track of
religious rites and ceremonies, he burst asunder the chains which
for ages past had held in bondage the nations of the earth. He
soared aloft and brought to light the hidden treasures of the
Almighty. He bid defiance to the superstitious dogmas and the
combined wisdom of the world, laid the foundation for man's
eternal happiness and revived the tree of liberty.

I was frequently called out by the Prophet Joseph to the
performance of various duties. There was to be held a conven-
tion of anti-Mormons in Carthage. I was required by the Prophet
to form one of their number. With a promise of my fidelity to
God, he assured me that not a hair of my head should fall to the
ground, and if I followed the first impressions of my mind, I should
not fail in the accomplishment of every object that I undertook.
At times, when to all human appearance inevitable destruction
awaited me, God would provide the means of escape.

When first I entered Carthage, I was interrogated by Joseph
Jackson, Mike Barns, and Singleton as to what business I had there.
I replied that I had business at the recorder's office. They being
suspicious of deception, went with me to the office. After examin-

ing the title of a certain tract of land, many impertinent questions were asked me which I promptly answered. Then a low-bred backwoodsman from Missouri began to boast of his powers in the murder of men, women and children of the Mormon Church, and the brutal prostitution of women while in the state of Missouri. He claimed that he had followed them to the state of Illinois for that purpose.

Without considering the greatness of their numbers, I felt like chastising him for his insolence. Just then, he made a desperate thrust at my bowels with his hunting knife, which penetrated all my clothing without any injury to my person. Nerved as it were with angelic power, I prostrated him to the earth, and with one hand seized him by the throat, and with the other drew his knife.

I afterward sat in council with delegates from different parts of the country and secured the resolutions passed by that assembly. I then returned in safety to Nauvoo, but not without a close pursuit by demons in human shape. I prayed to God that the strength of my horse would hold out in order that I might bear to the Prophet the information which I had obtained. But as I entered Nauvoo, my horse fell on his side in the mud, due to my urging him on to such a tremendous speed. We were entirely out of danger. Covered with mud by reason of the fall, I rushed into the presence of the Prophet and gave him a minute detail of all that had come under my observation during that short mission.

At length the evil day appeared and the dark cloud burst with fury over the Prophet's head. He appeared once more at the head of his favorite legion. They, however, surrendered the public arms and he gave himself a sacrifice for the people. Well I remember his saying, "Although I possessed the means of escape, yet I submit without a struggle and repair to the place of slaughter."

I saw the forms of court and heard the many charges against him, which were refuted by plain and positive testimony.

During that time, he received the promise of protection from Thomas Ford, then governor of the state, that he should go with him to Nauvoo. But the governor went to that place without fulfilling this promise.

After his departure, the few Saints that were left in Carthage were expelled at the point of the bayonet. Not, however, until the Prophet, from the jail window, exhorted them for the sake of their own lives to go home to Nauvoo. I well remember those last words of exhortation, and the long and lingering look on the den of infamy, for I did not consider it safe with such a guard. Thus, the Prophet, his brother Hyrum, Willard Richards, and John Taylor were left alone in the hands of those savage persons.

The afternoon previous to the martyrdom we hurried to Nauvoo to announce the coming of the Prophet, as was agreed by the governor. But with him came not the beloved Prophet, and this soon convinced the people that treachery of the foulest kind was at work.

On his return to Carthage, Governor Ford met George D. Grant bearing the sad news of the slaughter at the jail. Whereupon the cowardly curse arrested Grant and took him back to Carthage, in order to give himself time to escape. Thus, the distance of eighteen miles was traveled over three times before the sorrowful news of the Prophet's death reached his friends.

Autobiography of Gilbert Belnap, Brigham Young University Library, pp. 30-37.

Mary Ellen Kimball

The last time I saw the Prophet, he was on his way to Carthage jail. He and his brother Hyrum were on horseback, also Brothers John Taylor and Willard Richards. They stopped opposite Sister Clawson's house, at the house of Brother Rosecrans. We were on the porch and could hear every word he said. He asked for a drink of water. Some few remarks passed between them which I do not remember. But one sentence I well remember. After bidding goodbye, he said to Brother Rosecrans, "If I never see you again, or if I never come back, remember that I love you."

This went through me like electricity. I went in the house and threw myself on the bed and wept like a whipped child. And why this grief for a person I had never spoken to in my life, I could not tell. I knew he was a servant of God, and could only think of the danger he was in, and how deeply he felt it, for I could see that he looked pale.

The Juvenile Instructor, XXVII, (August 15, 1892), pp. 490-491.

Dan Jones

In the summer of 1842, I entered into an arrangement with a Mr. Moffat of Augusta, Iowa, to build a boat which we named the "Maid of Iowa." That winter I was baptized at St. Louis. In the spring I took a load of Saints from St. Louis to Nauvoo, where I first saw the Prophet. Patting me on the shoulder from behind, in the midst of the crowd on board, he said, "God bless this little man."

The news of my embracing Mormonism injured my influence as a steamboat captain. Mr. Moffat finally complained to Joseph of sustaining an injury by my embracing "Mormonism." That touched the fibres of his noble and generous soul. When I returned to Nauvoo, Joseph informed me that the unkind conduct of Mr. Moffat had won me his friendship, and that he had concluded to buy Mr. Moffat's interest in the boat, if I would take him for a partner.

On June 12, 1844, Joseph Smith was standing on the portico of the Mansion House, awaiting the remains of my little son who had died, to be brought out to be buried. He was accosted by the sheriff of Hancock County with a writ to appear before a magistrate in Carthage. He expostulated in vain for the privilege of paying the last debt of honor to the sacred dead.

Joseph having been honorably acquitted before Justice D. H. Wells, other attempts were then made to take the Prophet to Carthage. On Monday the 24th, hundreds gathered before the Mansion House early in the morning. In their midst, with head erect, towering above the rest, the Prophet stood gazing alternately on the devoted city and its much loved citizens. He listened to the entreaties of the throng not to give himself up or he would be murdered. A few brave-hearted men proposed to escort him to the West. Others, up north would have him go, while a fearless tar (sailor) proffered him a safe passage on a steamboat to whither he would go. A smile of approbation lit up the Seer's countenance. His lovely boys, hanging on to his skirts, urged on the suite and cried, "Father, O Father don't go to Carthage. They will kill you."

Not least impressive were the pleadings of his mother: "My son, my son, can you leave me without promising to return? Some forty times before have I seen you from me dragged, but never before without saying you would return; what say you now, my son?"

He stood erect, like a beacon among roaring breakers, his gigantic mind grasping still higher. The fire flashed in his eye. With hand uplifted on high, he spoke, "My friends, nay, dearer still, my brethren, I love you. I love the city of Nauvoo too well to save my life at your expense. If I go not to them, they will come and act out the horrid Missouri scenes in Nauvoo. I may prevent it. I fear not death. My work is well nigh done. Keep the faith and I will die for Nauvoo."

With some thirty or forty others who chose to follow, Joseph and Hyrum ascended the hill. When near the sacred spot—the Temple—the Prophet paused. He looked with admiration first on that, then on the city, and remarked, "This is the loveliest place and the best people under the heavens. Little do they know the trials that await them."

On the 25th, I carried some documents to Carthage, to be used in the Prophet's trial. There I heard Wilson Law, in endeavoring to get a warrant against Joseph for treason, declare that in preaching from Daniel 2:44, the Prophet said that the kingdom referred to therein was already set up, and that he (Joseph) was the king over it! (Wonder if Daniel himself was not more treasonable for predicting it?) The defendants, having given bail to appear at the quarter sessions, were released to return to Nauvoo.

But before the Prophet could leave I went downstairs, in Hamilton's Hotel, where I overheard the leaders of the mob say that they did not expect to prove anything against him, but that they had eighteen accusations, and as one failed they would try another to detain him there. Joseph Jackson replied, when I told them to desist from their cruel persecutions, that they had worked too hard to get "Old Joe" to Carthage to let him get out of it alive. Pointing to his pistols, he said, "The balls are in there that will decide his case."

I repaired upstairs and informed Joseph Smith what I had heard. He said, "They are going to take me to prison without a guard; you will not leave me, will you?"

To this I replied that, to the contrary, I had come to die with him.

Now the rush of heavy treads up the stairs drew our attention, and the stentorian voice of an officer demanded the prisoners. The "Carthage Greys" then escorted them to prison.

Being dark, the Prophet asked me to get inside the prison somehow. Colonel Markham was on one side, with a hickory club, while I was on the other, outside the guard. We parried off the guns and bayonets of the drunken rabble who tried to break the ranks to stab the prisoners. The prison doors being open before a light was produced, I rushed between the guard and the door and found my way into the farthest cells unhindered, followed by the defendants.

Amusing conversation on various interesting topics engaged us till late. After prayer, which made Carthage prison into the gate of heaven for a while, we lay promiscuously on the floor.

After breakfast, we were removed to an upstairs room, the entrance to which was up a flight of stairs from the front prison door, which was guarded by soldiers, by alternate four hours. The Prophet appeared extremely anxious, by his injunctions to the messengers who left for Nauvoo, to send out testimonies to exonerate his brother Hyrum.

A portion of us were alternately preaching to the guards, at which the Prophet, Patriarch and all took turns, and several were relieved before their time was out because they were proselyted to the belief of the innocency of the prisoners. Frequently they admitted they had been imposed upon by the tales of the mobs, and more than once was it heard, "Let us go home, boys, for I will not fight against these men."

About the middle of the afternoon, the sheriff came to take the prisoners to the courthouse to be tried, followed by drunken mobs armed and threatening. The Prophet put on his hat and, followed by all of us, walked boldly into their midst. He politely locked arms with the worst mobocrat he could see, whereas Hyrum patterned after him by clenching the next worse one, followed by Elders Richards and Taylor, escorted by a guard. The mobocrat's side was the best protection from the leveled rifles of the surrounding bushhiders. Colonel Markham on one side, myself on the other, with our "switches" parried off the crowding rabble.

In the evening, they were again escorted to the prison amidst the whooping, hallooing and denunciations of infuriated thousands, some of whom tauntingly upbraided him for not calling a legion of angels to release him, and to destroy his enemies, inasmuch as he pretended to have miraculous power. Others asked him to prophesy when and what manner of death awaited him, professing themselves to know all about it. In fact, the situation forcibly reminded us of the taunting and jeering of the Jews to our holy and meek Redeemer, so similar the words and actions of the mob proved their spirits to be.

During the evening, the Patriarch read and commented upon extracts from the Book of Mormon, the imprisonments and deliverance of the servants of God for the gospel's sake. Joseph bore a powerful testimony to the guards of the divine authenticity of the Book of Mormon, the restoration of the gospel, the ministration of angels, and the establishment of the kingdom of God again upon the earth, for the sake of which he was at that time incarcerated in the prison, and not because he had violated any law of God or man.

Late, we retired to rest, Joseph and Hyrum on the only bedstead, while four or five lay side by side on mattresses on the floor, Dr. Richards sat up writing until his last candle left him in the dark. The report of a gun, fired close by, caused Joseph (whose head was by a window) to arise, leave the bed, and lay himself by my side in close embrace. Soon after, Dr. Richards retired to the bed; and while I thought all but myself and heaven asleep, Joseph asked in a whisper if I was afraid to die.

"Has that time come, think you? Engaged in such a cause, I do not think that death would have many terrors," I replied.

"You will see Wales and fulfill the mission appointed you ere you die," he said.

I believed his word and relied upon it through the trying scenes which followed. All the conversation evinced a presentiment of an approaching crisis. At midnight I was awakened by heavy treads, as of soldiery close by, and I heard a voice under the window whispering, "Who, and how many shall go in?"

Upon arising, I saw a large number of men in front of the prison, and gave the alarm as they rushed up stairs to our door. We had taken the precaution to fortify ourselves by placing a chair, the only defence, against the door, which one of the brethren seized for a weapon, and we stood by the door awaiting their entrance. Hearing us, they hesitated when Joseph, with a "Prophet's voice," called out, "Come on, ye assassins. We are ready for you, and would as willingly die now as at daylight."

Hearing this, they retired again and consulted, advanced and retreated alternately, evidently failing to agree, until morning.

Early in the morning of the 27th of June, the Prophet requested me to descend and interrogate the guard as to the cause of the intrusion upon us in the night. The sergeant, whose name was Worrell, I think, of the Carthage Greys, replied in a very bitter spirit, "We have had too much trouble to bring 'Old Joe' here to let him ever escape alive, and unless you want to die with him you better leave before sundown. You are not a d - - n bit better than him for taking his part."

I endeavored to cool him down, but he insisted the more, "You'll see that I can prophesy better than 'Old Joe', that neither he nor his brother, nor anyone who will remain with them, will see the sun set today."

Joseph and Hyrum were all this time listening unobservedly at the head of the stairs, and on my return they desired me to go and inform Governor Ford of all that I had heard; which I did. The governor replied, "You are unnecessarily alarmed for your friends' safety, sir. The people are not that cruel."

I returned to the prison and sought to enter, but the guard would not let me in. I was then handed a letter from Joseph Smith, with a request to take it to Mr. Browning, of Quincy, forthwith. The guard being aware of the letter, informed the mob "that Joe had sent orders to raise the Nauvoo Legion to rescue him." This drew the mob around me, and they demanded the letter, which I utterly refused to give to them. When some would take it by force, others objected. The mob disagreed among themselves. While some said I should not leave the place alive, others swore that I should not stay there longer. At this, the former party said that if I left then I should not reach Nauvoo alive, and about a dozen started off with rifle in hand to waylay me where the road runs through the woods. Having previously ordered my horse, which was already in the street, I took advantage of their disagreement. No sooner was I in the saddle than both spurs were to work, and a race horse and rider were enveloped in a cloud of dust, with balls whistling by me. That night I heard of the death of Joseph and Hyrum Smith.

> Dan Jones, "The Martyrdom of Joseph and Hyrum Smith," written January 20, 1855, handwritten manuscript in the Church Historian's Library, Salt Lake City, Utah.

John Taylor

During the early period of his ministry, Joseph Smith was ignorant of letters as the world has it, but he was the most profoundly learned and intelligent man that I ever met in my life, and I have traveled hundreds of thousands of miles, been on different continents and mingled among all classes and creeds of people. Yet I have never met a man so intelligent as he was. Where did he get his intelligence from? Not from books, not from the logic or science or philosophy of the day, but he obtained it through the revelation of God.

The principles which he had, placed him in communication with the Lord, and not only with the Lord, but with the ancient apostles and prophets; such men, for instance, as Abraham, Isaac, Jacob, Noah, Adam, Seth, Enoch, and Jesus, and the Father, and the apostles that lived on this continent, as well as those who lived on the Asiatic continent. He seemed to be as familiar with these people as we are with one another.

I am reminded of a circumstance that occurred in Missouri, which shows the kind of feeling that Joseph Smith possessed. At Far West, a mob had come against us, placing themselves in position to give us battle; and there were not more than about two hundred of us in the place. We had one fellow who was taken with a fit of trembling in the knees, and he ordered our people to retreat. As soon as Joseph heard this sound, he exclaimed, "Retreat! Where in the name of God shall we retreat to?"

He then led us out to the prairie, facing the mob, and placed us in position. And the first thing we knew a flag of truce was seen coming towards us. The person bearing it said that some of their friends were among our people, for whose safety they felt anxious. The mob wished these parties to come out, as they were going to destroy every man, woman and child in the place.

Joseph Smith sent word back by this messenger. Said he, "Tell your general to withdraw his troops or I will send them to hell."

I thought that was a pretty bold stand to take, as we only numbered about two hundred to their thirty-five hundred. But they thought we were more numerous than we really were. It may be that our numbers were magnified in their eyes. But they took the hint and left, and we were not sorry.

I was with Joseph Smith a great deal during his life, and was with him when he died. During one of our conversations in the Carthage Jail, Dr. Willard Richards remarked, "Brother Joseph, if it is necessary that you die in this matter, and if they will take me in your stead, I will suffer for you."

At another time, when conversing about deliverance, I said, "Brother Joseph, if you will permit it, and say the word, I will have you out of this prison in five hours, if the jail has to come down to do it."

My idea was to go to Nauvoo, and collect a force sufficient, as I considered the whole affair a legal farce, and a flagrant outrage upon our liberty and rights. Brother Joseph refused.

Elder Cyrus H. Wheelock came in to see us, and when he was about leaving, drew a small pistol, a six-shooter, from his pocket, remarking at the same time, "Would any of you like to have this?"

Brother Joseph immediately replied, "Yes, give it to me," whereupon he took the pistol, and put it in his pantaloons pocket.

Brother Wheelock went out on some errand, and was not suffered to return. The report of the governor having gone to Nauvoo without taking the prisoners along with him caused very unpleasant feelings, as we were apprised that we were left to the tender mercies of the Carthage Greys.

We looked upon it not only as a breach of faith on the part of the governor, but also as an indication of a desire to insult us, if nothing more, by leaving us in the proximity of such men. The prevention of Wheelock's return was among the first of their hostile movements.

Colonel Markham went out, and he was also prevented from returning. He was very angry at this, but the mob paid no attention to him. They drove him out of town at the point of the bayonet, and threatened to shoot him if he returned.

We all of us felt unusually dull and languid, with a remarkable depression of spirits. In consonance with those feelings, I sang a song that had lately been introduced into Nauvoo, entitled, "A Poor Wayfaring Man of Grief." The song is pathetic, and the tune quite plaintive, and was very much in accordance with our feelings at the time, for our spirits were all depressed, dull, and gloomy, and surcharged with indefinite ominous forebodings.

After a lapse of some time, Brother Hyrum requested me again to sing that song. I replied, "Brother Hyrum, I do not feel like singing."

He remarked, "Oh, never mind; commence singing, and you will get the spirit of it."

At his request, I did so.

Soon afterwards I was sitting at one of the front windows of the jail, when I saw a number of men, with painted faces, coming around the corner of the jail, and aiming towards the stairs. The other brethren had seen the same, for, as I went to the door, I found Brother Hyrum Smith and Dr. Richards already leaning against it. They both pressed against the door with their shoulders to prevent its being opened, as the lock and latch were comparatively useless.

While in this position, the mob, who had come upstairs and tried to open the door, probably thought it was locked and fired a ball through the keyhole.

At this Dr. Richards and Brother Hyrum leaped back from the door, with their faces towards it. Almost instantly another ball passed through the panel of the door, and struck Brother Hyrum on the left side of the nose, entering his face and head. At the same instant, another ball from outside entered his back, passing through his body and striking his watch. The ball came from the back, through the jail window, opposite the door, and must, from its range, have been fired from the Carthage Greys, who were placed there ostensibly for our protection, as the balls from the firearms, shot close by the jail, would have entered the ceiling, we being in the second story, and there never was a time after that when Hyrum could have received the latter wound.

Immediately, when the ball struck him, he fell flat on his back, crying as he fell, "I am a dead man!"

He never moved afterwards.

I shall never forget the deep feeling of sympathy and regard manifested in the countenance of Brother Joseph as he drew nigh to Hyrum and, leaning over him, exclaimed, "Oh! my poor, dear brother Hyrum!"

He, however, instantly rose, and with a firm, quick step, and a determined expression of countenance, approached the door, and pulling the six-shooter left by Brother Wheelock from his pocket, opened the door slightly, and snapped the pistol six successive times. Only three of the barrels, however, were discharged. I afterwards understood that two or three were wounded by these discharges, two of whom, I am informed, died.

I had in my hands a large, strong hickory stick, brought there by Brother Markham and left by him, which I had seized as soon as I saw the mob approach; and while Brother Joseph was firing the pistol, I stood close behind him.

As soon as he had discharged it he stepped back, and I immediately took his place next to the door, while he occupied the one I had done while he was shooting.

Brother Richards, at this time, had a knotty walking-stick in his hands belonging to me, and stood next to Brother Joseph a little farther from the door, in an oblique direction, apparently to avoid the rake of the fire from the door.

The firing of Brother Joseph made our assailants pause for a moment. Very soon after, however, they pushed the door some distance open, and protruded and discharged their guns into the room, when I parried them off with my stick, giving another direction to the balls.

It certainly was a terrible scene. Streams of fire as thick as my arm passed by me as these men fired, and, unarmed as we were, it looked like certain death. I remember feeling as though my time had come, but I do not know when, in any critical position, I was more calm, unruffled, energetic, and acted with more promptness and decision. It certainly was far from pleasant to be so near the muzzles of those firearms as they belched forth their liquid flames and deadly balls. While I was engaged in parrying the guns, Brother Joseph said, "That's right, Brother Taylor, parry them off as well as you can."

These were the last words I ever heard him speak on earth.

Every moment the crowd at the door became more dense, as they were unquestionably pressed on by those in the rear ascending the stairs, until the whole entrance at the door was literally crowded with muskets and rifles, which, with the swearing, shouting, and demoniacal expressions of those outside the door and on the stairs, and the firing of the guns, mingled with their horrid oaths and execrations, made it look like pandemonium let loose, and was, indeed, a fit representation of the horrid deed in which they were engaged.

After parrying the guns for some time, which now protruded farther and farther into the room, and seeing no hope of escape or protection there, as we were now unarmed, it occurred to me that we might have some friends outside, and that there might be some chance of escape in that direction, but here there seemed to be none. As I expected them every moment to rush into the room— nothing but extreme cowardice having thus far kept them out— as the tumult and pressure increased, without any other hope, I made a spring for the window which was right in front of the jail door, where the mob was standing, and also exposed to the fire of the Carthage Greys, who were stationed some ten or twelve rods off. The weather was hot; we all of us had our coats off, and the window was raised to admit air. As I reached the window, and was on the point of leaping out, I was struck by a ball from the door about midway of my thigh, which struck the bone and flattened out almost to the size of a quarter of a dollar, and then passed on through the fleshy part to within about half an inch of the outside. I think some prominent nerve must have been severed or injured, for as soon as the ball struck me, I fell like a bird when shot, or an ox when struck by a butcher, and lost entirely and instantaneously all power of action or locomotion. I fell upon the window sill, and cried out, "I am shot!"

Not possessing any power to move, I felt myself falling outside of the window, but immediately I fell inside, from some, at that time, unknown cause.

When I struck the floor, my animation seemed restored, as I have seen it sometimes in squirrels and birds after being shot. As soon as I felt the power of motion I crawled under the bed, which was in a corner of the room, not far from the window where I received my wound. While on my way and under the bed, I was wounded in three other places.

It would seem that immediately after my attempt to leap out of the window, Joseph also did the same thing, of which circumstance I have no knowledge only from information. The first thing that I noticed was a cry that he had leaped out of the window. A cessation of firing followed, the mob rushed downstairs, and Dr. Richards went to the window. Immediately afterward I saw the doctor going towards the jail door, and as there was an iron door at the head of the stairs adjoining our door which led into the cells for criminals, it struck me that the doctor was going in there, and I said to him, "Stop, Doctor, and take me along."

He proceeded to the door and opened it, and then returned and dragged me along to a small cell prepared for criminals.

Brother Richards was very much troubled, and exclaimed, "Oh! Brother Taylor, is it possible that they have killed both Brother Hyrum and Joseph? It cannot surely be, and yet I saw them shoot them."

Elevating his hands two or three times, he then exclaimed, "Oh Lord, my God, spare Thy servants!"

He then said, "Brother Taylor, this is a terrible event"; and he dragged me farther into the cell, saying, "I am sorry I can not do better for you."

Taking an old filthy mattress, he covered me with it, and said, "That may hide you, and you may yet live to tell the tale, but I expect they will kill me in a few moments!"

While lying in this position, I suffered the most excruciating pain.

Soon afterwards Dr. Richards came to me, informed me that the mob had precipitately fled, and at the same time confirmed the worst fears that Joseph was assuredly dead.

I felt a dull, lonely, sickening sensation at the news. When I reflected that our noble chieftain, the Prophet of the living God, had fallen, and that I had seen his brother in the cold embrace of death, it seemed as though there was a void or vacuum in the great field of human existence to me, and a dark gloomy chasm in the kingdom, and that we were left alone. Oh, how lonely was that feeling! How cold, barren, and desolate! In the midst of difficulties he was always the first in motion; in critical positions his counsel was always sought. As our Prophet he approached our God, and obtained for us his will; but now our Prophet, our counselor, our general, our leader, was gone, and amid the fiery ordeal that we then had to pass through, we were left alone without his aid, and as our future guide for things spiritual or temporal, and for all things pertaining to this world, or the next, he had spoken for the last time on earth.

Journal of Discourses, XXI, pp. 94, 163; XXIII, pp. 36-37; *History of the Church,* VII, pp. 100-106.

Biographical Sketches

LUCY DIANTHA MORLEY ALLEN was born at Kirtland, Ohio, October 4, 1815, the daughter of Isaac Morley; baptized at Kirtland, November 15, 1830; figured in the events of Church history until her death at Orderville, Utah, in 1908.

WILLIAM MOORE ALLRED was born in Bedford County, Tennessee, December 24, 1819; baptized in Monroe County, Missouri, and was associated with the Saints until his death in 1901.

JOHN F. BELLOWS was born in Wayne County, Illinois, May 24, 1825; baptized in Morgan County, Illinois, May 8, 1843; associated with the Church in Illinois and Utah, where he was an Indian War veteran; died in 1894.

GILBERT BELNAP was born in Hope, Newcastle District, Canada, December 22, 1821; baptized September 11, 1842; associated with the Church in Illinois and Utah, serving as a ward bishop in Utah and a missionary to the Indians on the Salmon River in Idaho; died in 1899.

JOHN M. BERNHISEL was born in Tyrone Township, Cumberland County, Pennsylvania, June 23, 1799; baptized in New York City about 1837 and served there as a bishop before moving to Nauvoo in 1843. Trained as a medical doctor, he later became Utah's first delegate to the United States Congress; died at Salt Lake City in 1881.

HENRY WILLIAM BIGLER was born in Harrison County, Virginia (now West Virginia), August 28, 1815; baptized in July, 1837; associated with the Saints in Missouri and Illinois, and later became a member of the Mormon Battalion, a missionary to the Sandwich Islands, and a pioneer of southern Utah, where he died at St. George in 1900.

JAMES B. BRACKEN, SR., was born in Hamilton County, Ohio, January 14, 1816; baptized in Clinton County, Indiana, March 10, 1832, and was associated with the Saints until his death in Panguitch, Utah, in 1900.

BENJAMIN BROWN was born in Queensburg, New York, September 30, 1794; associated with the Church as a missionary and as a ward bishop in Utah.

HARRISON BURGESS was born at Putnam, Washington County, New York, September 3, 1814; baptized October 1, 1832, was a member of Zion's Camp, and was ordained to the First Quorum of the Seventy in 1835; figured in the events of Church history until his death in Pine Valley, Utah, in 1883 after serving there as a ward bishop.

MARGARETTE McINTIRE BURGESS was born in Indiana County, Pennsylvania, March 22, 1837; baptized about 1845, and was associated with the Saints until her death at St. George, Utah, in 1919.

PETER HARDEMAN BURNETT was born in Nashville, Tennessee, November 15, 1807; a lawyer, he became Joseph Smith's legal counsel in Missouri and later the first governor of California.

WILLIAM FARRINGTON CAHOON was born in Harpersfield, Ashtabula County, Ohio, November 7, 1813; baptized at Kirtland, Ohio, October 16, 1830, and became a member of the First Quorum of the Seventy in 1835; helped build the Kirtland Temple; crossed the plains to Utah in 1849, and died there in 1883.

ANSON CALL was born at Fletcher, Franklin County, Vermont, May 13, 1810; baptized at Kirtland, Ohio; associated with the Church in Ohio, Missouri, Illinois, and Utah, where he served as a ward bishop and a counselor in a stake presidency.

ANGUS M. CANNON was born in Liverpool, England, May 17, 1834; baptized at Nauvoo in 1844; associated with the Saints in pioneering Utah; manager of *Deseret News* and mayor of St. George, Utah; stake president and patriarch.

JOHN M. CHIDESTER was born at Pompey, Onondaga County, New York, January 22, 1809; baptized in Michigan in June, 1832; became a member of Zion's Camp and figured in the events of Church history until his death at Washington, Utah, in 1893.

ZEBEDEE COLTRIN was born at Ovid, Seneca County, New York, September 7, 1804; baptized in Ohio, January 9, 1831, and became a member of the First Council of the Seventy in 1835; figured in the events of Church history in Ohio, Illinois, and Utah, where he was ordained a patriarch.

HOWARD CORAY was born in Dansville, Steuben County, New York, May 6, 1817; baptized in Illinois, March 25, 1840; did clerical work for Joseph Smith in Nauvoo; associated with the Church as a missionary and a clerk in the Presiding Bishop's Office in Salt Lake City, Utah, where he died in 1908.

HENRIETTA COX was born in Mansfield, Lolland County, Connecticut, March 8, 1835; baptized in 1844; associated with the Church in Illinois and Utah, where she died in 1917.

JESSE W. CROSBY was born in Yarmouth, Nova Scotia, Canada, November 25, 1820; baptized June 24, 1838; a close neighbor to Joseph Smith in Nauvoo; prominent in pioneering southern Utah, where he died in 1893.

PHILO DIBBLE was born at Peru, Massachusetts, January 6, 1806; baptized at Kirtland, Ohio, October 16, 1830, and figured prominently in the events of Church history until his death at Springville, Utah, in 1895.

ADDISON EVERETT was born in Orange County, New York, October 10, 1805; baptized in New York State, September 1, 1837, and served as a ward bishop in Salt Lake City, Utah, before he was called to pioneer southern Utah, where he died at St. George in 1885.

RACHEL RIDGEWAY GRANT was born at Hornerstown, New Jersey, March 7, 1821; married Jedediah Morgan Grant, and was the mother of Heber Jedy Grant, the seventh President of the Church; died in Salt Lake City, Utah, in 1909.

SARAH ANN GREGORY HALES was born at Barnes, Alleghany County, New York, January 16, 1823; baptized in Pennsylvania about 1838, and was associated with the Saints until her death at Huntington, Utah, in 1908.

LEVI W. HANCOCK was born in Hampden County, Massachusetts, April 7, 1803; baptized at Kirtland, Ohio, November 16, 1830, and became a member of the First Council of the Seventy in 1835; served as a police officer in Nauvoo, chaplain of the Mormon Battalion, a patriarch, and a pioneer of southern Utah.

MOSIAH L. HANCOCK was born at Kirtland, Ohio, April 9, 1834, a son of Levi W. Hancock; baptized in Nauvoo, Illinois, April 10, 1842, and became a veteran of the Black Hawk War and an early settler in southern Utah and Arizona, where he died in 1907.

JOHN W. HESS was born in Franklin County, Pennsylvania, August 24, 1824; baptized in March, 1834, and later served as a member of the Nauvoo Legion, a member of the Mormon Battalion, a ward bishop in Utah, and a member of a stake presidency.

EDWIN HOLDEN was born at New Salem, Massachusetts, June 4, 1807; baptized July 14, 1839, and moved west with the Church to Utah, where he died in 1894.

OLIVER B. HUNTINGTON was born at Watertown, Jefferson County, New York, October 14, 1823; baptized at Kirtland, Ohio, in October, 1836, and figured in the events of Church history until his death in Springfield, Utah, after serving as a missionary to England and being ordained a patriarch.

WILLIAM HUNTINGTON was born at Grantham, New Hampshire, March 28, 1784; baptized in April, 1835, and became a member of the high council at Kirtland; appointed chairman of the committee to remove the Saints from Missouri in 1839, and president of the Mt. Pisgah Stake, Iowa, in 1846, where he died.

"AUNT" JANE JAMES was a Negro born at Wilton, Fairfield County, Connecticut, May 11, 1821; baptized about 1839, and worked as a maid in Joseph Smith's home at Nauvoo; associated with the Saints in Illinois and Utah.

BENJAMIN F. JOHNSON was born at Pomfret, Chatauqua County, New York, July 28, 1818; baptized at Kirtland, Ohio, in March, 1835, and was associated with the Saints in Ohio, Missouri, Illinois (where he was made a member of the General Council, or Council of Fifty), and the West, where he was ordained a patriarch before his death in Mesa, Arizona, in 1905.

JOEL HILLS JOHNSON was born at Grafton, Massachusetts, March 23, 1802; baptized in Ohio, June 1, 1831, and later became a ward bishop and a patriarch; figured in the events of Church history in Ohio, Missouri, Illinois, and Utah, where he died in 1882.

LUKE S. JOHNSON was born at Pomfret, Windsor County, Vermont, November 3, 1807; baptized by Joseph Smith at Kirtland, Ohio, May 10, 1831, and became a member of the Quorum of the Twelve in 1835; excommunicated in 1838, but later returned to the Church and died in Utah in 1861.

DAN JONES was born in Flintshire, Wales, August 4, 1811; baptized at St. Louis, Missouri, in 1843; one of the greatest of the early missionaries in respect to convert baptisms, and recognized as the founder of the Welsh Mission. As a pioneer, he helped settle Manti, Utah; died in 1861.

WILLIAM E. JONES was born at Buckley, North Wales, April 6, 1817; baptized in North Wales, June 27, 1841, and was associated with the Saints in Illinois and Utah, where he died at Gunlock, Washington County, in 1898.

HEBER C. KIMBALL was born at Sheldon, Franklin County, Vermont, June 14, 1801; baptized in April, 1832, and became a member of the Quorum of the Twelve Apostles in 1835, and a counselor to Brigham Young in the First Presidency in 1847.

LUCY WALKER KIMBALL was born in Peacham, Caledonia County, Vermont, April 30, 1826; baptized at Ogdensburgh, New York, in her ninth year; sealed to Joseph Smith in 1843, married to Heber C. Kimball, 1845; temple worker in Logan and Salt Lake City, Utah.

MARY ELLEN KIMBALL was born in Charleston, Montgomery County, New York, October 5, 1818; baptized in Utica, Oneida County, New York, 1842; a wife of Heber C. Kimball, she was associated with the Church in Illinois and Utah.

SARAH M. KIMBALL was born at Phelps, Ontario County, New York, December 29, 1818; first president of the Utah Suffrage Association, and a counselor in the general Relief Society presidency in Utah; died in 1898.

JOSEPH KNIGHT, JR., was born in Vermont, June 22, 1808, and resided at Colesville, Broome County, New York, where his father's family was among the first to believe the testimony of Joseph Smith, even before the Prophet obtained the Nephite record; served as an acting bishop at Winter Quarters and Council Bluffs, Iowa, and was a pioneer of Utah.

LYDIA BAILEY KNIGHT was born at Sutton, Worchester County, Massachusetts, June 9, 1812; baptized at Mt. Pleasant, Upper Canada (now Ontario), October 24, 1833, and later married Newell Knight; figured in the events of Church history until her death at St. George, Utah, where she was a temple worker in the St. George Temple.

NEWELL KNIGHT was born in Vermont, September 13, 1800, and resided at Colesville, Broome County, New York, where he was baptized in 1830; figured prominently in the events of the Church in Missouri and Illinois; died in northern Nebraska in 1847.

CHARLES LAMBERT was born in Kirk Deighton, York, Yorkshire, England, August 30, 1814; baptized at Lincolnshire, England, July 12, 1843; worked on the Nauvoo Temple, and was associated with the Church in Utah until his death in 1892.

MARY ALICE CANNON LAMBERT was born in Liverpool, England, December 9, 1828, a sister to George Q. Cannon; baptized June 14, 1840; associated with the Church in Illinois and Utah, where she died in 1920.

CHRISTOPHER LAYTON was born in Thorncut, Northhill, Bedfordshire, England, March 8, 1821; baptized in England, April 12, 1843; associated with the Church in Illinois and Utah; member of the Mormon Battalion, bishop, stake president and patriarch; died at Salt Lake City in 1898.

JAMES LEECH was born in Pilling Lane, Lancashire, England, May 2, 1815; baptized in Nauvoo, Illinois, November, 1841, associated with the Church in Illinois and Utah.

MARY ELIZABETH ROLLINS LIGHTNER was born in Livingston County, New York, April 9, 1818; baptized at Kirtland, Ohio, October, 1830, and moved with the Saints to Missouri, Illinois, and Utah.

LOUISA Y. LITTLEFIELD was born in Hector, Tomkins County, New York, May 1, 1822; baptized at Kirtland, Ohio, in 1834, and married Lyman O. Littlefield; associated with the Saints in Ohio, Missouri, Illinois, and Utah.

DANIEL D. McARTHUR was born at Holland, Erie County, New York, April 8, 1820; baptized in Missouri in July, 1838, and later became president of the St. George Stake, in Utah, where he was an early pioneer.

ALEXANDER McRAE was born in Anson County, North Carolina, September 7, 1807; baptized in Ripley County, Indiana, June, 1837; associated with the Church as a missionary and as a ward bishop in Utah, where he died in 1891.

WANDLE MACE was born at Johnstown, Montgomery County, New York, February 19, 1809; baptized in New York City, winter, 1837 or 1838, and served as the presiding elder of the New York City Branch; associated with the main body of the Saints in Illinois and Utah, where he helped settle the southern part of the state.

SUSAN E. J. MARTINEAU was born at Kirtland, Ohio, July 11, 1836, daughter of Joel H. Johnson; baptized July 11, 1844, and was associated with the Saints until her death at Salt Lake City, Utah, in 1921.

CHRISTOPHER MERKLEY was born in Williamsburg, Dundas County, Ontario, Canada, December 18, 1808; baptized July 27, 1837; helped build the Nauvoo, Salt Lake, and Logan temples; Indian War veteran, and missionary eight times; died in Salt Lake City, Utah, in 1893.

SAMUEL MILES was born at Attica, Genesee County, New York, April 8, 1826; baptized at Portage, Ohio, in April, 1836; figured in the events of Church history in Ohio, Missouri, and Illinois; became a member of the Mormon Battalion, and was a pioneer of southern Utah before his death at St. George, Utah, in 1910.

GEORGE MILLER was born in Orange County, Virginia, November 25, 1794; baptized in Illinois in 1839, and was sustained as a general bishop at Nauvoo, where he also became a member of the General Council, or Council of Fifty.

CALVIN W. MOORE was born at Palmer, Hampden County, Massachusetts, July, 1829; baptized at Kirtland, Ohio, in 1835, and became a ward bishop in Utah, after his experiences with the Saints in Ohio, Missouri, Illinois, and as a member of the Mormon Battalion.

WILLIAM G. NELSON was born in Jefferson County, Illinois, June 10, 1831; associated with the Saints in Illinois and in the West, where he served as a ward bishop and a member of the high council at Oxford, Idaho.

MARY A. NOBLE was born at Levonia, Livingston County, New York, October 19, 1810, the daughter of Alva Beaman, an early acquaintance of the Smith family in New York in whose home the Prophet hid the gold plates for a time before moving to Harmony, Pennsylvania; married Joseph B. Noble and was associated with the Saints until her death in Salt Lake City in 1851.

DAVID OSBORN was born in Greenbrier County, Virginia; baptized in Green County, Iowa, July, 1835, and figured in Church history in Missouri, Illinois, and Utah, where he died in 1895.

JAMES PALMER was born in Dymock, England, August 6, 1820; baptized April 30, 1840; associated with the Church in Illinois and Utah, where he died in 1905.

MRS. PALMER was an early resident of the Palmyra-Manchester area in New York, who later lived in Monroe, Sevier County, Utah, with her daughter who taught in the Presbyterian schools of the state. (See "Guest Editor's Prologue," BYU Studies, Spring 1969, p. 235.)

SARAH M. POMEROY was born at Rose, Wayne County, New York, November 4, 1834, the daughter of Thomas Colburn; married Francis M. Pomeroy and was associated with the Saints until her death at Mesa, Arizona, in 1926.

PARLEY P. PRATT was born April 12, 1807, at Burlington, New York; baptized September 1, 1830, and became a member of the Quorum of the Twelve Apostles in 1835; assassinated May 13, 1857, at Van Buren, Arkansas.

JANE SNYDER RICHARDS was born in Pamelia, Jefferson County, New York; married to Franklin D. Richards; a member of the Relief Society in Nauvoo and on the general board of the Relief Society in Utah from 1888-1910; died in 1912.

JOSEPH LEE ROBINSON was born in Shaftsburg, Vermont, February 18, 1811; baptized at Bonneville, New York, August 13, 1836; associated with the Church as a bishop, high council member and patriarch; died at Uintah, Weber County, Utah, in 1893.

JAMES HENRY ROLLINS was born at Lima, Livingston County, New York, May 27, 1816; baptized in Jackson County, Missouri, June 1, 1832, and later became a ward bishop in Utah, after figuring in the events of Church history in Missouri and Illinois.

EDWIN RUSHTON was a convert immigrant from England; arrived in Nauvoo, April 13, 1843; served as a lieutenant in the Nauvoo Legion, and as a counselor in a ward bishopric in Utah.

ORLANDO SAUNDERS was an early resident of the area of Palmyra, New York, interviewed in March, 1881, by E. L. and William H. Kelley, of Michigan.

BATHSHEBA W. SMITH was born near Shinnston, Harrison County, West Virginia, May 3, 1822; baptized there, August 21, 1837; married George A.

Smith; present at the organization of the Female Relief Society in Nauvoo, and later its fourth general president in Utah, where she died in 1910.

GEORGE A. SMITH was born at Potsdam, St. Lawrence County, New York, June 26, 1817; baptized September 10, 1832, and became a member of the Quorum of the Twelve Apostles, April 26, 1838, and a counselor in the First Presidency to Brigham Young in 1868.

JESSE N. SMITH was born at Stockholm, St. Lawrence County, New York, December 2, 1834; baptized August 13, 1843, and later became president of the Snowflake Stake, Snowflake, Arizona, after associating with the Saints in Ohio, Missouri, and Illinois.

JOHN LYMAN SMITH was born November 17, 1829; baptized in Kirtland, Ohio, at the age of eight; president of the Swiss and Italian Mission from 1856 to 1857; died at St. George, Utah, 1898.

LUCY M. SMITH was born at Bethel, Oxford County, Maine, February 9, 1817; baptized August 12, 1837; the wife of George A. Smith, she was associated with the Church in Illinois and Utah, where she died in 1892.

ELIZA R. SNOW was born at Becket, Berkshire County, Massachusetts, January 21, 1804; baptized at Kirtland, Ohio, April 5, 1835; sealed to Joseph Smith as a plural wife in 1842; served as the second president of the Relief Society and figured prominently in the events of Church history as a poetess and a writer until her death at Salt Lake City in 1889.

EUNICE BILLINGS SNOW was born in Mentor, Ohio, January 3, 1830, daughter of Titus Billings, who was among the earliest converts in that area; married George W. Snow, and was associated with the Saints until her death at Provo, Utah, in 1914.

LORENZO SNOW was born at Mantua, Ohio, April 3, 1814; baptized at Kirtland, Ohio, June, 1836, and became a member of the Quorum of the Twelve Apostles, February 12, 1849, and the fifth President of the Church in 1898.

DR. JOHN STAFFORD was an early resident of New York State, interviewed in March, 1881, by E. L. and William H. Kelley, of Michigan.

EDWARD STEVENSON was born May 1, 1820, at Gibraltar, Spain; baptized December 20, 1833, at Far West, Missouri, and later became a member of the First Council of the Seventy; crossed the plains eighteen times, and the Atlantic Ocean nine times, before his death at Salt Lake City in 1897.

ANDREW J. STEWART was born in Jackson, Monroe County, Ohio; baptized at Fox River township, Van Buren County, Iowa, February 18, 1844; associated with the Church in Illinois and Utah, and served as president of the Australian Mission, 1857-1858; died in 1911.

JOHN TAYLOR was born at Milnthorpe, Westmoreland, England, November 1, 1808; baptized in Toronto, Ontario, Canada, May 9, 1836; became a member of the Quorum of the Twelve Apostles in 1838, and the third President of the Church in 1880.

JOSEPH TAYLOR, SR., was born in Warren County, Kentucky, June 4, 1825; baptized in Ray County, Missouri, summer, 1835, and was associated with the Saints in Missouri, Illinois, and Utah, where he died in 1900.

THOMAS H. TAYLOR was an early resident of Manchester, New York, who engaged in several of the reform movements during the first half of the nineteenth century; interviewed in March, 1881, by E. L. and William H. Kelley, of Michigan.

WILLIAM TAYLOR was born in Hale, Westmoreland, England, September 2, 1823; baptized 1836; a brother of President John Taylor; associated with the Church as a home missionary and a missionary to Germany; died in Utah in 1910.

JAMES P. TERRY was born in Horn District, Albion, Upper Canada (now Ontario); migrated to Nauvoo in 1842 or 1843, and was associated with the Saints in Illinois and Utah.

MERCY R. THOMPSON was born at Honeydon, Bedfordshire, England, June 15, 1807; baptized in the vicinity of Toronto, Canada, May 21, 1836, and later married Robert B. Thompson, one of the Prophet's personal clerks at Nauvoo; died at Salt Lake City, Utah, in 1893.

DANIEL TYLER was born at Semproneous, New York, November 23, 1816; baptized at Springfield, Pennsylvania, January 16, 1833; became a member of the Mormon Battalion, served as president of the Swiss and Italian Mission, and was ordained a patriarch in Utah, where he died in 1906.

WILLIAM HOLMES WALKER was born in Peacham, Caledonia County, Vermont, August 28, 1820; baptized September, 1835; was a member of the Mormon Battalion, a missionary, a temple worker, and a patriarch in the Church.

EMMELINE BLANCHE WELLS was born at Petersham, Worcester County, Massachusetts; associated with the Church in Illinois and Utah; editor of the *Woman's Exponent*, she became the fifth general president of the Relief Society.

MARY C. WESTOVER, as a child, knew Joseph Smith in Nauvoo; associated with the Church in Illinois and Utah.

ELIZABETH ANN WHITNEY was the wife of Bishop Newel K. Whitney, affectionately called "Mother Whitney"; baptized at Kirtland, Ohio, in November, 1830, and became a counselor to Emma Smith in the presidency of the Relief Society at Nauvoo; died in Salt Lake City, Utah, in 1882.

HELEN MAR WHITNEY was born in Mendon, Monroe County, New York; baptized about 1836 in Missouri; oldest daughter of Heber C. Kimball, and mother of Apostle Orson F. Whitney; wrote extensively in behalf of the Latter-day Saints; died at Salt Lake City in 1896.

ORANGE L. WIGHT was born in Alleghany County, New York, November 29, 1823, the son of Lyman Wight; baptized in Jackson County, Missouri, October 4, 1832, and was associated with the main body of the Saints in Ohio, Missouri and Illinois.

MARY ANN WINTERS was born in Coomb, Hampshire, England, February 20, 1820; a stepdaughter of Parley P. Pratt, she was associated with the Church in Illinois and Utah, where she died in 1912.

WILFORD WOODRUFF was born at Avon, Connecticut, March 1, 1807; baptized at Richland, New York, December 31, 1833, and became a member of the Quorum of the Twelve Apostles in 1839, and the fourth President of the Church in 1889.

ANDREW WORKMAN was born in Bourbon County, Kentucky, July 15, 1824; baptized in Overton County, Tennessee, in March, 1842; a member of the Mormon Battalion and the first white settler of Virgin City, Washington County, Utah.

SARIAH A. WORKMAN was born at Amhurst, Lorain County, Ohio, February 18, 1832, a daughter of Joel H. Johnson; baptized June, 1841; married Andrew J. Workman and was associated with the Saints until her death at Hurricane, Utah, in 1925.

BRIGHAM YOUNG was born at Whitingham, Vermont, June 1, 1801; baptized at Mendon, New York, April 14, 1832, and became a member of the Quorum of the Twelve Apostles in 1835, and the second President of the Church in 1847.

EMILY D. PARTRIDGE YOUNG was born in Painesville, Geauga County, Ohio, February 28, 1824; baptized in Independence, Jackson County, Missouri; daughter of Bishop Edward Partridge, she was sealed to Joseph Smith as a plural wife; associated with the Church in Ohio, Missouri, Illinois, and Utah, where she died in 1899.

Index

- A -

Adam-ondi-Ahman, 40, 86, 105-106
Addison, Everett, 14
Allen, Joseph, 32
Allen, Lucy Diantha Morley, 31
Allred, William Moore, 140
Apocrypha, 86
Apostles, the Twelve
  are a sign of true succession, 119
  receive keys of kingdom, 26, 35, 88,
  96
Apostleship, conferred by
  Peter, James and John, 15
Atchison, General, 70-71, 110

- B -

Baldwin, Caleb, 108
Baptism, 50
  for the dead, 123, 155
Barlow, Watson, 109
Basset, Herman, 18
Beaman, Alva, 15
Behunnin, Isaac, 53-54
Bellows, John F., 169
Belnap, Gilbert, 180
Bennett, John C., 135
Bernhisel, Dr. John M., 158, 160, 176
Bigler, Henry William, 100
Billings, Father, 27
Blood sacrifices, 62
Boggs, Gov. Lilburn, 78, 171
Book of Mormon, 3-5, 7, 15-16, 22-23,
  42-43, 99, 101, 126, 155
Booth, Ezra, 29
Bracken, James B., Sr., 78
Brown, Benjamin, 125
Brown, Eliza, 49
Burgess, Harrison, 46
Burgess, Margarette McIntire, 127
Burgess, Wallace, 127
Burk, John, 75
Burnett, Peter Hardeman, 112

- C -

Cahoon, William Farrington, 132
Call, Anson, 105

Cannon, Angus M., 163
Carter, Gideon, 52
Carter, John, 20
Carthage, Illinois, 151, 153, 180-192
Charity and liberality, 62
Chidester, John M., 55
Clark, General, 71
Clayton, William, 140, 161, 173
Colborn, Thomas, 171
Coltrin, Zebedee, 18, 27, 47
Copley, Leman, 18
Coray Howard, 133
Cowdery, Oliver, 6-7, 12-15, 28, 38, 75
Cox, Henrietta, 147
Crosby, Jesse W., 143
Curtis, Levi, 128

- D -

Daniels, Cyrus, 109
Davidson, James, 8, 12
Dibble, Philo, 61, 66
Doniphan, Gen. Alexander, 110
Douglas, Stephen A., 134

- E -

Ephraim, blood of in Europe, 86

- F -

Farr, Olive Hovey, 139
Feast of the Poor, 40
First Vision, 1
Follett, King, discourse, 167
Ford, Gov. Thomas, 149, 181
Fordham, Elijah, 82-83

- G -

Garden of Eden, 86
Gift of Tongues, 28-29, 36
Gilbert, Sidney, 74
Goddard, Stephen, 167
Gods, plurality of, 151
Grant, George D., 182
Grant, Rachel Ridgeway, 126
Green, Evan, 19
Green, Harvey, 18

- H -

Hale, Isaac, 15
Hales, Sarah Ann Gregory, 124
Hall, Levi, 7
Hancock, Joseph, 66, 69
Hancock, Levi W., 17
Hancock, Mosiah L., 102
Harris, Martin, 23-24
Haun's Mill, 52-53
Healings. *See* Smith, Joseph, heals
Hess, John W., 101
Higbee, Elias, 175
Higbee, Isaac, 70
Hinkle, George M., 79
Hoit, Henry, 114
Holden, Edwin, 16
Holeman, David, 109
Holman, Joshua, 73-74
Hunter, Edward, 77
Huntington, Dimick, 65-66
Huntington, Oliver B., 62
Huntington, William D., 109, 128
Hyde, Charles, 79

- I -

Indians, 95-96, 126, 166, 175
Invention and improvement, spirit of,
     among the Saints, 62

- J -

Jackson, Joseph, 148
James, Jane, 158
Johnson, Benjamin F., 88
Johnson, Father, 67-68
Johnson, Joel H., 29, 99
Johnson, Mrs. John, 60-61
Johnson, Luke S., 29
Johnson, Lyman, 16, 19
Jones, Dan, 182
Jones, William E., 162
Journal writing, 65

- K -

Keys of the kingdom, 26, 35, 88, 96
Killian, Capt. John, 52-53
Kimball, Heber C., 34, 36, 38, 130,
     175-176
Kimball, Hiram, 130
Kimball, Lucy Walker, 137
Kimball, Mary Ellen, 182
Kimball, Sarah M., 130
Kirtland Temple, 29, 40, 46, 90
Knight, Joseph, Jr., 5
Knight, Joseph, Sr., 7-8
Knight, Lydia Bailey, 42
Knight, Newell, 6, 71, 79
Knight, Polly, 7
Knowlton, Martha, 136

- L -

Lamanites, 20, 126, 175
Lambert, Charles, 172
Lambert, Mary Alice Cannon, 168
Law, William, 123
Law, Wilson, 184
Layton, Christopher, 174
Leech, James, 141
Legal trials of Joseph Smith, 6, 8-15,
     70-71, 101, 149-150, 183
Liberty Jail, 104-105, 108-112
Lightener, Mary Elizabeth Rollins, 23
Littlefield, Louisa Y., 46
Lyman, Amasa, 77

- M -

McArthur, Daniel D., 73
McRae, Alexander, 108
Mace, Wandle, 115
Markham, Colonel Stephen, 185, 189,
     191
Marriage, Joseph Smith's counsel on,
     139-140, 145
Marriott, John, 174
Marsh, Mrs. Thomas B., 67
Martineau, Susan E. J., 99
Masonry, 107
Merkley, Christopher, 121
Miles, Samuel, 98
Milican, Lucy, 150
Miller, George, 113
Mobs, against Joseph Smith and the
     Saints, 6-7, 12-15, 18, 30, 36,
     70-71, 78-79, 84, 90, 102-103, 106,
     111, 125, 154, 161, 163, 181ff
Morley, Isaac, 22, 27, 31-32

- N -

Nauvoo Expositor, 179
Nauvoo Legion, 153, 167
Nauvoo Temple, 120, 123, 130-131,
     162, 179
Nelson, William G., 118
Nickerson, Freeman, 42-45
Nickerson, Moses, 42-45
Noah's ark, location of, 65
Noble, Joseph B., 83-84, 91
Noble, Mary A., 15

- O -

Osborn, David, 101
Orton, Roger, 46

- P -

Page, Hiram, 13
Palmer, James, 154
Palmer, Mrs., 1
Parker, J. D., 160

Partridge, Bishop Edward, 38
Patriarchal blessing meeting, the first, 40
Patten, David, 52, 78
Peck, Hezekiah, 7
Penniston, William 111
Plural marriage, 57-58, 93, 123, 140
Pomeroy, Sarah M., 171
Pratt, Parley P., 5, 40, 58, 166
Prayer, true order of, 123
Praying, Joseph Smith's counsel on, 100
Preaching, Joseph Smith's counsel on, 100

- R -

Records of the Church, to remain with true successors of Joseph Smith, 119
Reid, John, 8, 12, 14
Relief Society, 41, 123, 131
Reynolds, Governor, 81
Richards, Jane Snyder, 165
Richards, Willard, 49, 87, 130, 179, 182, 185-186, 189-193
Richmond Jail, 59-60, 101
Rigdon, Sidney, 4-5, 16, 28, 30, 42-43, 67-68, 86, 104-105, 108, 112, 134
Ripley, Alanson, 109
Robinson, Colonel G. W., 70
Robinson, Ebenezer, 164
Robinson, James Henry, 74
Robinson, Joseph Lee, 164
Rockwell, Porter, 79, 117, 171
Rocky Mountains, 81, 95, 107, 124, 165, 179
Roundy, Shadrach, 107, 160
Rushton, Edwin, 170

- S -

Sacrament, change from wine to water, 13
Salsbury, Jenkins, 114
Saunders, Orlando, 2
School of the Prophets, 28, 38
Scott, Jacob, 18
Scriptures, expounded by Joseph Smith
See Smith, Joseph, expounds the scriptures.
Seer stones, 13
Seventies, 35
Sherwood, Henry G., 77
Slavery, 160
Smith family, attributes of, 1-4
Smith, Bathsheba W., 122
Smith, David, 151
Smith, Don Carlos, 114
Smith, Emma, 13, 25, 41, 88, 91, 120, 127-129, 131-132, 138, 141, 143, 146-147, 149, 152-153, 158-159, 171
Smith, Freeborn, 151
Smith, George A., 47, 75

Smith, Hyrum, 17, 46-47, 49, 55-56, 67, 75, 90, 104-105, 108-111, 121, 150, 153, 161-162, 179, 182, 186-187, 190
Smith, Jesse, 48, 75, 99
Smith, John Lyman, 146
Smith, Joseph
   ability of, as financier, 147
   borrows baby for Emma, 127-128
   burial of, 170
   candidate for U.S. presidency, 178
   character traits of, 49, 56, 59, 73, 88-89, 98-99, 112, 119-120, 149 157-158, 165, 176-177, 180
   charity of, 49, 89, 184
   chastizes the rich, 102
   compassion of, 38, 53-54, 75-76, 86-87, 89, 92, 138, 165, 166, 175
   confesses weaknesses, 87
   corrects scriptures, 87
   counsel of, on
      keeping journals, 65
      marriage, 139-140, 145
      praying, 100
      preaching, 100
      staying with the Twelve, 119
   courage of, 139, 188
   death of, 97, 104, 151, 153, 168, 170-171, 182-192
   eagerness of, to be helpful, 17, 22
   escapes from law, 148-149, 169
   expounds the scriptures, 62, 117-118, 120, 134
      baptism, 87
      birth by water and spirit, 50-51
      blood sacrifices, 62
      charity and liberality, 62
      Daniel, 2, 100
      Parable of the ten talents, 94
      plurality of gods, 151
      rewards and punishments, 62
   generosity of, 71, 89, 121-122, 142, 148, 150, 158-159
   grief of, at loss of friends, 149-150
   heals, 118, 132
      Benjamin Brown, 125
      Margarette M. Burgess, 127
      Sarah Ann Gregory Hales, 124
      Wm. Huntington, 128-129
      Mrs. John Johnson, 60-61
      Luke Johnson's mother, 30
      Heber C. Kimball, 38-39
      many saints in Nauvoo, 82-83, 91, 103
      Wm. Nelson's son, 119
      Newell K. Whitney, 39
   honesty of, 7, 121, 145, 171-172
   honors parents, 88
   hospitality of, 41, 138-139, 158-159
   illiteracy of, in youth, 4
   intelligence and knowledge of, 4, 56-57, 87, 95, 120, 164, 176, 188

interprets Lamanite remains, 20
joviality of, 4, 98
gives keys of kingdom to the Twelve,
    26, 35, 88, 96
last words of, 191
in Liberty Jail, 104-105, 108-112
is loved by Saints, 89, 166, 168
love of, for children, 46, 99, 101-102,
    127, 151, 154, 166, 175
love of, for home life, 88, 99-100,
    152, 177
makes a marriage match, 137
motto of, 88
parades in Nauvoo, 153, 167
physical description of, 29, 42, 58-59,
    80, 116, 122, 154, 159
plainness of, as youth, 7
plans western trek, 179
pleads law, 64
power of example of, 95
praises Christian martyrs, 85
prayers of, their eloquence, 24, 51-52,
    147
preaches, 44, 67, 116, 154, 162-163,
    174
  ancient order of Abraham, 123
  baptism for the dead, 123
  to Indians, 126, 175
  last sermon, 172
  parable of the Good Samaritan, 115
  plan of salvation, 177-178
  true order of prayer, 123
prophesies, 25-26, 45, 52, 66-67,
    70-73, 81-82, 85, 95-96, 102,
    105, 107, 109, 111, 119, 123,
    141, 146-147, 167, 174, 180-181
  Civil War, 87, 155
  Dan Jones' mission to Wales, 186
  destruction of Eastern cities, 39
  establishment of world government
    by priesthood, 177-178
  expulsion from Nauvoo, 63
  freedom of slaves, 160
  future of Relief Society, 41
  meteor shower, 69
  Saints in Rocky Mountains, 64, 81,
    95, 107, 124, 139, 165
  temples in Rocky Mountains, 165
  suffering of Missourians, 64-65
pursued by mobs. See Mobs.
radiance of countenance of, when
    inspired, 23, 34, 46, 65, 68,
    85-86, 107, 143, 166-167
rebukes evil spirits, 23, 27, 32, 66-67,
    79, 176
rebukes Sidney Rigdon, 91
receives home teachers, 132-133
refinement of, 157
reluctance of, to judge quickly,
    144-145
reputation of, in youth, 1-7
in Richmond Jail, 59-60, 101
social ease of, 119, 120, 133-134

speaking style of, 32-33, 35, 81,
    116-117, 164
sports and amusements of, 6, 16, 32,
    86, 89, 98, 103, 112-113,
    117-118, 130, 135, 140
sternness and firmness of, 31, 73-74,
    79, 86, 111, 120, 149, 158,
    162-163
studies Greek and Latin, 101
sufferings of, 19, 48
teaching excellence of, 35, 87-88,
    95-96, 164
tenderness of, 86-87
testimony of, 26, 43, 67, 101-102,
    155, 163, 172, 186
tests friends, 103-104
tests new Saints, 170
on trial, 7-12, 14-16
visions of, 28, 46, 50, 67-68, 107,
    167-168
weariness of, at end of life, 97
work habits of, 1, 5, 17, 143, 147-148
Smith, Julia, 152
Smith, Lucy Mack, 1, 116, 150, 153
Smith, Samuel, 114
Smith, Sylvester, 19-21, 36-37
Smith, William, 51-52, 75
Snow, Eliza R., 33, 56, 131
Snow, Erastus, 100, 109-110
Snow, Eunice Billings, 152
Snow, Lorenzo, 32, 57
Stafford, Dr. John, 4
Stevenson, Edward, 85
Stewart, Andrew J., 178
Stoal, Josiah, 8-9
Stringham, Julia, 7
Stymore, Mr., 10-11

- T -

Taylor, John, 104, 115, 160, 182, 185,
    188
Taylor, Joseph, Sr., 141
Taylor, Thomas H., 3
Taylor, William, 160
Temples, 29, 40, 46, 90, 120, 123,
    130-131, 162, 165, 179
Terry, James P., 162
Thompson, Charles, 49
Thompson, Jonathan, 9
Thompson, Mercy R., 119
Thompson, Robert B., 119, 135, 137
Tongues, speaking in, 34, 36, 45
Turley, Theodore, 49, 155
Tyler, Andrew, 50
Tyler, Daniel, 49
Tyler, Elizabeth Comins, 50

- U -

United Order, 178
Urim and Thummim, 85

- V -

Visions, 1-2, 28, 67, 107, 167-168

- W -

Walker, Cyrus, 134
Walker, Wm. Holmes, 147
Wells, Daniel H., 183
Wells, Emmeline Blanche, 156
West, the. *See* Rocky Mountains.
Westover, Mary C., 167
Wheelock, Cyrus H., 189-190
Whitlock, Harvey, 17-18, 27
Whitmer, David, 30
Whitmer, John, 22-23
Whitmer, Peter, Sr., 13
Whitney, Elizabeth Ann, 39
Whitney, Helen Mar, 175
Whitney, Newell H., 19, 39-40, 61, 78

Wight, Lyman, 17-18, 22, 27, 47, 55, 86, 104, 108
Wight, Orange L., 104
Williams, Frederick G., 75
Winters, Mary Ann, 166
Wood, Joseph, 133
Woodruff, Wilford, 80, 84, 87
Workman, Andrew, 150
Workman, Sariah A., 99

- Y -

Young, Brigham, 16, 34, 36, 49, 178
Young, Joseph, 16, 34, 36

- Z -

Zion's Camp, 19, 21-22, 25, 26-28, 47, 55, 69-70, 75, 80, 90